SYMBOLIC COMPUTATION
Computer Graphics – Systems and Applications

Managing Editor: J. Encarnação

Editors: K. Bø J. D. Foley R. A. Guedj
P. J. W. ten Hagen F. R. A. Hopgood M. Hosaka
M. Lucas A. G. Requicha

Springer-Series
SYMBOLIC COMPUTATION
Computer Graphics – Systems and Applications

J. Encarnação, E. G. Schlechtendahl:
Computer Aided Design. Fundamentals and System
Architectures. IX, 346 pages, 183 figs., 1983

G. Enderle, K. Kansy, G. Pfaff:
Computer Graphics Programming. GKS – The Graphics
Standard. Second, revised and enlarged edition. XXIII,
651 pages, 100 figs., 1987

J. Encarnação, R. Schuster, E. Vöge (eds.):
Product Data Interfaces in CAD/CAM Applications.
Design, Implementation and Experiences. IX, 270 pages,
147 figs., 1986

U. Rembold, R. Dillmann (eds.):
Computer-Aided Design and Manufacturing. Methods and
Tools. Second, revised and enlarged edition. XIV,
458 pages, 304 figs., 1986

Y. Shirai:
Three-Dimensional Computer Vision. XII, 297 pages,
313 figs., 1987

D. B. Arnold, P. R. Bono:
CGM and CGI. Metafile and Interface Standards
for Computer Graphics. XXIII, 279 pages,
103 figs., 1988

David B. Arnold   Peter R. Bono

CGM and CGI

Metafile and Interface Standards
for Computer Graphics

With 103 Figures

Springer-Verlag
Berlin Heidelberg New York
London Paris Tokyo

Dr. David B. Arnold
University of East Anglia, School of Information Systems
Norwich NR4 7TJ, UK

Dr. Peter R. Bono
Peter R. Bono Associates, Inc.
P.O. Box 648, Gales Ferry, CT 06335, USA

ISBN 3-540-18950-5 Springer-Verlag Berlin Heidelberg New York
ISBN 0-387-18950-5 Springer-Verlag New York Berlin Heidelberg

This work is subject to copyright. All rights are reserved, whether the whole or part of the material is concerned, specifically the rights of translation, reprinting, reuse of illustrations, recitation, broadcasting, reproduction on microfilms or in other ways, and storage in data banks. Duplication of this publication or parts thereof is only permitted under the provisions of the German Copyright Law of September 9, 1965, in its version of June 24, 1985, and a copyright fee must always be paid. Violations fall under the prosecution act of the German Copyright Law.

The use of registered names, trademarks, etc. in this publication does not imply, even in the absence of a specific statement, that such names are exempt from the relevant protective laws and regulations and therefore free for general use.

© Springer-Verlag Berlin Heidelberg 1988
Printed in Germany

Printing: Druckhaus Beltz, Hemsbach; Bookbinding: Schäffer, Grünstadt
2145/3140-543210

Foreword

We have written this book principally for users and practitioners of computer graphics. In particular, system designers, independent software vendors, graphics system implementers, and application program developers need to understand the basic standards being put in place at the so-called Virtual Device Interface and how they relate to other industry standards, both formal and *de facto*.

Secondarily, the book has been targetted at technical managers and advanced students who need some understanding of the graphics standards and how they fit together, along with a good overview of the Computer Graphics Interface (CGI) proposal and Computer Graphics Metafile (CGM) standard in particular. Part I, Chapters 1, 2, and 3; Part II, Chapters 10 and 11; Part III, Chapters 15, 16, and 17; and some of the Appendices will be of special interest.

Finally, these same sections will interest users in government and industry who are responsible for selecting, buying and installing commercial implementations of the standards. The CGM is already a US Federal Information Processing Standard (FIPS 126), and we expect the same status for the CGI when its development is completed and it receives formal approval by the standards-making bodies.

Formal standards documents are–by design–very precise, containing little explanatory matter and few examples. Standards usually contain no tutorial material and are somewhat dry. The requirement for precision makes graphics standards documents very long and complex. In short, they are nearly unreadable, except by those who have spent several years contributing to their development! Consequently, much of the material in the book is designed to *supplement* the material contained in the standards documents.

The book is designed to be read prior to, but *in conjunction with*, the formal documents. In order that the book be self-contained, considerable material from the formal standard itself is repeated in the book, but we have tried to incorporate the material in a more interesting, less pedantic fashion.

Extensive examples and figures are used to illustrate important features, capabilities, and concepts. Discussions of current commercial implementations are also included. Consequently, the book is well suited as a textbook to supplement commercial short courses or units on computer graphics in college and university curricula. However, in this first edition, no exercises are included with the text.

The CGM has been formally approved and published by both the International Standards Organization (ISO 8632) and by the American National Standards Institute (ANSI/X3.122). The CGI, on the other hand, is still under development. Yet, many functions defined in the CGI have already surfaced in commercial products–both hardware and software. These functions are stable and are being used to provide device-independent programming interfaces to graphics equipment. Part II, Chapter 11, describes some of these CGI implementations, while Part II, Chapter 16, describes implementations of the CGM.

The first edition of this book documents the state of the CGI standard (ISO DP9636; ANSI/X3.161) as of December, 1987. We have worked hard to keep the production time short so that the book is available as early as possible. In particular we have supplied camera-ready Apple LaserWriter typescript to Springer-Verlag. When the CGI becomes technically frozen and is published as an official ISO and ANSI standard, we will prepare a revised version that reflects the final standard. At that time, we should also have new material that reflects Addenda to the CGM now under development (see Part III, Chapter 17).

Standards are developed by committee, and decisions are arrived at by consensus. The current state of the CGI and the CGM reflects the collective efforts of literally hundreds of individuals from over a dozen countries. Their efforts, in turn, have been built on the prior efforts of hundreds more who contributed to either, or both of, the ACM-SIGGRAPH-sponsored Core System and the Graphical Kernel System (ISO 7942), the first formally-approved graphics standard. We wish to acknowledge the contributions of all these people.

Given the contributions of so many, it is hazardous to cite by name those few who have made special contributions. Nevertheless, we would be remiss if we did not mention specifically Chris Osland, who led the international task force that developed the CGM; Lofton Henderson, who was the document editor for the CGM; and Andrea Frankel, who is the document editor of the CGI. Many others have made significant personal and intellectual contributions to the resulting standards. They and their colleagues know who they are, and they have our gratitude and admiration.

By writing this book, we hope that many more people will come to appreciate the importance of these standards. The CGI and the CGM have the potential to facilitate international trade, help hold down rapidly increasing software development costs, and contribute toward improving human productivity–all necessary conditions for improving everyone's standard of living.

David B. Arnold
Norwich
England

Peter R. Bono
Gales Ferry, Connecticut
United States of America

January, 1988

*This book is dedicated to our families–
our wives, children, and parents–
whose support and encouragement
have permitted us to attain
the level of knowledge and competence
required to write this book.*

*In particular we remember Molly Arnold,
who set us all an example
in her celebration of life and living,
but died on 28th December 1987,
just before this project was brought to completion.*

Table of Contents

Part I: The Computer Graphics Interface

Chapter 1: Introduction to Computer Graphics Standards   3

1.1	Overview of Various Graphics Standards	3
1.1.1	A Reference Model	3
1.1.2	The Application Programmer Interface	7
1.1.3	The Virtual Device Interface	9
1.1.4	Developments in the Reference Architecture	9
1.2	Organization of the Book	10

Chapter 2: The Computer Graphics Interface   11

2.1	What is the CGI?	11
2.2	Purpose	11
2.3	Uses and Benefits	12
2.4	Design Requirements	13
2.5	Design Criteria	14
2.6	Relationship with Other Standards	15
2.6.1	CGI Data Encodings Standard	15
2.6.2	CGI Language Binding Standards	15
2.6.3	Relationship of CGI Data Encoding and Language Binding Standards	16
2.6.4	Relationship with GKS	17
2.6.5	Relationship with GKS-3D and PHIGS	17
2.6.6	Relationship with the CGM	17
2.6.7	Relationship with Window Managers	18
2.6.8	Relationship with PostScript	19
2.6.9	Relationship with ISO Register of Graphical Items	19
2.7	Main Concepts	19
2.7.1	The CGI Pipeline	20
2.7.2	The CGI State Model	22
2.7.3	Interrogation and Inquiry	22
2.7.4	CGI Error Philosophy	22

Chapter 3: Elementary CGI Output and Attribute Functions   23

    3.1   Introduction   23
    3.2   Line Class Graphic Objects   25
       3.2.1   Line Class Primitives   25
       3.2.2   Attributes of Line Class Primitives   26
    3.3   Polymarker Primitive and Attributes   27
    3.4   Text   28
       3.4.1   Introduction to Text Primitives and Attributes   28
       3.4.2   Font Description Coordinate System   29
       3.4.3   Character Expansion Factor and Character Spacing   30
       3.4.4   Character Orientation   31
       3.4.5   Text Path   31
       3.4.6   Text Alignment   32
       3.4.7   Text Precision   33
    3.5   Filled Area Primitives   34

Chapter 4: Control and Error Handling   39

    4.1   Virtual Device Management   39
       4.1.1   Managing a Dialogue Session   39
       4.1.2   Managing the Display Surface   41
       4.1.3   Controlling Deferral Modes and Regeneration   42
       4.1.4   Classes of CGI Devices   42
    4.2   Characteristics of Output Devices   43
    4.3   Coordinate Space Control   45
    4.4   Clipping Control   48
    4.5   Error Model   49
       4.5.1   Error Classification Scheme   49
       4.5.2   Mechanism for Error Reporting   51
    4.6   Interrogation and Inquiry   52
    4.7   Interrogation and Negotiation   53
    4.8   Miscellaneous Control   53

Chapter 5: The Raster Functions in the CGI   55

    5.1   Introduction   55
    5.2   Representation and Storage of Bitmaps   56
    5.3   Bitmap Data Structure   58
    5.4   Control of Bitmap Manipulations   58
    5.5   Pixel Array   62
    5.6   BITMAP Interior Style   63
    5.7   Displayable Bitmaps   63

Chapter 6: Synchronous Input   65

6.1	Introduction	65
6.2	Logical Input Devices and Their Measures	65
6.3	Coordinate Systems for Stroke and Locator	67
6.4	CGI Input Model	68
6.5	Triggers	68
6.6	Request Input	69
6.7	Echoing, Prompting, and Acknowledgement	70
6.8	Setting Initial Conditions for Devices	71

Part II: Advanced Features of the CGI

Chapter 7: Segmentation in the CGI   75

7.1	Introduction	75
7.2	Segments in the CGI	78
7.3	Creation of Segments	79
7.4	Segment Attributes	80
7.5	Segment Display	82
7.6	Segment Manipulations	83
7.7	Pick Input and Segmentation	85
7.8	Segment Interrogations and Inquiries	86
7.9	Segment Storage Overflow Handling	86

Chapter 8: Further CGI Output and Attribute Functions   87

8.1	Introduction	87
8.2	Additional Line Class Primitives	87
8.2.1	DISJOINT POLYLINE	88
8.2.2	CIRCULAR ARC CENTRE BACKWARDS	88
8.2.3	ELLIPTICAL ARC	89
8.3	Further Text Primitives	89
8.3.1	APPEND TEXT	89
8.3.2	The RESTRICTED TEXT Primitive	90
8.4	Additional Filled Area Primitives	92
8.5	Closed Figures	93
8.6	Controlling Edge Visibility	94
8.7	Cell Array Primitive	94
8.8	Generalized Drawing Primitive	95
8.9	Output and Attribute Control Functions	96
8.9.1	Specification Modes and Colour Definition	96
8.9.2	Transparency	97
8.9.3	Setting Bundle Table Contents	97
8.10	Save and Restore Primitive Attributes Settings	98

Chapter 8: (Cont)

8.11	Inquiry and Interrogation	98
8.12	New CGI Pipeline Model	99
8.13	Fonts and Character Sets	102

Chapter 9: Asynchronous Input   103

9.1	Introduction	103
9.2	Event Input	104
9.3	Event Queue Management	105
9.4	Echo Request Input Mode	106

Chapter 10: CGI Conformance and Constituency Profiles   109

10.1	Purpose	109
10.2	Conformance and Constituency Profiles	109

Chapter 11: Implementations of the CGI   117

11.1	Overview	117
11.2	Traditional Output Primitives and Attributes	118
11.3	Raster Graphics Capabilities	119
11.4	Control	119
11.5	Segmentation	119
11.6	Input	120
11.7	Hardware Manifestations of the CGI	121

Part III: The Computer Graphics Metafile

Chapter 12: CGM Concepts and Purposes   131

12.1	Metafiles	131
12.1.1	GKS Metafiles	131
12.1.2	The Computer Graphics Metafile	132
12.2	A Reference Model for Data Interchange	134
12.3	Purposes of Metafiles	136
12.3.1	Picture File Transfer and Storage	136
12.3.2	Product Definition Data Base Transfer and Storage	137
12.3.3	Transaction Recording	138
12.3.4	Symbol Libraries	139

Chapter 13: CGM Elements — 141

13.1	Delimiter Elements	141
13.2	Metafile Descriptor Elements	146
13.3	Picture Descriptor Elements	153
13.4	Control Elements	156
13.5	CGM Tailoring	159
13.6	Graphical Primitive Elements	160
13.7	Attribute Elements	163
13.8	Escape and External Elements	170
13.9	Metafile Defaults	171

Chapter 14: CGM Encodings — 173

14.1	Binary Encoding	173
14.1.1	Overview	173
14.1.2	List of Binary Encoding Metafile Element Codes	177
14.1.3	Binary Encoding Defaults	180
14.2	Clear Text Encoding	180
14.2.1	Overview	180
14.2.2	List of Clear Text Encoding Derived Element Names	181
14.2.3	Clear Text Encoding Defaults	184
14.3	Character Encoding	185
14.3.1	Overview	185
14.3.2	List of Character Encoding Metafile Element Codes	186
14.3.3	Character Encoding Defaults	188
14.4	Private Encodings	189

Chapter 15: Relationship of the CGM to Other Standards — 193

15.1	CGI	193
15.2	GKS	193
15.3	Registration of Graphical Items	195
15.4	Office Document Architecture	195
15.5	Standard Generalized Markup Language	197

Chapter 16: Implementations of the CGM — 199

16.1	CGM Exporters	200
16.1.1	On Mainframes, Minicomputers, and Workstations	200
16.1.2	On Personal Computers and in Hardware	201
16.2	CGM Importers	202
16.2.1	On Mainframes, Minicomputers, and Workstations	202
16.2.2	On Personal Computers and in Hardware	202
16.3	CGM Editors	203
16.4	NCGA GraphNet'88	203
16.5	Practical Considerations	204

XVI   Table of Contents

Chapter 16: (Cont)

    16.5.1 Barriers to Interchange   204
    16.5.2 Using Outside CGMs   206
    16.5.3 Issues for the Application Developer   207

Chapter 17: Future Extensions to the CGM   209

    17.1 The CGM as a GKS Metafile   209
    17.2 Global Segments   212
    17.3 New Elements from the CGI   215
    17.4 3D Elements   216
    17.5 Other Requirements   216
        17.5.1 Purpose   217
        17.5.2 Scope   218
        17.5.3 Suggested New Elements   218

Part IV: The Appendices

Appendix A: Glossary   227

Appendix B: Bibliography   235

    B.1 Standards Documents   235
    B.2 Books   236
    B.3 Journal Articles   237

Appendix C: The Standards-Making System   241

    C.1 Standards Bodies   241
    C.2 The ANSI Process   243
    C.3 The ISO Process   244
    C.4 Standards Status   246

Appendix D: CGI Description Tables and State Lists   249

    D.1 Device Description Table   249
    D.2 Output Description Table   251
    D.3 Attributes Description Table   252
    D.4 Raster Description Table   254
    D.5 Segmentation Description Table   254
    D.6 Input Description Table   255
    D.7 Echo Output Description Table   256
    D.8 Output State List   257

Appendix D (Cont)

D.9	Control State List	260
D.10	Raster State List	261
D.11	Segmentation State List	261
D.12	Logical Input Device State List	262
D.13	Event Queue State List	263
D.14	Echo Entity State List	263

Appendix E: CGI Functions and Parameterization 265

E.1	Introduction and Conventions	265
E.2	Part 2 Functions	265
E.2.1	Virtual Device Management	265
E.2.2	Coordinate Space Control	265
E.2.3	Error Handling	266
E.2.4	Miscellaneous Control	266
E.3	Part 3 Functions	266
E.3.1	Graphical Primitives	266
E.3.2	Attribute Functions	267
E.3.3	Output and Attribute Control Functions	268
E.4	Part 4 Functions	268
E.4.1	Segment Manipulation	268
E.4.2	Segment Attributes	269
E.4.3	Segment Interrogations	269
E.5	Part 5 Functions	269
E.5.1	Logical Input Device Functions	269
E.5.2	Echo Output Functions	270
E.6	Part 6 Functions	270
E.6.1	Output and Attributes	270
E.6.2	Raster Control Functions	271
E.6.3	Raster Inquiry Functions	271

Appendix F: TOP CGM Application Profile 273

F.1	What is an Application Profile?	273
F.2	The Technical Office Protocols Organization	273
F.3	TOP Version 3.0	274
F.4	Constraints on the Metafile Contents	275
F.5	Constraints on Generators and Interpreters	278

List of Figures

1.1	The major components of the graphics support environment	3
1.2	Typical arrangement c.1975	4
1.3	Mapping the current standards projects onto typical applications	5
1.4	Graphics pipelines feeding a window manager	9
2.1	Valid Models of CGI Generators and Interpreters	16
2.2	Schematic Output Pipeline for the CGI	21
3.1(a)	Simple use of bundle tables	24
3.1(b)	Adding the ASFs to the example in Fig 3.1(a)	25
3.2(a)	Polyline primitive	25
3.2(b)	Circular Arc 3 Point	26
3.2(c)	Circular Arc Centre	26
3.3	Polymarker primitive and predefined types	27
3.4	Simple use of the Text primitive	28
3.5	Font description coordinate system	30
3.6	Effect of Character Spacing attribute	30
3.7	Effect of Character Expansion Factor	31
3.8	Non-orthogonal Character Baseline and Up Vector	31
3.9	Effect of Text Path Attribute	32
3.10	Text Alignment Parameters	33
3.11	Continuous Text Alignment values	33
3.12	Text precisions	34
3.13	Polygon primitive types	35
3.14	Simple geometric Fill Area primitives	36
3.15	Circular Arc Close Fill Area primitives	36
3.16	Interior styles for Fill Area primitives	38
4.1(a)	Effects of initialising the CGI	40
4.1(b)	Assembly of CGI page	40
4.1(c)	Effect of End Page for Hardcopy Devices	41
4.1(d)	Effect of End Page for softcopy devices	41
4.1(e)	Effect of RESET TO DEFAULTS	42
4.2(a)	Buffering and Deferral Mode ASTI	43
4.2(b)	Buffering and Deferral Mode ASTI	43
4.2(c)	Buffering and Deferral Mode ASTI	44

4.2(d)	Buffering and Deferral Mode ASAP	44
4.2(e)	Buffering and Deferral Modes (BNI)	44
4.2(f)	Buffering and Deferral Mode BNI	45
4.3(a)	Coordinate systems defined by VDC Extent	46
4.3(b)	Alternative systems defined by point order	46
4.4(a)	Isotropic mapping control	47
4.4(b)	Effect of anisotropic mapping from Fig 4.4(a)	47
4.5	Mirrored final image via Viewport specification	48
4.6(a)	Normal clipping	49
4.6(b)	View surface clipping everything off the screen	49
5.1	Positions of segment store and bitmaps in the graphics pipeline	55
5.2	Types of bitmap	57
5.3	Writing to, and displaying from, Mapped Bitmaps	57
5.4(a)	The Source Destination Bitblt	59
5.4(b)	The Tile Three Operand Bitblt	61
5.5	Mapping truth tables to values of Drawing Mode 3	62
5.6	The Pixel Array primitive	63
6.1	Coordinated use of separate OUTPUT and INPUT CGIs	66
6.2	State model for REQUEST and SAMPLE modes	69
6.3	Processes used in REQUEST mode	69
7.1	Generic model of data stores in graphics systems	75
7.2 (a)	Graphics objects do not affect the system's state when displayed	76
7.2 (b)	Example of segments defining graphics objects	77
7.2 (c)	Storing executable commands	77
7.3	Incomplete objects as segment definitions	78
7.4	Transforming primitives' reference points only	81
7.5(a)	Definition of a simple CGI segment	84
7.5(b)	Copy without inheritance	84
7.5(c)	Copy with inheritance	85
7.6	Effect of bundle changes between segment definition and display	85
8.1	The DISJOINT POLYLINE primitive	88
8.2	CIRCULAR ARC CENTRE BACKWARDS	88
8.3	ELLIPTICAL ARC primitive	89
8.4	Use of APPEND TEXT primitive	90
8.5	Simple use of RESTRICTED TEXT primitive	91
8.6	Use of RESTRICTED TEXT and APPEND TEXT	91
8.7	The ELLIPSE primitive	92
8.8	ELLIPTICAL ARC CLOSE primitive	92
8.9	Closed Figures as a way of constructing Filled Areas	94

8.10	Use of individual edge visibility flags	95
8.11	The CELL ARRAY primitive	95
8.12	GENERALIZED DRAWING PRIMITIVE	96
8.13	Use of transparency	97
8.14	Saving and restoring individual attributes	98
8.15	Effect of not saving and restoring bundle representations	98
8.16(a)	The new CGI pipeline model	100
8.16(b)	The new CGI pipeline model (continued)	101
9.1(a)	State model of Logical Input Device in Event Mode	104
9.1(b)	Processes active during Event Input	104
9.2	Event Queue states and transitions	106
9.3	State model of Echo Request Mode operation	107
9.4	Stages in remote echoing operations	108
9.4(a)	Initialize input device and Echo Request	108
9.4(b)	Initialize Echo Output, set modes and 1st value	108
9.4(c)	Send Echo Request	108
9.4(d)	Measure changed, value returned	108
9.4(e)	Value echoed	108
9.4(f)	Send Echo Request	108
9.4(g)	Trigger fired	108
9.4(h)	Value returned to application and echoed to operator	108
12.1	Generating and interpreting metafiles	132
12.2	CGM file structure	133
12.3	Levels of data interchange	135
13.1	CGM state diagram	142
13.2(a)	Different character set; same font index	150
13.2(b)	Same character set; different font index	150
14.1(a)	Format of a short-form command header	175
14.1(b)	Format of a long-form command header	175
14.2	Partitioned POLYLINE with 50 points	176
14.3	Example of a short-form string	177
C.1	Proposed Working Group Structure for ISO/IEC JTC1/SC24	246

List of Tables

4.1	Error classification scheme in the CGI	50
4.2	CGI error detection, reaction and reaction reporting by class	51
5.1	Drawing Mode v Logical Operation	60
10.1	GKS constituency profiles	110
11.1	Comparison of CGI functionality by supplier	122
13.1(a)	CGM elements	143
13.1(b)	CGM elements (cont)	144
14.1	Suggested minimum capabilities for a CGM interpreter	191
C.1	Programme of Work for ISO/IEC JTC1/SC24	247
D.1-14	CGI Description Tables and State Lists	249

PART I

The Computer Graphics Interface

Chapter 1

Introduction to Computer Graphics Standards

1.1 Overview of Various Graphics Standards

1.1.1 A Reference Model

Functional standards specify a model of a system, a set of operations on the model, and the *externally visible* effects of these operations. Such standards do not specify how these effects are to be implemented. In short, standards codify the exchange of information across an interface between two functional units and specify *what* is to be exchanged, but not *how* the functional units carry out their operations.

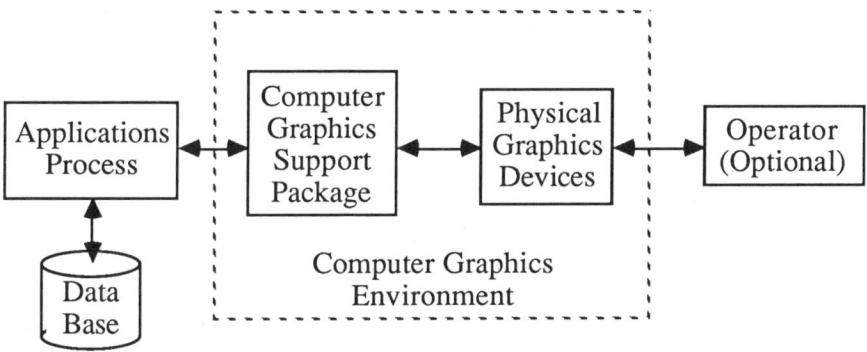

Fig. 1.1. The major components of the graphics support environment

Figure 1.1 is a very simple model of a computer graphics operating environment. The model emphasizes that a graphics application process interacts with physical graphics devices and human operators via a computer graphics environment. It also shows that the application may get information from an external product definition data base. The model is extremely schematic and, with the possible exception of using the term "database," is a schematic representation of the use of graphics systems over the past 20 years. At the time when the work on graphics standards got underway (*c*. 1975) this model might have been associated with the arrangement in Fig. 1.2. This shows the applications package communicating through a graphics package (usually at that time a library of FORTRAN routines) and via the operating system on the host computer over a serial line to a remote terminal. The graphics package was typically divided into a device independent "front-end" and device dependent "back-end" or device driver. Depending on the affluence of the system's owner the terminal might have had some local intelligence, although the majority would have been unintelligent devices.

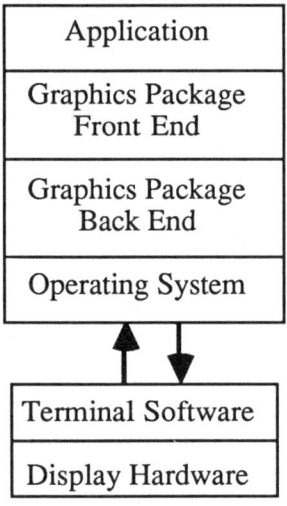

Fig. 1.2. Typical arrangement *c*.1975

Figure 1.3 identifies the generic interfaces within this model by partitioning the environment into a support package level and a workstation level and by naming the interfaces significant for graphics standards. It shows a very similar underlying architecture to Fig. 1.2, but the expectation of the single graphics device has been replaced with the concept of multiple active workstations each of which may have different capabilities ranging from input-only devices to intelligent interactive workstations. Obviously the layer of device dependent software needs to be adjusted to support such radically different environments and the application software will need to be able to inquire the capabilities of the underlying system in order to maximise its efficiency in using the underlying hardware. It is however very noticeable that essentially the same interfaces as were present in the earlier model are still present on the pipeline to any individual device. These are usually called the Applications Programmer Interface (API) and the Virtual Device Interface (VDI).

Chapter 1: Introduction to Computer Graphics Standards 5

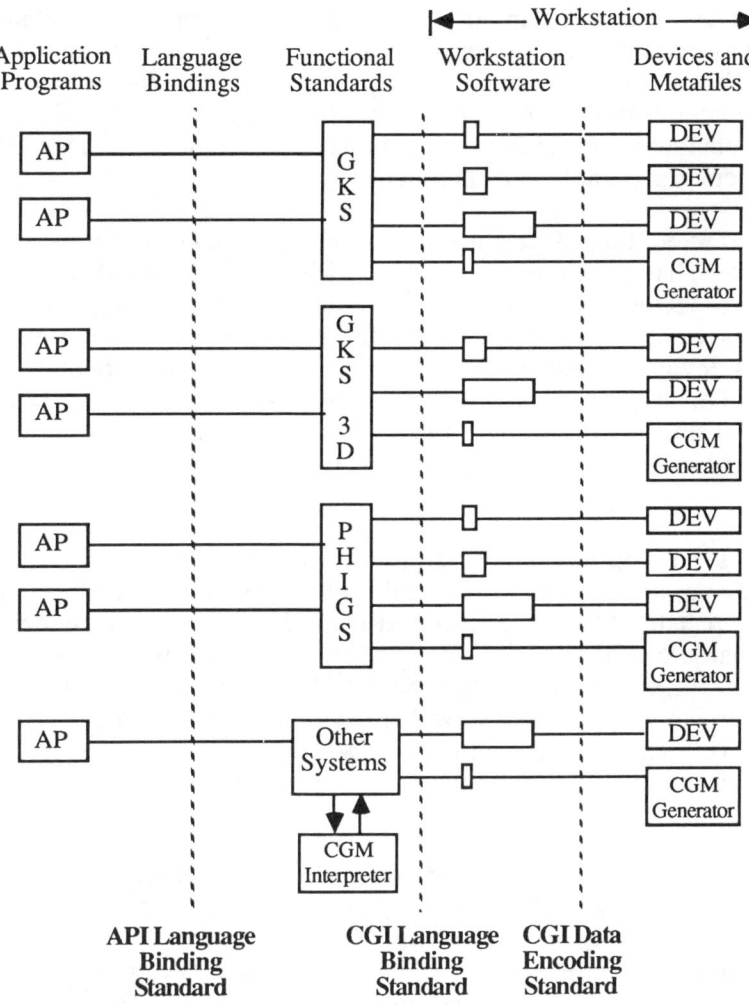

Fig. 1.3. Mapping the current standards projects onto typical applications

Figure 1.3 also shows the position of the current range of graphic standardisation projects in this sort of schematic organisation. It shows two sorts of standardisation efforts. The first is represented by the boxes and shows a piece of hardware or software capable of interpreting or generating a sequence of commands at the interfaces. Included in this category are the definitions of the functionality of graphics systems such as GKS and PHIGS but, more importantly to this text, this category also includes the specification within the CGI of the actions required of a CGI interpreter–the externally visible effects referred to above. The second type of standard is represented by the dotted lines crossing the connections between these boxes and shows an interface at which the syntax of a sequential set of commands has been defined by a standard. These are obviously closely related to the functionality supported by the pieces of hardware, but in the case of the CGM, for example, the standard defines the file format and not the operation of the generator or interpreter of that format. Similarly the language binding standards for GKS specify the appearance of the GKS functions in the particular programming languages.

Standards at both interfaces provide *device independence* for the user of the standard. That is, the user can deal with one or more abstract graphics devices (or *virtual devices*) with a full range of input and output capabilities. The "messy details" of the particular hardware capabilities of any particular graphics device are hidden from the user. Instead, implementations of the standards must emulate any required facilities not directly supported by the hardware. Furthermore, the implementations mask the peculiarities of the particular command sets used to communicate specific orders to the graphics devices.

A user of the Applications Programmer Interface standards may therefore be using only a software simulation of some features which are indistinguishable in their description from those features provided directly by the hardware of the graphics system. Users at this level are using the standard facilities because they wish to be isolated from the vagaries of particular hardware. If they wish to combine this with highly efficient operations, then either the underlying system must be closely tuned to the standard functionality or they must make extensive use of adaptive code and inquiry functions.

In contrast, the user of a standard at the virtual device interface (VDI) level has either opted to abandon extensive protection from the lower levels of the system or is in fact attempting to use the standard in supporting implementations of the higher level Applications Programmer Interface (API). Standards at this level are therefore provided with the more sophisticated programmer in mind. The "user" in a production environment is more typically a piece of code which uses the standard functionality to control a piece of hardware.

To highlight this difference, the system calling CGI functions is usually refered to as the *client,* in contrast to the user of a standard at the API level who is usually thought of as an applications programmer. The person controlling the interactive system is normally referred to as the *operator*.

To exchange pictures among diverse applications and across separate programming environments, information can be captured at an interface and placed in a *graphical metafile*, a formatted disk or magnetic tape file containing graphical commands and data. These files can be transmitted over telephone lines and computer networks to be stored and processed at remote sites or reused locally as a library of prespecified pictures.

1.1.2 The Application Programmer Interface

The Application Programmer Interface (API) is represented by three major graphics standards projects: **GKS**, **GKS-3D**, and **PHIGS**. These API standards are typically implemented as a collection of external procedures or subroutines that a programmer can link with his application code to obtain graphical input and cause pictures to be displayed on graphical output devices.

The API standards are not directly suitable for picture exchange. However, each standard has an associated storage mechanism (an archive file or graphical metafile) that can be used to exchange graphical information between systems using the same standard. The API standards are briefly described below. Their associated metafiles are described in Part III of this book.

GKS. The Graphical Kernel System (GKS) consists of nearly 200 user interface routines that give a programmer the ability to create graphical output and accept graphical input from a wide variety of graphical devices. These include black-and-white and colour displays, printers, plotters, and camera systems of varying resolutions, as well as mice, data tablets, keyboards, joysticks, and digitizers. Only 2D primitives are used to describe pictures, although 3D renderings can be created by the application by first performing the 3D to 2D mapping itself before calling the GKS functions.

A GKS implementation typically provides programming access to GKS from such high-level programming languages as Fortran, Pascal, Ada, and C. Unlike the ACM-SIGGRAPH Core System, the GKS family of standards defines the exact appearance (syntax) of GKS functions and data types in each of these programming languages.

GKS's purpose is to allow the creation of *views* of objects. Each view is described to GKS by a succession of primitives and attributes that may be grouped into segments for later viewing, without the client's having to respecify the primitives and attributes in the segment. As a whole, segments may be made invisible and highlighted, assigned priority, made detectable, and translated, rotated, and scaled, but the individual contents of segments may not be modified. Consequently, GKS is a pure viewing system; GKS does not keep any graphical model or graphical data base for the application program.

GKS-3D. The project to specify extensions to GKS for defining and viewing three-dimensional objects is nearly complete. Like GKS, GKS-3D is restricted to viewing objects: no modelling is performed by a GKS-3D implementation. This limitation in GKS and GKS-3D keeps the size, complexity, and cost of the implementation down and meets the needs of at least 80% of the graphics applications today, including much of the needs of business graphics, statistical and engineering graphics, project management, and mapping. In addition to providing functions for obtaining the usual perspective and orthographic projections of objects specified in 3D Cartesian coordinates, GKS-3D also provides functions to access hidden-line and hidden-surface algorithms that may be available in certain workstations or provided by the implementation to all GKS-3D workstations.

PHIGS. The Programmer's Hierarchical Interactive Graphics System (PHIGS) is an emerging standard specifying an application programmer's interface to a rich, device-independent graphics environment. PHIGS is designed to support such important applications as CAD/CAE/CAM, command and control, molecular modelling, simulation, and process control. PHIGS emphasizes the support of applications needing a highly dynamic, highly interactive operator interface and expects rapid screen update of the complex images to be performed by the display system.

PHIGS provides all the *viewing* capabilities of GKS-3D in a compatible manner, but, in addition, PHIGS supports the creation, modification, and viewing of a geometric *model*, which is maintained by the PHIGS implementation. Stored in an area called the Central Structure Store, PHIGS elements are structured into hierarchies, with structures calling other structures and with offspring structures inheriting attributes from parent structures. Once created, or while being created, PHIGS structures can be marked for display on one or more workstations. A powerful feature of the system is the provision to allow scanning and selective editing of the contents of structure store, which is provided to allow the results of interactive sequences to be displayed without completely redefining the displayed structures.

The principal purpose of an API standard is to provide portability for an application program across a wide range of operating systems, programming languages, and interactive graphics devices. Consequently, programs written to an API standard at one facility can be exchanged with another facility and used with only minor modifications needed to tailor the software to the implementation differences allowed by the standard.

Furthermore, as hardware CPUs and peripherals are upgraded and replaced, software written to an API standard will survive and need not be rewritten. Indeed, the software performance should improve, assuming that the new hardware is more capable than the old hardware and that new graphics hardware will be developed taking the graphics standards into consideration.

1.1.3 The Virtual Device Interface

The Virtual Device Interface (VDI) is internal to the graphics system and concerns system programmers, independent software vendors, peripheral device manufacturers, graphics controller board makers, and graphics chip makers. These clients require device independence without sacrificing performance.

The **CGI** (Computer Graphics Interface) standard is designed to specify the exchange of information at the VDI, while the related **CGM** (Computer Graphics Metafile) standard serves to capture the descriptions of pictures at the level of the CGI. These two standards are the subject of this textbook.

1.1.4 Developments in the Reference Architecture

Probably the most obvious change in the architecture of systems with graphics capabililties in the last five years has been the acceptance of the window paradigm of interactive system use and the rapid growth in the number and variety of such systems in the marketplace. While these do change the underlying architecture of the system supporting the graphics application, they do not affect the existence of interfaces within the system equivalent to the API and VDI (Fig. 1.4). Their most profound effect is on the assumptions that the resources available to the devices in any of the standard graphics systems are fixed. This assumption will have to be adapted in the revision of the standards to allow a window manager to alter the allocation of facilities dynamically.

Windowing systems also present a challenge to the lower level graphics standards in that they raise the question of whether or not these standards are capable of supporting the window manager's requirements of the graphics environment. This challenge has not been taken up in the first set of graphics standards.

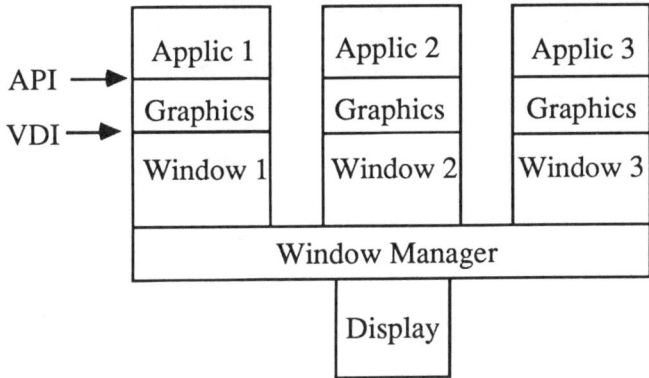

Fig. 1.4. Graphics pipelines feeding a window manager

1.2 Organization of the Book

The book is divided into three parts. The first two parts deal with the CGI and the third part with the CGM. Six appendices are provided to add useful detail, without distracting from the flow of the narrative.

You have just completed Chapter 1, which has provided an overview of all the computer graphics standards. Chapter 2 introduces the CGI–explaining its role and describing the potential benefits that will accrue when the CGI is accepted as a formal standard. Chapter 2 also introduces the concepts of the CGI, without overwhelming you with too much technical detail. Chapters 3 through 6 comprise the remainder of Part I and describe in detail most of the basic facilities of the CGI. Output Primitives and Attributes, Control, Raster, and Input are each the subject of a separate chapter in Part I.

Part II introduces the more advanced features of the CGI. Chapter 7 introduces the notion of a graphical *segment*, a group of primitives and attributes that can be manipulated as a single entity. Chapter 8 describes the remaining Output Primitives and Attributes available to the CGI client and adds more detail to the outline of the CGI pipeline model given in Chapter 2. More advanced input capabilities are covered in Chapter 9.

Chapter 10 introduces the notion of *conformance*: it explains what behaviour an implementation of the CGI must demonstrate in order to be able to be called a conforming CGI implementation. Finally, Chapter 11 completes Part II by briefly describing some early implementations based on the CGI.

Part III focusses on the CGM. Chapter 12 introduces the concept of a graphical metafile and explains the varied uses of a CGM. Chapter 13 details the semantics of the CGM elements, while Chapter 14 explains the three standardized syntaxes (known as *encodings*). Chapter 15 describes CGM's relationships with other standards. Chapter 16 describes the first commercially-available implementations of the CGM standard and discusses matters of practical concern to the prospective implementer or user. Finally, Chapter 17 describes some ongoing work to extend the CGM in a number of different directions.

Six appendices, including a Glossary and a Bibliography, complete the book.

Chapter 2

The Computer Graphics Interface

2.1 What is the CGI?

The Computer Graphics Interface is a standard functional and syntactic specification for the exchange of device independent data and associated control information between systems with graphical functional capabilities. These systems may be peer graphics systems or may be device dependent graphics device drivers.

The CGI defines an idealized abstract graphics device capable of accepting input and generating, storing, and manipulating pictures. It contains elements for generating graphical primitives; controlling the appearance of graphical primitives; inquiring graphics device capabilities, characteristics, and states; controlling graphics devices; generating and controlling groups of primitives called segments; and obtaining graphical input. The CGI also contains functions that are specifically targetted at the creation, manipulation, and display of raster bitmaps. The current version of the CGI supports only 2D output primitives and controls only one output device.

2.2 Purpose

The purpose of the CGI is to serve as a standardized, device independent interface for graphics package implementers to write to. When supported in hardware by peripheral device manufacturers, the burden of writing device drivers will be greatly eased. Furthermore, just as with applications written to GKS, implementations written to the CGI will be able to take advantage of new hardware without having to be rewritten or extensively modified. Thus, the developer's investment is protected, and any application layered on top of the CGI shares this same benefit. With hardware products having a lifespan of barely one year (because new, less costly, faster, and higher-resolution devices usually appear within a year of the initial product offering), writing to the CGI instead of to the hardware pays enormous dividends to the developer and end-user (consumer) alike.

Clearly the amount of graphics processing that can be transferred to a graphics device depends on the device's capabilities. A successful CGI definition must therefore allow control of a range of capabilities from simple devices with no input or display list capabilities to more sophisticated devices incorporating higher level primitives and other features. Because the CGI is intended to support a range of other graphics systems, the system controlling the CGI interface (known as the *client*) will be responsible for more or less of the device dependent operations, depending upon the capabilities of the target device.

2.3 Uses and Benefits

The CGI will simplify the development and implementation of graphics applications. A standardized interface will encourage uniform access to the graphics devices supported by an implementation. A reduction in overall development and life cycle costs should result.

The CGI promotes the interchange of software among installations. By isolating the device-dependent aspects of any graphics system, modularity is encouraged, thus promoting increased portability. A standardized set of functions, access mechanisms, and terminology allow developers and users to move between installations with minimal retraining.

Educational benefits also accrue. The standard set of CGI functions uses standard terminology. Consequently, both the academic and industrial communities can develop instructional programs concentrating on programming techniques and methodologies based on the standard set of functions rather than having to emphasize the idiosyncracies of each device.

With the trend towards lower hardware costs and higher software costs, the following economic benefits should be realized by users of the CGI standard:

- The CGI encourages transporting of software between installations, thereby reducing the costs associated with "reinventing."

- The CGI protects the large software investment made by both users and vendors because the software will not be rendered obsolete by the introduction of new graphics devices.

- The CGI allows developers to focus on higher-level graphics functions and applications instead of device-level functions, thus improving the developer's productivity.

- Use of the CGI reduces maintenance costs of software systems because the standard encourages modularity.

- The user gains vendor independence because any system designed to use a particular CGI device can more easily be changed to use some other CGI device.

- Vendors writing to the CGI will be able to interface easily to a broad range of customer systems because of the device-independence supported by the CGI.

- Using the CGI allows users, OEMs, and turnkey vendors to take advantage of new, lower-cost or higher-performance hardware designs. The total systems hardware cost can be reduced because system redesign will not be necessary.

2.4 Design Requirements

The CGI was developed with the following design requirements in mind:

- The CGI should provide a set of functions for the description of a *wide range of pictorial information*.

- The CGI should provide a set of functions for the necessary session control of a *wide range of graphics devices*.

- The CGI should address the more usual and essential features found on graphical devices *directly* and should provide access to less common facilities via an *escape mechanism*.

- The design of the CGI should not preclude *extension* at a later stage to cover facilities currently not standardized by the CGI.

- The CGI should be *usable* by implementations of the Graphical Kernel System (ISO 7942; ANSI/X3.124). In particular, the CGI should include functionality to support the various levels of a GKS workstation in an efficient and concise manner, but without compromising the ability of the interface to support non-GKS systems in an efficient and concise manner.

- The CGI should address the needs of different applications that have conflicting requirements for:

    - allocation of processing burden between host and device,
    - speed of generation and interpretation of functions,

- readability of the device protocol,
- editability and manipulation of graphical entities, and
- ease of transfer through different transport mechanisms.

2.5 Design Criteria

With these requirements in mind, a number of criteria were formulated to help decide between different design possibilities. These criteria are discussed in the following.

Completeness. In any area of the standard, the functionality specified by the CGI should be complete and self-contained.

Conciseness. Redundant functions or parameters should be avoided.

Consistency. Contradictory functions should be avoided.

Extensibility. The ability to add new functions and generality to the CGI should not be precluded.

Fidelity. The minimal results and characteristics of functions should be well defined.

Implementability. A function should be able to be efficiently supported on most host systems and graphics hardware.

Orthogonality. Independent functions for separate and noninteracting activities should be provided.

Predictability. The CGI standard should be written such that the recommended or proper use of standard functions guarantees the results of using a particular function.

Standard Practice. Only those functions that reflect existing practice, that are necessary to support existing practice, or that are necessary to support standards being developed concurrently should be standardized.

Usefulness. The standardized CGI functions should be powerful enough to perform useful tasks.

Well-structured. The number of assumptions that functions make about each other should be minimized. A function should have a well-defined interface and a simply-stated unconditional purpose. Multi-purpose functions and side effects should be avoided.

2.6 Relationship with Other Standards

The graphics standards reference model presented in Chap.1 shows the relationship between the different modules that comprise the reference model. The CGI is located between the workstation software of a graphics system and a device or graphics metafile. On the system side, the CGI has to interface in a concise and efficient manner with GKS. Extension of the CGI functionality to cover the additional functionality provided by GKS-3D and PHIGS can be added at a later stage, if required. On the device side, the CGI must be able to support interpretation of the CGM metafile in a straightforward way. Furthermore, it should be possible to generate a CGM metafile through the CGI, with minimal addition of non-CGI functions by deduction or separate communication.

In the paragraphs that follow, the relationship of the CGI standard to other standards is more fully detailed.

2.6.1 CGI Data Encodings Standard

Several specific data-stream *encodings* of the CGI functions will appear in a standard separate from the CGI Functional Description standard. Encodings are specific representation syntaxes of the functions intended to exactly describe a data stream connecting a graphics system and the devices it supports.

The data stream encodings of the CGI are based on the encoding principles of the corresponding data stream encodings of the CGM. Furthermore, where functions are identical in parameterization and equivalent in semantics, the encodings will be identical. However, the capabilities of the CGI are not identical with those of the CGM, so that specific encodings will differ in detail in those areas where the CGI and the CGM differ functionally.

Character, binary, and clear text data stream encodings of the CGI will be provided eventually, but, as of December, 1987, no such encodings have been agreed upon by the ISO Subcommittee responsible for computer graphics standards. See Chap. 14 for a detailed discussion of these encoding methods in the context of the CGM.

2.6.2 CGI Language Binding Standards

Two different approaches are recognized as possible for the mapping of CGI functions to language procedures: a *multi-procedure* mapping, or library, and a *single entry point* mapping. Whereas an objective for language binding interfaces at the application level (as in GKS or PHIGS) may be a one-to-one mapping to language procedures, the workstation device interface may be handled by a single entry point interface.

It is expected that two standards will be developed, one for each of these types of procedural bindings. Both of the language binding standards will have the same document structure, with a separate part for each programming language. Currently, the languages being considered for procedural bindings of the CGI are Fortran, Pascal, Ada, and C.

2.6.3 Relationship of CGI Data Encoding and Language Binding Standards

The primary context for the use of a CGI is over a serial interface in which a CGI generator is driving a CGI interpreter, which is controlling the device (Fig. 2.1). Thus, where a CGI implementation is in a high level language (e.g., supplied as a library of routines), this implementation is based on the assumption that the library of routines communicates with the underlying device (whether a CGI device or not) via a linearly-encoded data stream. Some of the functions of the CGI make sense only when viewed in the context of this sort of a model. For example, functions are provided to allow the client to control the number of bits used to represent the various data types. This is unlikely to be of interest in improving the efficiency of a parameter passing mechanism in a high level language, but it is of considerable interest if it can be used to minimise the number of data bits to be transmitted to a remote device. Thus, the routine may be used by the CGI generator but not affect future calls to the high level language interface. Instead, it may well be used by the generator to control the number of data bits transmitted to the remote device.

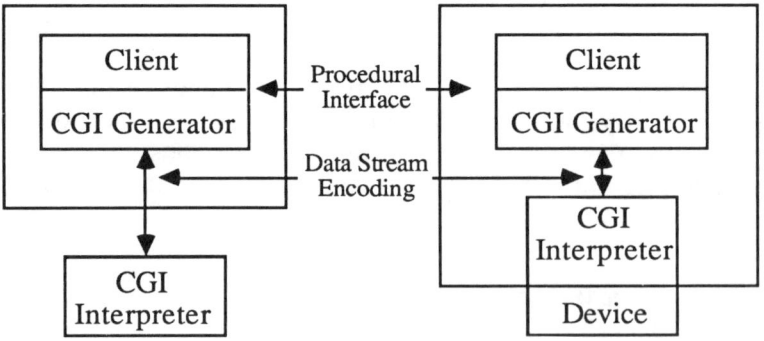

Fig. 2.1. Valid Models of CGI Generators and Interpreters

2.6.4 Relationship with GKS

The CGI standard draws extensively for its model of a graphics system on GKS. GKS communicates with the devices connected to it via the GKS workstation interface. If the devices are at the functional level of this interface, the CGI must be able to support this communication on the same level; that is, all functions at the GKS workstation interface must be expressable in terms of CGI functions without loss of meaning. For more simple devices, the GKS workstation functions are converted to a series of functions at a more primitive level. Therefore, the CGI must also contain lower level functions.

It is expected that GKS implementations should be able to use the CGI as their internal interface between the device-independent code and the device-dependent code. Where possible and appropriate, the CGI defaults and the preferred behaviour of functions have been specified to align with GKS.

2.6.5 Relationship with GKS-3D and PHIGS

The CGI can be extended to contain functional capabilities addressing specific requirements of GKS-3D and PHIGS. However, until GKS-3D and PHIGS are approved standards, no work on three-dimensional extensions to CGI is planned. The CGI should be appropriate to support that level of the GKS-3D or PHIGS pipeline where the third dimension has been dropped as the data is routed to a 2D device.

2.6.6 Relationship with the CGM

The CGI standard draws extensively for its model of a graphics picture on the Computer Graphics Metafile standard (ISO 8632; ANSI/X3.122).

It should be possible to generate a CGM through the CGI and to interpret a CGM through the CGI in a straightforward way. Therefore the CGI output and attribute functions are a superset of the CGM output and attribute functions, and there is also a close relationship between control functions in the two standards.

The data stream encodings of the CGI are based on the encoding principles of the corresponding data stream encodings of the CGM. Furthermore, where functions are identical in parameterization and equivalent in semantics in the two standards, the encodings will be identical.

2.6.7 Relationship with Window Managers

It is rather difficult to discuss the relationship of ISO standards projects to window management, when there is, at present, not even an approved ISO project on windowing systems. The nearest project would appear to be the new Terminal Management work item, which mentions windowing systems as one of the paradigms for the multifaceted operations of which the workstation is capable. There has, however, been a project within a task group of ANSI X3H3 discussing the Display Manager and its relationship to existing graphics standards, and most of the conclusions here are based on those discussions.

As outlined in Chap. 1, the window paradigm for interactive working will impact the underlying device architecture assumed by all members of the family of graphics standards. At present, all the standards are based on an explicit expectation that the resources available to a graphics device are dedicated and static. There is no mechanism to allow the window manager to interrupt an established CGI session to indicate that resources have been changed (for example, the operator has resized the window in which the CGI's display is being shown). Even were there such a mechanism, the interrelation would still need some considerable clarification (e.g., does the resize operation change the size of the CGI's display surface, or does the window manager maintain a separate record of the complete virtual surface and its contents, which is then only partially displayed on the physical display surface at any one time?).

If and when window standards do come into the ISO arena, it is likely that their clients will maintain a separate command stream direct to the display manager independently of the graphics commands being sent to the virtual workstation running in a window. It would then be on this data stream that the window manager informed the *client*, rather than the implementation of the graphics system, of relevant resource changes. The client would then be expected to react appropriately to take into account the changed resources.

In parallel to the work of X3H3, it is likely that the X system will be presented via the "fast-track" procedure for adoption at the DIS stage within ISO (see Appendix C for the relevance of this mechanism). The essential problem with this approach is that X contains not just those aspects concerned with the control of multiple windows, but also a series of graphics generating functions, which occupy a very similar position in the applications pipeline to the CGI in the reference model outlined above, but with some important differences. As such the two should be reviewed together, but the ability to do this will be severely impaired if the proponents of X are successful in by-passing the normal ISO review process.

The relationships described above all concern the use of the CGI to feed graphics to a window of the windowing system. The other possible relationship is that of regarding the windowing system as a sophisticated application, which runs on a single set of dedicated graphics hardware–the exact definition of the CGI's client. In these circumstances, if the CGI has the correct facilities to support such a client, there is no reason why the CGI should not support a portable windowing environment. However, at the time we were writing this book, the windows "community" has yet to input into the CGI processing any requirements that might allow this scenario to be addressed, and the first version of the CGI has not, and will not, be designed with support of a windowing client as a primary objective.

2.6.8 Relationship with PostScript

Another system receiving considerable interest in the standards arena is PostScript™, which is a page composition language and, as such, overlaps with both the CGI and the CGM. From the point of view of the standards process, the overlap with CGI is rather spurious, because there are obvious differences of intent between an output-only page description language and an interactive system like the CGI. There are, however, some proposals to add input functionality to the definition of PostScript; this would obviously increase the overlap. It should, however, be easier to ensure that the output functionality is based on the CGI, if the eventual work in this area is properly reviewed by the page description language groups within ISO/IEC JTC1/SC18. The relationship between Office Document Architecture standards and the CGM is already well established and should set a precedent for future cooperation involving standards with a graphics component.

2.6.9 Relationship with ISO Register of Graphical Items

For certain functions, the CGI defines value ranges as being reserved for registration or future standardization. The values and their meanings will be defined using the procedures established for coordinating registration across graphics standards. These *Procedures for Registration of Graphical Items* have been approved by ISO and are being administered by the US National Bureau of Standards, functioning as an ISO Registration Authority.

It is intended that the CGI's usage of registered values (such as line and marker types) be identical with their usage in other graphics standards.

2.7 Main Concepts

The objective of the CGI is to provide for the description and communication of graphical information between a client program and a virtual graphics device in a device-independent manner. To accomplish this, the CGI standard, which is formally divided into six interrelated Parts, defines the form (syntax) and functional behaviour (semantics) of a set of functions that may occur in a CGI session. The Part structure of the CGI will occasionally be referred to in this book. The CGI functions are divided into several types as described below:

- Control Functions (described in Part 2 of the standard), which specify the modes of operation of certain other functions; which specify the address space to be used; which select the protocols for exchange of data; which provide for session initialization and termination; and which control the device's operation.

- Output Primitive Functions (Part 3), which describe the visual components of a picture on the virtual graphics device.

- Attribute Functions (also in Part 3), which further describe and elaborate the appearance of output primitive functions.

- Raster Functions (Part 6), which can be used to generate and manipulate bit-mapped images targetted for display on raster devices.

- Segmentation Functions (Part 4), which can be used to store and manipulate groups of primitives and their attributes.

- Input Functions (Part 5), which provide the CGI client with the ability to obtain graphical input from the virtual graphics device in different ways and to control the form and timing of that acquisition of information.

- External Functions (Part 2), which communicate information not directly related to the generation of a graphical image.

- Escape Functions (Part 2), which permit device-dependent or implementation-dependent features to be accessed by the client through the CGI in a device-independent manner. These functions are not otherwise standardized, but they may be registered so that communities of users can share in the definition of these otherwise implementation-dependent features.

2.7.1 The CGI Pipeline

Figure 2.2 shows a schematic version of the graphics pipeline recently adopted by the CGI project. When detailed, this pipeline is much more explicit than the pipeline included in the other graphics standards and shows the state of the graphics data at each point in the pipeline. It is still being refined and the latest detail is included in Chap. 8. A particular feature of this model is that it helps to demonstrate the interrelation between the various parts of the standard and to highlight the potential conflicts. This has direct impact on the analysis of the states of the CGI system, because the setting of the state variable is represented typically by the setting of a switch in the pipeline.

The output pipeline begins with an area where compound primitives are assembled (for example, closed figures or compound text–see Chap. 8). Beyond this, the primitive's attributes are bound (see Chap. 3) and, if a segment is being defined, the primitive is routed to be added to the segment's definition (see Chap. 7). If the segment is being drawn to the display, the primitive is also passed further down the pipeline where it collects the data defining the representation of its attributes on the workstation in use. If a raster bitmap is being defined (see Chap. 5), the primitive will be rendered into the pixel store and be combined with the image already stored in pixel format. Finally, the pixels are displayed on the screen either directly or by passing through a colour lookup table (see Chap. 8).

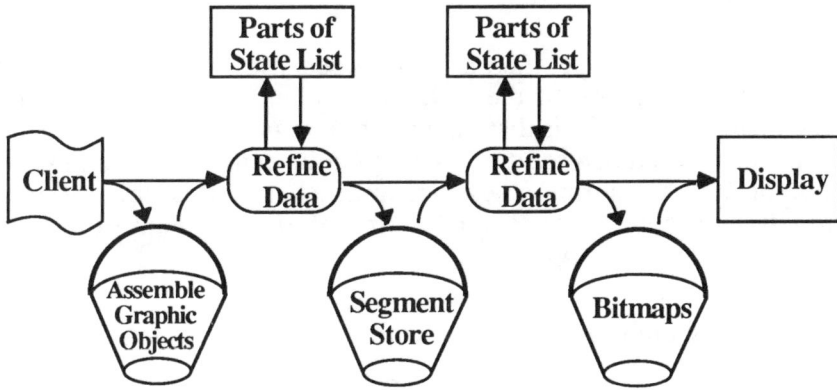

Fig. 2.2. Schematic Output Pipeline for the CGI

The input pipeline really only interacts with this model in the cases of LOCATOR, STROKE and PICK input classes (see Chap. 6). The principal components of the input pipeline involve the inverse transformation of data from the raw device coordinates of STROKE and LOCATOR inputs to positions in Virtual Device Coordinates (VDC) and the redisplay of this positional information by introducing the echo information into the output.

Echo information is displayed conceptually at the very last stage of the pipeline and does not, therefore, end up stored in segments or in bitmaps but is transient. The echo for PICK input will normally use the contents of a segment to reflect the segment identifier and pick identifier chosen by the PICK operation.

2.7.2 The CGI State Model

The review of the current draft CGI standard has led to adoption of the concept of minimal state constraints on the client, who is, after all, meant to be a sophisticated user. The implication of this is that, unless there are states in which the use of particular functions would lead to unstable or ill-defined states in the CGI itself, functions should not be prohibited. However, it also means that functions may be permitted in circumstances where they may not damage the state of the system, but their use does not make a lot of sense. An example of this might be a SELECT DRAWING BITMAP when a segment is partially defined. Does the whole segment definition get sent to the new display bitmap or are the parts that are sent restricted to new primitives being added to the segment definition? The implication is that the CGI is intended for the sophisticated client, and unsophisticated or unknowledgeable use is liable to lead to circumstances not predicted by the client.

2.7.3 Interrogation and Inquiry

Both of these types of operation are concerned with returning information from the implementation of the CGI to the client. The distinction made between them in DP 9636 is that interrogation returns information about the capabilities of the implementation, while inquiry returns information about the state of the CGI during a session. In practical terms, this means that interrogation is equivalent to an inquiry of the contents of the fixed Description Tables (see App. D).

2.7.4 CGI Error Philosophy

The error philosophy is closely related to the philosophy regarding the generation of state constraints. In other words, the intention is that there should be very few error conditions, but that those which remain as error conditions are necessary for some classes of client and therefore rigidly controlled.

Errors in the CGI are classified in seven classes of increasing level of severity. For more trivial errors, a conforming implementation may not even be required to detect the error. In addition, a second part of the error philosophy is that the CGI will be used to support implementations of systems that require a very efficient service and that, once a system is thoroughly debugged and installed, there will only be occasional (and probably fatal) errors requiring error checking and release of a new debugged version. Provision is therefore made to allow error detection and reporting to be suppressed in the installed version of systems based on CGI.

Chapter 3

Elementary CGI Output and Attribute Functions

3.1 Introduction

Part 3 of the CGI describes the functions that define graphic objects. This includes both the primitives' geometry and the attributes that affect the final rendering of the objects on the display surface. The Part also defines a few control functions provided specifically to affect the behaviour of the other functions in the Part. This is by far the largest Part of the CGI and many of the functions are identical or correspond closely to CGM functions.

In addition Part 3 defines the Output Description Table and State List, which may be inquired within any CGI implementation. As for other Parts, the functions to perform these inquiries depend on the binding or encoding used, but generic rules are provided for converting the State Lists and Description Tables into a definition of the functions to be bound.

Although the output primitives and attribute functions are grouped into sections in the draft CGI standard, they will be considered together here with the primitives being considered along with their attributes. Primitives in the CGI are divided into five classes:

- Line functions
- A marker function
- Text functions
- Filled area functions
- A cell array function.

In addition, there is the Generalized Drawing Primitive, which is intended to allow access to any "native" primitives on a device that are not directly addressed by other primitives.

24   Part I: The Computer Graphics Interface

The reader should note that these are not the only functions that can cause visible effects at the display surface. For example, the bitblt functions of Part 6 of the CGI (see Chap. 5) include a pixel array function, which routes client-defined image portions directly to the device's bitmaps, and control functions, which force updating of the display, will also cause visible effects.

Associated with each class of output primitive is a set of attributes. For most attributes the client can control whether a modal value (called the INDIVIDUAL value) or an entry from a table, which accesses all the different attributes for any class (the BUNDLE table) via a single bundle index, is used. Strictly speaking the bundle index in this case is defined as the attribute (the distinction is important because the settings of attributes are stored in segments, but the contents of bundle representations are not). The choice of which source is used for any attribute is controlled by the use of Aspect Source Flags, which may be set to either INDIVIDUAL or BUNDLED for each attribute independently. The ASFs themselves are also defined as attributes. Figure 3.1(a) shows the simplest use of the bundle table mechanism, while when adding the ASF mechanism we get the situation in Fig. 3.1(b).

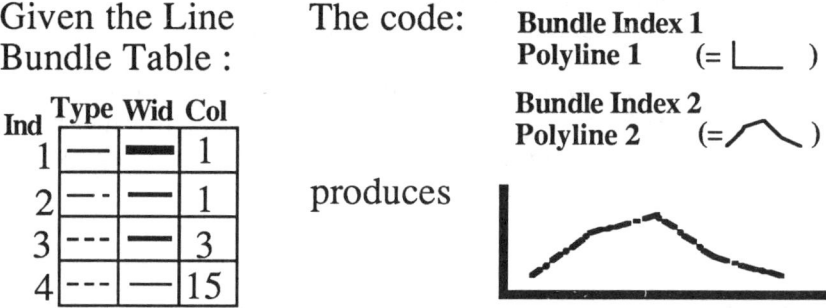

Fig. 3.1(a). Simple use of bundle tables

The origins of this technique for distinguishing the source of attribute values lie in the development of GKS where some aspects were felt to be essentially workstation independent in an environment of multiple active workstations. Because the reason for this distinction was the feeling that geometric attributes were a characteristic of the picture and should not vary between workstations, but be transformable, INDIVIDUAL attributes are sometimes also called geometric attributes. This model of the differing types of attribute has been carried forward to the CGI work, although the CGI supports only a single workstation, removing some of the rationale from the original approach. Supporting the model directly in the CGI permits a GKS implementation to move more of the graphics pipeline to the virtual device.

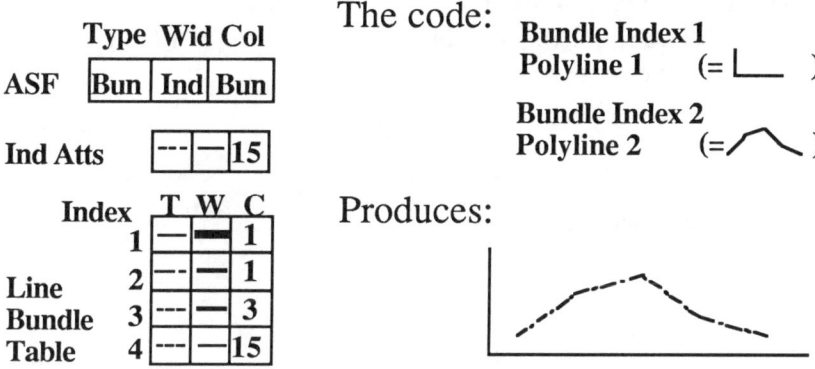

Fig. 3.1(b). Adding the ASFs to the example in Fig. 3.1(a)

3.2 Line Class Graphic Objects

3.2.1 Line Class Primitives

The six primitives in this class are:

- POLYLINE, which draws a set of connected lines through successive points given in a point list (Fig. 3.2(a)).

- CIRCULAR ARC 3 POINT, which generates a circular arc from the two end points and one other point on the arc (Fig. 3.2(b)).

- CIRCULAR ARC CENTRE, which generates a circular arc from centre point, radius and two radial vectors defining start and end vectors (Fig. 3.2(c)).

- DISJOINT POLYLINE, CIRCULAR ARC CENTRE BACKWARDS and ELLIPTICAL ARC (see Chap. 8).

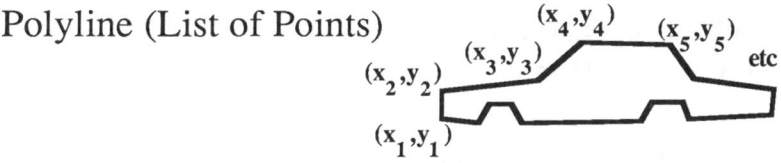

Fig. 3.2(a). Polyline primitive

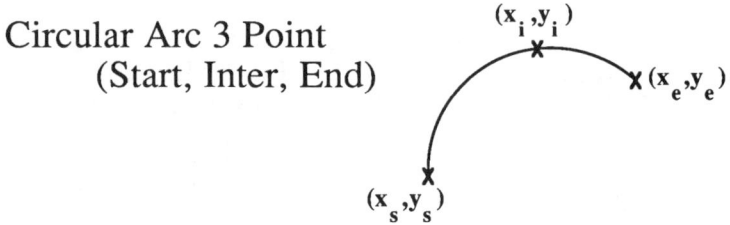

Fig. 3.2(b). Circular Arc 3 Point

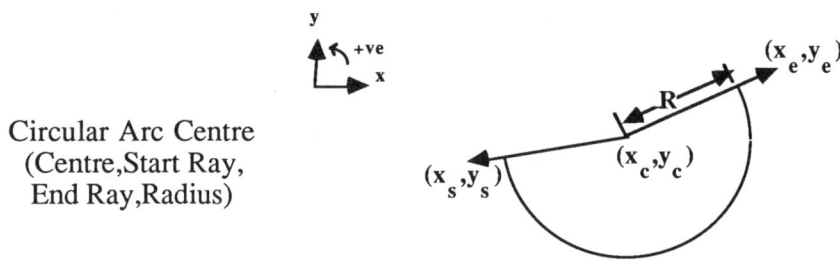

Fig. 3.2(c). Circular Arc Centre

The sense of the arcs is defined such that Circular Arc Centre draws the arc by following the circle in a positive angular direction defined by VDC Extent (see Fig. 4.3) from start ray to end ray. The different parameterizations of Circular Arcs have their applicability in different circumstances. The Circular Arc 3 Point is useful where an arc needs to be defined, but the centre of the circle may lie outside the device's VDC space. Circular Arc Centres are useful in some geometric constructions. Note that, in DP 9636, Circular Arc Centre and Circular Arc 3 Point were transformed differently by segment transformations, but this situation has been corrected by more recent decisions, and the primitives are now all transformed as in GKS by transforming the loci of points given by the primitive's definition.

3.2.2 Attributes of Line Class Primitives

Each primitive in the Line Class is rendered using four attributes, plus the associated ASFs (see Fig. 3.1):

- LINE TYPE (e.g., *solid*, *dotted*, etc.)
- LINE WIDTH (see Sect. 8.9 for details)
- LINE COLOUR (see Sect. 8.9 for details)
- A LINE BUNDLE INDEX for selecting an entry from the line bundle table.

For any attribute, a number of values are predefined in the standard. For example, five line types are predefined as in the CGM Standard:

1 : solid
2 : dash
3 : dot
4 : dash dot
5 : dash dot dot

Other positive numbers are reserved to be used to extend the standard by registration of other styles; negative numbers are available to allow implementations to provide private styles.

In general, when dimensions are defined by scaling factors, the standard defines the actual size as that which is closest to the product of the nominal size of the object and the scaling factor requested. Where colour tables are used, they all reference a single colour table.

3.3 Polymarker Primitive and Attributes

The only primitive in the marker class is POLYMARKER, which takes a list of points and displays a marker at each point. Figure 3.3 shows an example using the same point list as in Fig 3.2(a) and assuming marker index 3 is the currently selected marker type.

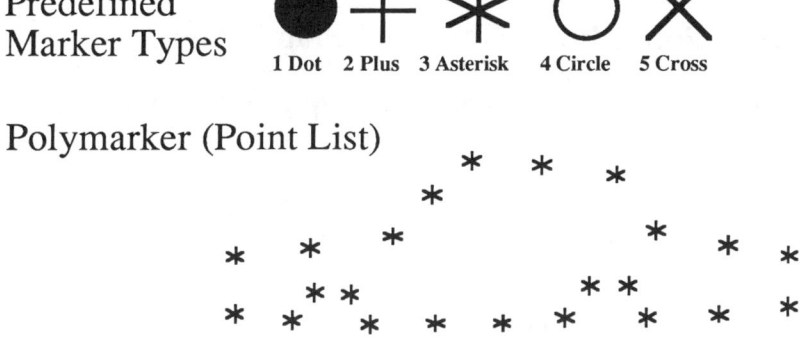

Fig. 3.3. Polymarker primitive and predefined types

Markers are rendered according to the following attributes, plus the associated ASFs (see Fig. 3.1):

- MARKER TYPE (e.g., triangles, circles, asterisks, etc.)
- MARKER SIZE (See Sect. 8.9 for details)
- MARKER COLOUR (See Sect. 8.9 for details)
- A MARKER BUNDLE INDEX for selecting an entry from the marker bundle table.

3.4 Text

3.4.1 Introduction to Text Primitives and Attributes

Three primitives comprise the text class:

- TEXT (Fig. 3.4(a))
- RESTRICTED TEXT
- APPEND TEXT.

Only the simple TEXT primitive is described in this chapter; the others are described in Chap. 8. This means that examples in this chapter are restricted to using the value *final* for the second parameter of the TEXT function.

Text(Point, Final/Non-final Flag,String)

eg   Text((X,Y),"Final","Sample Text String")

Sample Text String

(X,Y)

Fig. 3.4. Simple use of the Text primitive

The text string is rendered according to the text attributes, which are not all available as both individual (modal) and bundled attributes:

- Text attributes available only individually:
  - CHARACTER HEIGHT
  - CHARACTER ORIENTATION
  - TEXT PATH
  - TEXT ALIGNMENT
  - CHARACTER SET INDEX (See Sect. 13.7 for details)
  - ALTERNATE CHARACTER SET INDEX (See Sect. 13.7)
  - TEXT BUNDLE INDEX.

- Text attributes available either individually or bundled:
  - TEXT FONT INDEX
  - TEXT PRECISION
  - CHARACTER EXPANSION FACTOR
  - CHARACTER SPACING
  - TEXT COLOUR.

It should be obvious just from the length of this list that Text is a complex area, and it is the most complex of the primitives in the CGI. The TEXT primitive itself is a list of indices to a character set, which by its nature defines a complex shape covering an area of the picture. Also associated with the basic primitive is a reference point in VDC, but obviously there are many ways of mapping the set of characters relative to this point.

3.4.2 Font Description Coordinate System

Every character in a font is described in a character box (Fig. 3.5), the extremes of which are referred to as "left," "right," "top," and "bottom." At the midpoint between left and right is "centre," and "half" lies midway between top and bottom. In addition there are two other reference points on the vertical axis, called "base" and "cap." For proportionally spaced fonts the distance from left to right will vary from character to character, but, with the exception of kerns, all visible parts of the character must lie within this box, which is called the *character body*. The CHARACTER HEIGHT attribute refers to the distance between base and cap lines along the CHARACTER UP VECTOR (i.e., not necessarily perpendicular to the direction of writing).

3.4.3 Character Expansion Factor and Character Spacing

Fonts are assumed to be designed such that a text string composed of character bodies which abut, either horizontally or vertically, will give properly spaced characters. It is therefore assumed that a certain amount of space is built into each character in its definition. The CHARACTER SPACING function specifies any additional space to be added, as a fraction of the current CHARACTER HEIGHT (Fig. 3.6).The CHARACTER EXPANSION FACTOR specifies the deviation from the aspect ratio of the original font design (Fig. 3.7).

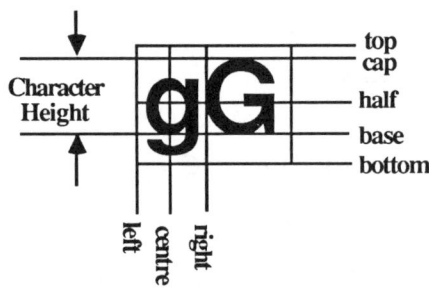

Fig. 3.5. Font description coordinate system

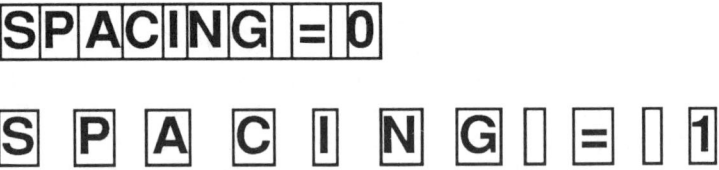

Fig. 3.6. Effect of Character Spacing attribute

Character Expansion Factor(1)

Character Expansion Factor(2)

Character Expansion Factor(.5)

Fig. 3.7. Effect of Character Expansion Factor

3.4.4 Character Orientation

The CHARACTER ORIENTATION function specifies two vectors, a character up vector and a character baseline vector. These vectors need not be orthogonal and, if they are not, *skewed characters* will generally result. Since character height is measured along the character up vector, the perpendicular distance will be less than that set by the character height function (Fig. 3.8).

Fig. 3.8. Non-orthogonal Character Baseline and Up Vector

3.4.5 Text Path

This attribute controls the "direction of writing" and may take one of four values–*up, down, left,* or *right*. Note that this attribute relates to the relative positioning of successive character bodies in the string. For example, *up* means "place successive character bodies above each other" (along the character up vector); the others are also specified relative to the character baseline or character up vector (Fig. 3.9).

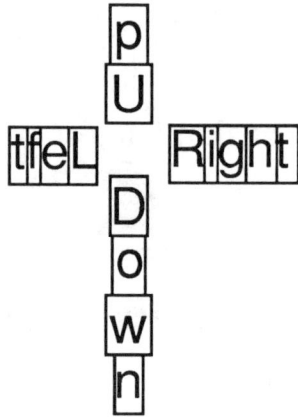

Fig. 3.9. Effect of Text Path Attribute

3.4.6 Text Alignment

Having defined all the geometric aspects of the text primitive, the size and shape of the text string (the text extent) can be calculated and the string can be displayed. The text alignment controls the positioning of the text extent rectangle relative to the text position, as given in the TEXT primitive definition (Fig. 3.4). Text alignment operates either discretely via horizontal alignments *left, centre, right* or *normal horizontal* and vertical alignments *top, cap, half, base, bottom,* or *normal vertical*, or *continuous* offsets in terms of numbers of character heights can be specified numerically. Both "normal" values are defined as variable values depending upon text path. A combination of the horizontal and vertical alignments defines a position on the text extent rectangle (Fig. 3.10). There is an interaction between the interpretation of the alignment parameters and the text path. This interaction is predictable, although a more complex problem than might be expected at first glance.

For Text Path *left* or *right*:

TOPLINE	=	TOPLINE farthest from baseline
CAPLINE	=	CAPLINE " " "
HALFLINE	=	HALFLINE " " "
BOTTOMLINE	=	BOTTOMLINE farthest from baseline
LEFT	=	Leftmost edge of leftmost character body
RIGHT	=	Rightmost " " " " "
CENTRE	=	Halfway between left and right edges

A similar table applies for Text Path *up* and *down*.

Chapter 3: Elementary CGI Output and Attribute Functions   33

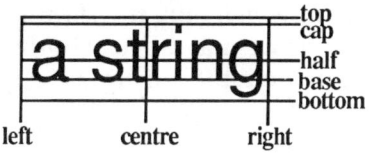

Text Alignment (Centre,Top,0,0)
Text((X,Y),"Final",
       "Top Centre")

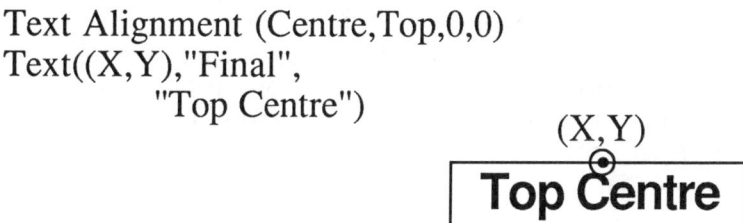

Fig. 3.10. Text Alignment Parameters

In addition, either or both alignments can take the value *continuous*, which uses a second argument (real data type) of the alignment to define the number of "normalised" text extent rectangles of an offset from the text position given in the text primitive along the character up and character base vectors (Fig. 3.11).

Text Alignment(Left,Continuous Vertical,0,0)
Text((X,Y),"Final","First Line")
Text Alignment(Left,Continuous Vertical,0,2.0)
Text((X,Y),"Final","Second Line")

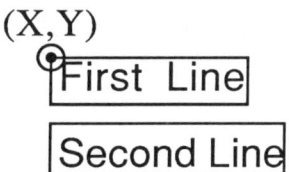

Fig. 3.11. *Continuous* Text Alignment values

3.4.7 Text Precision

The text attributes mentioned so far describe a complex set of intended effects, with the expectation that not every system will be able to meet the complete specification. Three levels of realisation of the text requested are recognised by the CGI (Fig 3.12):

- *string* precision, in which only the starting point of the text string is guaranteed. The string may appear horizontal from that point and the manner in which the string is clipped is implementation dependent.

- *character* precision, in which the start point of each character is guaranteed giving the effect of character strings at an angle etc., but the individual characters are not guaranteed to have the correct size, skew or orientation. Characters wholly inside or outside a clipping rectangle are handled correctly, but those partially intersected by the clipping rectangle are clipped in an implementation dependent manner.

- *stroke* precision, in which the CGI will display the primitive accurately with respect to all attributes, and clipping will be to the accuracy of the device.

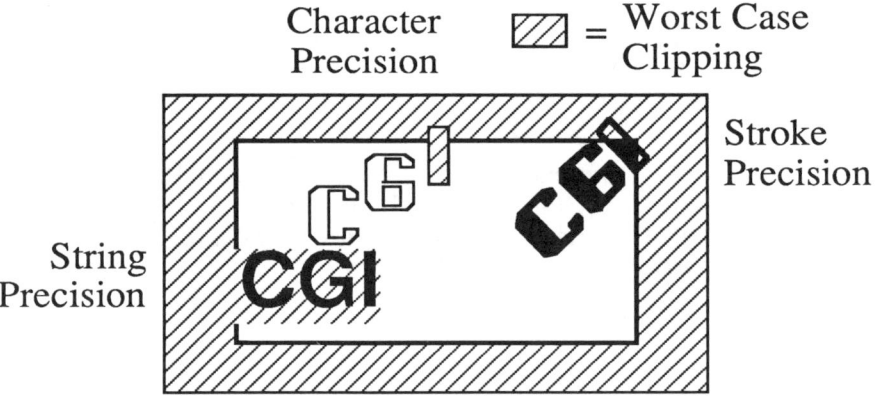

Fig. 3.12. Text precisions

The text precision attribute supplied by the client is a measure of the amount of tolerance the client would like in rendering the text, but a CGI can be conforming without supporting the full text model as described above. If the CGI implementation cannot support the requested value of text precision, it will use the next best available precision and will return this value in response to an inquiry as to the current text precision.

3.5 Filled Area Primitives

There are eight primitives and one composition technique that are subject to the filled area attributes, as follows:

- POLYGON, which generates an area defined by a set of bounding edges derived from a list of points (Fig. 3.13).

- POLYGON SET, which generates a number of areas, defined from a set of points and flags that indicate whether the associated point closes an individual polygon and whether the edge defined by the point will be drawn or not (Fig. 3.13).

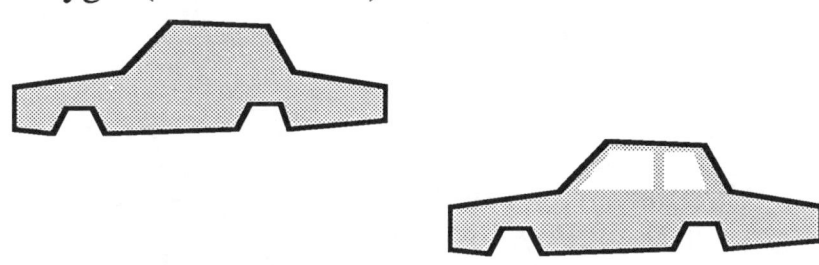

Fig. 3.13. Polygon primitive types

- RECTANGLE, which draws a rectangle parallel to VDC axes (Fig. 3.14). Note that according to DP 9636, if a rectangle were stored in a rotated segment, then only the defining corners are rotated and the rectangle's aspect ratio will change.

- CIRCLE (Fig. 3.14).

- CIRCULAR ARC 3 POINT CLOSE draws a circular arc made into an area by closing the arc with either a chord joining the end points (*chord* closure), or two radii (*pie* closure). The circular arc is defined as in the CIRCULAR ARC 3 POINT line primitive (Fig. 3.15).

- CIRCULAR ARC CENTRE CLOSE, in which the area is defined as above, with the circle parameterization as in the CIRCULAR ARC CENTRE primitive (Fig. 3.15).

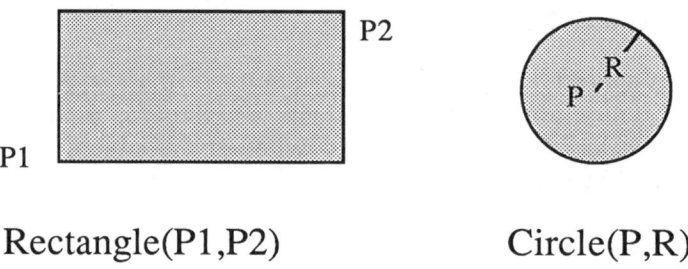

Fig. 3.14. Simple geometric Fill Area primitives

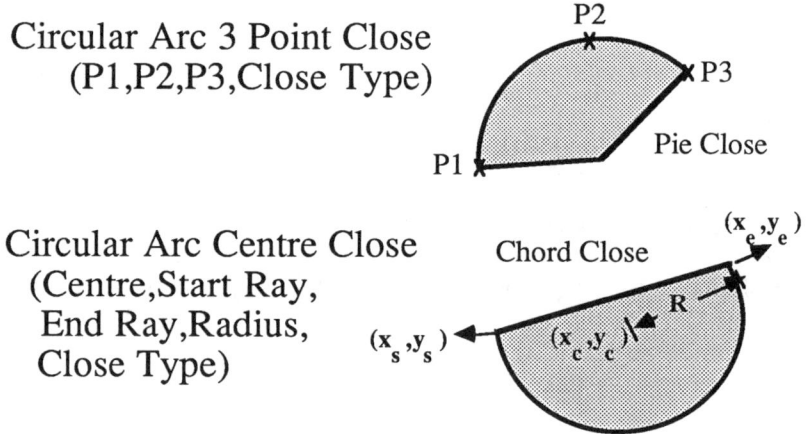

Fig. 3.15. Circular Arc Close Fill Area primitives

The filled area primitives are rendered using two groups of attributes, one controlling the rendering of the interior and the other the rendering of the edges. The filled primitive is treated as if the edge rendering takes priority over the display of the interior. Attributes affecting the interior are:

- Fill Area attributes available only individually:
    - FILL REFERENCE POINT
    - PATTERN SIZE
    - FILL BUNDLE INDEX.

- Fill area attributes available either individually or bundled:
    - INTERIOR STYLE
    - FILL COLOUR
    - HATCH INDEX
    - PATTERN INDEX
    - FILL BITMAP.

The use of these attributes is controlled by the INTERIOR STYLE, which may have one of five values defined in Part 3: *hollow, solid, pattern, hatch,* or *empty* (Fig. 3.16); an additional interior style *bitmap* is available where the implementation of the CGI supports raster operations (see Chap. 5).

Interior style *empty* displays nothing for the interior, but the edge of the area is subject to the edge attributes and visibility flags, as discussed below.

For interior style *hollow*, the boundary of the area is considered to be a rendering of the interior and is drawn using the currently selected fill colour with implementation dependent line type and line width.

Interior style *solid* describes the expected solid colour specified by the current fill colour.

Interior style *hatch* uses the current hatch index and fill colour to cross hatch the area. The internal description of the hatch pattern is implementation dependent, and the rendering of the gaps between hatch lines is subject to the transparency control (see Chap. 8).

Interior style *pattern* uses the current pattern index to access the description of the pattern in the pattern table. A pattern is defined as a rectangular array of colours by the PATTERN TABLE function (either as RGB values or as indices into a colour table). This pattern is repeated to fill the whole area, starting from the FILL REFERENCE POINT, with a repeat size given by the current pattern size. The fill reference point and the two vectors given in the PATTERN SIZE function define a parallelogram into which the whole pattern is mapped. On a raster device, with inherently limited resolution, the pixels of the display are allocated the colour definition of the cell containing their centre.

Interior style *bitmap* uses a client-defined bitmap portion to pattern fill, allowing the client to use other graphics primitives to assemble the pattern to be used. The methods of assembling the bitmap used for filling are described in Part 6 of the CGI. The fill bitmap is specified via an index.

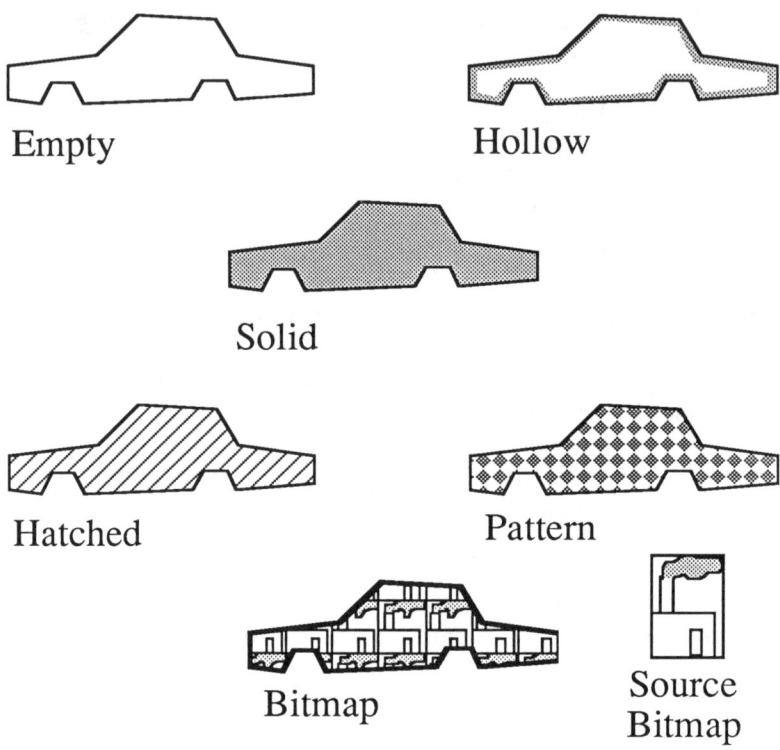

Fig. 3.16. Interior styles for Fill Area primitives

Attributes controlling the rendering of the edges of the filled area are all available either individually or bundled:

- EDGE TYPE
- EDGE WIDTH
- EDGE COLOUR.

which all operate identically to the equivalent line attributes. The bundle table containing these entries is controlled by an EDGE BUNDLE INDEX, which is a further attribute. These attributes are used to render the edges of the filled area if the EDGE VISIBILITY is set *on*. The POLYGON SET primitive definition contains an additional set of flags that indicate which edges of the boundary should be drawn and which remain invisible. These flags are used only if the edge visibility flag is *on*. A similar set of flags is assembled during the definition of a closed figure (see Chap. 8), but the edges of a closed figure also differ from other filled areas in that different attributes may be used for individual edges if an implementation supports this feature.

Chapter 4

Control and Error Handling

Part 2 of the draft CGI standard covers the topics of Control, Negotiation, and Error Handling, and the functionality is grouped into four sections:

- Virtual Device Management, concerned with managing the dialogue session and with global operations on the graphic image.

- Coordinate Space Control, for establishing correct transmission of coordinate information and for management of the coordinate space.

- Error Management, concerned with error detection, reporting, and reaction.

- Miscellaneous Control.

In addition, CGI Part 2 contains a definition of the Device Description Table, representing an implementation's capabilities in each area, and the Control State List, containing the current settings of all data items related to this part of the proposal. The entries in both are all inquirable, but the exact mechanism for the inquiries is left (as for all Parts) to the specific language bindings or data stream encodings. This allows the inquiry mechanism to exploit the relevant features in particular bindings; that is, a high-level language binding might return pointers to complete data structures, while a data encoding might return individual items at the lowest level of the data structure.

4.1 Virtual Device Management

4.1.1 Managing a Dialogue Session

The INITIALIZE function is provided to set up the system for a session of CGI use. The defaults are set, the display surface cleared, and any intermediate storage (e.g., segment and raster stores) emptied.

During a session, the RESET TO DEFAULTS function in DP 9636 returns all attribute values and specification modes to their defaults, but it does not affect the display surface or intermediate storage. However, this function is being reconsidered and may disappear in the next revision of the document.

The TERMINATE function ends the session of CGI use.

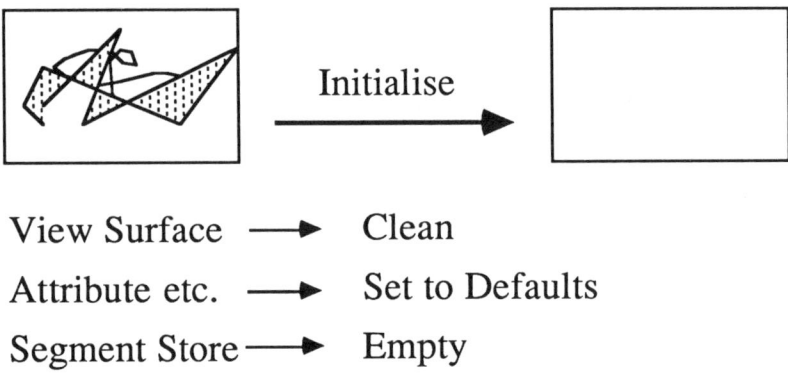

Fig. 4.1(a). Effects of initialising the CGI

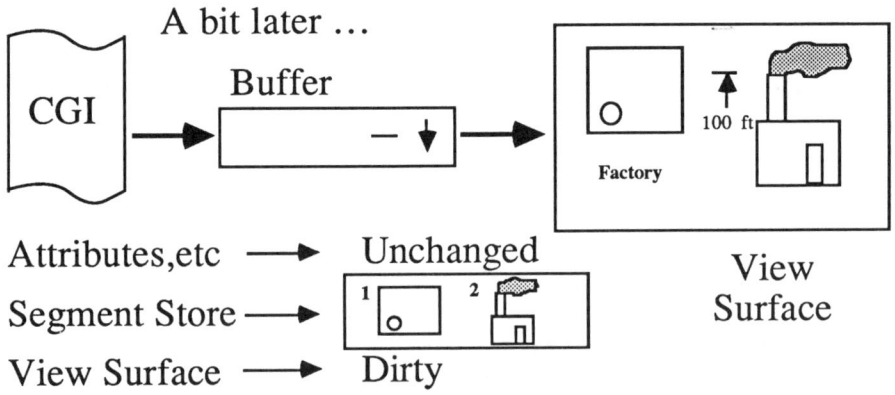

Fig. 4.1(b). Assembly of CGI page

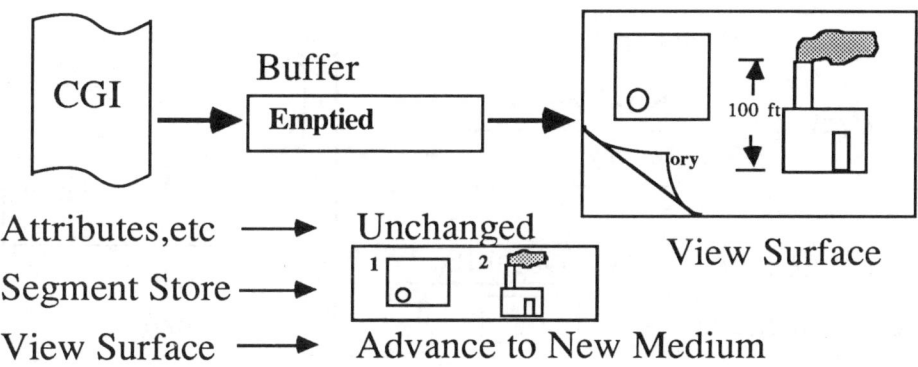

Fig. 4.1(c). Effect of End Page for Hardcopy Devices

4.1.2 Managing the Display Surface

The PREPARE VIEW SURFACE function provides the means to start a fresh image. It makes use of a parameter according to the type of device being used to decide whether a "clean" hardcopy display surface should be forced to advance or not. SET BACKGROUND COLOUR is used before a softcopy device is prepared for a new image and determines the background colour to be used when the surface is prepared. Finally, the END PAGE function forces an implicit MAKE PICTURE CURRENT and leaves the screen of a softcopy device unchanged, but it does advance the hardcopy output medium if the display surface is "dirty." Figures 4.1(a-e) illustrate the effects of these fundamental control functions.

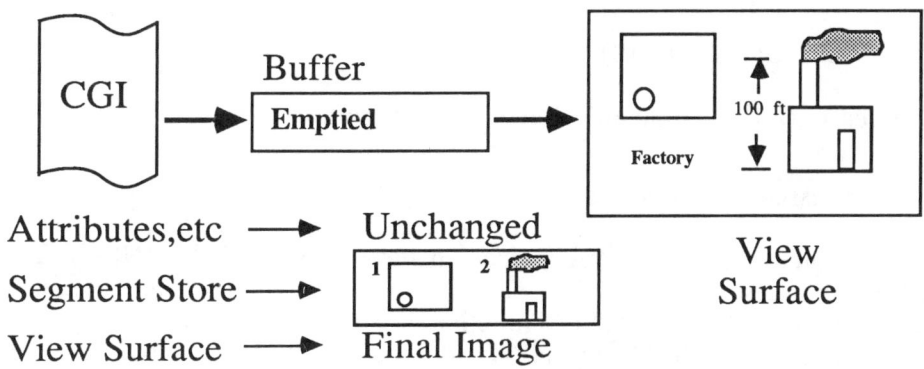

Fig. 4.1(d). Effect of End Page for softcopy devices

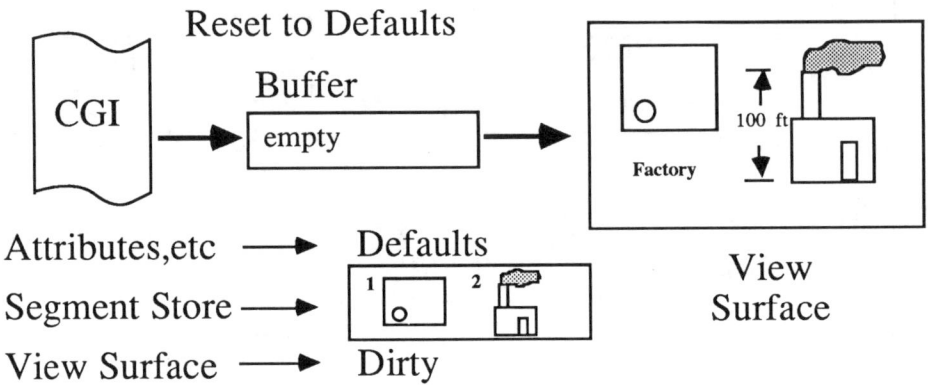

Fig. 4.1(e). Effect of RESET TO DEFAULTS

4.1.3 Controlling Deferral Modes and Regeneration

Functions are provided in this area to allow the client to advise the buffering system for the graphics output of the level of performance required and to make sure that the picture seen by the operator is complete at particular times. The functions DEFERRAL MODE and MAKE PICTURE CURRENT are used to accomplish this control. Three modes of deferral can be set:

- ASTI (meaning "At Some TIme")

- BNI (or "Before Next Interaction")

- ASAP (as normal!)

Figures 4.2(a-f) illustrate the effects of these modes.

4.1.4 Classes of CGIDevices

Three device classes are recognised in the CGI–OUTPUT, INPUT, and OUTIN classes. OUTPUT class devices accept only output data but can be used with the ECHO OUTPUT functionality as the output side of a pair of coordinated OUTPUT and INPUT devices. Similarly INPUT devices provide only INPUT data but may be coordinated as the input side of a coordinated pair. OUTIN devices provide interaction on a single device but may be used as either side of a coordinated pair of CGI devices for remote echoing. The possibilities are further elaborated in Chap. 9.

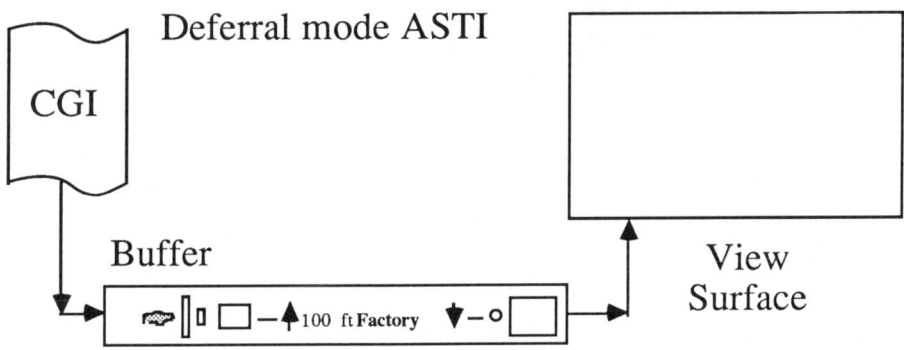

Fig. 4.2(a). Buffering and Deferral Mode ASTI

4.2 Characteristics of Output Devices

Output devices have one rectangular display surface and are categorised as Hardcopy or Softcopy on the basis of the medium that implements the display surface. The display surface of a hardcopy device is "replaced for each new image," while the display surface of softcopy devices are cleared "electronically." Given the variety of display technologies, the distinction between these types is still grey, but appears to be useful in a range of situations.

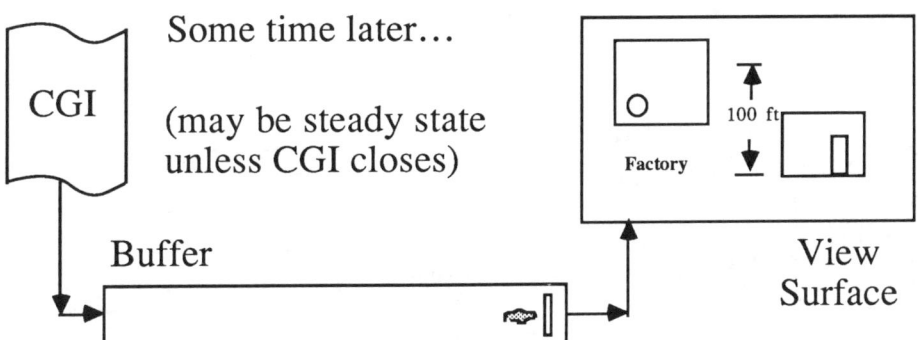

Fig. 4.2(b). Buffering and Deferral Mode ASTI

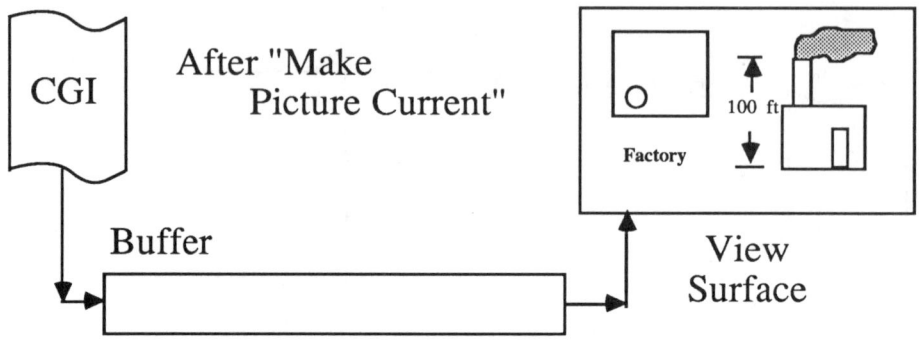

Fig. 4.2(c). Buffering and Deferral Mode ASTI

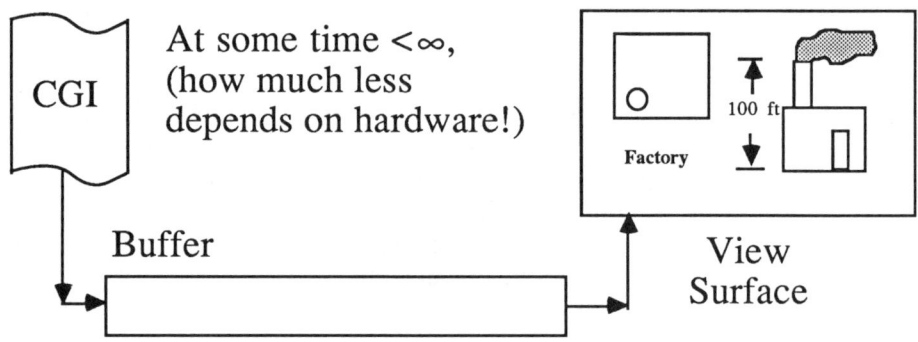

Fig. 4.2(d). Buffering and Deferral Mode ASAP

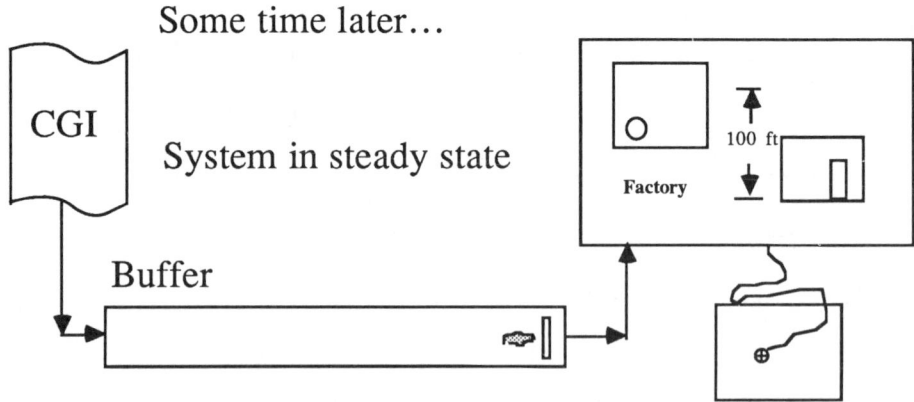

Fig. 4.2(e). Buffering and Deferral Modes (BNI)

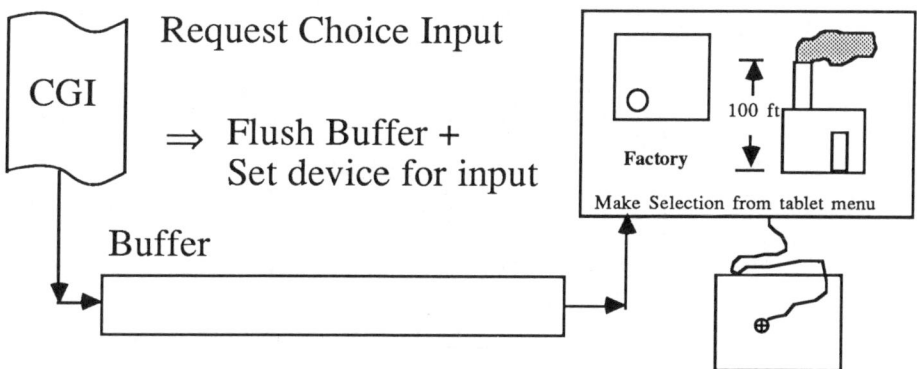

Fig. 4.2(f). Buffering and Deferral Mode BNI

4.3 Coordinate Space Control

Primitives, some attributes, and some viewing control data are specified in Virtual Device Coordinates, or VDC. VDC Space is continuous and infinite, while VDC Range is of finite precision and magnitude. VDC coordinates are related to Device Coordinates (DC) by a mapping from VDC EXTENT to DEVICE VIEWPORT. Isotropy in this mapping is expected, but not mandated, and may be ensured explicitly by a CGI command (DEVICE VIEWPORT MAPPING), or by interrogating display addressing units. VDC TYPE (*real* or *integer*) and VDC PRECISION may be set as well as the precisions of the other data types (see Sect. 4.8).

Specification of VDC extent is via two points in VDC and allows the sense of the axes on the display surface to be set. For each axis, positive is defined from the first specifying point toward the second. Positive angles go from the positive X-axis towards the positive Y-axis (see Fig. 4.3). Changing the VDC TYPE causes the VDC EXTENT to be set to the default appropriate to the new type.

The DEVICE VIEWPORT SPECIFICATION UNITS function selects units from one of three parameterisations: *% of display surface, mm with scale factor,* or *physical display address units*. The mapping depends on isotropy control. If isotropy is not forced, the mapping occurs directly, linearly in X and Y, but not necessarily uniformly. If isotropy is forced, the largest rectangle of correct aspect ratio is aligned in the Device Viewport according to horizontal and vertical alignment parameters. Forced isotropy and alignment values are all parameters of the DEVICE VIEWPORT MAPPING function (Fig. 4.4).

46   Part I: The Computer Graphics Interface

VDC extent (0,0,200,100)

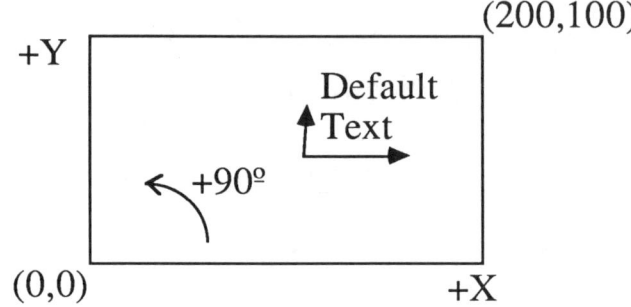

Fig. 4.3(a). Coordinate systems defined by VDC Extent

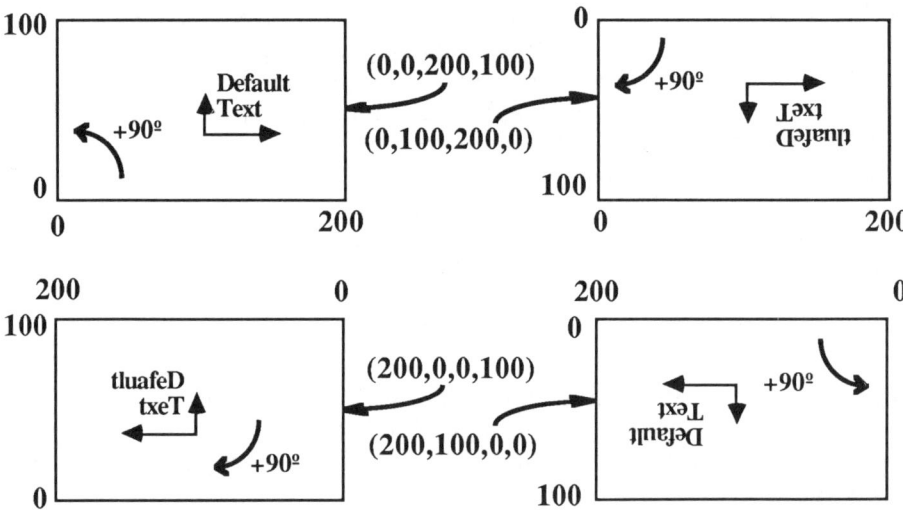

Fig. 4.3(b). Alternative systems defined by point order

Chapter 4: Control and Error Handling   47

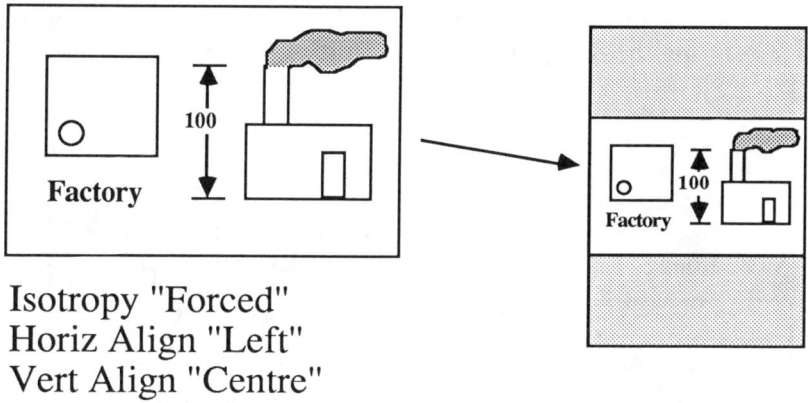

Isotropy "Forced"
Horiz Align "Left"
Vert Align "Centre"

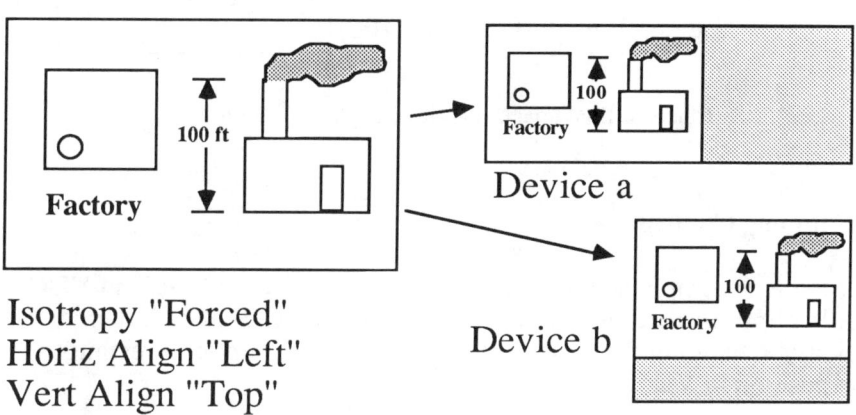

Isotropy "Forced"
Horiz Align "Left"
Vert Align "Top"

Fig. 4.4(a). Isotropic mapping control

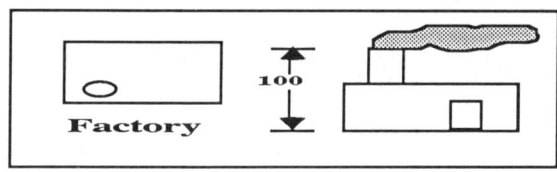

Fig. 4.4(b). Effect of anisotropic mapping from Fig 4.4(a)

Mirrored mapping of an entire image can be achieved by control of the order of specifying the device viewport defining corners (Fig. 4.5).

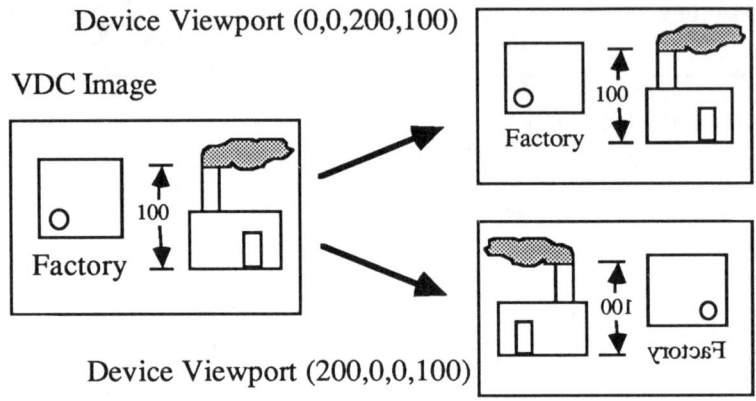

Fig. 4.5. Mirrored final image via Viewport specification

4.4 Clipping Control

Clipping is accomplished by specifying a CLIP RECTANGLE in VDC. The default clipping rectangle is defined as the VDC Extent but may be set explicitly. Changing the VDC Extent leaves the current clip rectangle in the same position in VDC space.

There are three modes of operation of clipping, the selection of which is controlled by the value of CLIP INDICATOR. These are:

- Clip to *clip rectangle*, which actually means the intersection of the clip rectangle with the viewport and the physical display bounds (Fig. 4.6(a)).

- Clip to *view surface*, which is equivalent to clip indicator *off* in the CGM (Fig. 4.6(b)).

- Clipping *off*, which means "really off," because all graphical primitives including those like CIRCLE–where the parameterisation points do not necessarily define the limits of the primitive's geometry and which may require further expansion–are nevertheless guaranteed not to overflow device limits. On devices which could be damaged by oversized images, it is recognised that the device is unlikely to trust itself to this mode of operation.

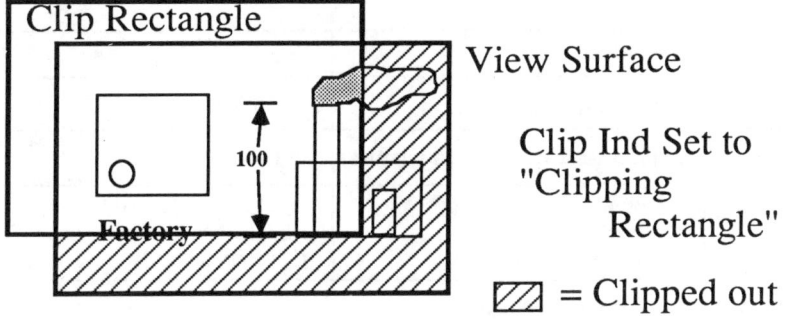

Fig. 4.6(a). Normal clipping

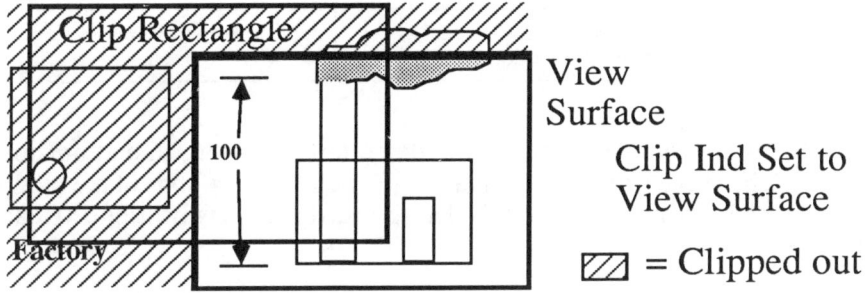

N.B. Clipping Indicator "Off" would be an error

Fig. 4.6(b). View surface clipping everything off the screen

4.5 Error Model

4.5.1 Error Classification Scheme

Classes of error are described in Part 1 of the draft CGI standard, and these seven categories are used throughout the draft (see Table 4.1). In this table, a *function* is a CGI element (e.g., linetype). A *feature* is some value of a function (e.g., linetype 5). *Request for* an unsupported feature may have a reasonable CGI response (e.g., linetype 8 mapped to linetype 1). *Use of* an unsupported feature may not be mappable–the error reaction may not be the same between request and use. At the level of the function, there is no difference between request and use. The model also includes a set of recommended behaviours by class.

Table 4.1. Error classification scheme in the CGI

Class	Description	Example
1	Invalid parameter description	Negative radius on CIRCLE
2	Request for Unsupported Feature	Set LINE_TYPE 8
3	Use of an Unsupported Feature	Set VDC_TYPE REAL when implementation handles INTEGERS only
4	Request for (and use of) an Unsupported Function	Any function not in a foundation profile
5	Disallowed use of function in certain states	Changing VDC_TYPE after first primitive has been specified
6	Internal CGI implementation failures	Overflowing buffers (strings, polygon vertices, etc.)
7	Failure requiring operator intervention	e.g., power failure

In Table 4.2, the requirements for detection, reaction, and reporting are shown. The standardised error reaction for classes 3, 4 and 5 takes the form "Ignore <what> until <when>". There are three possibilities for each of <what> and <when>; namely,

- possibilities for <what>:

    (a) Just this function;
    (b) All subsequent functions;
    (c) All subsequent functions in a special list.

- possibilities for <when>:
    (a) Until this function is set to a value supported by the implementation;
    (b) Until this state is exited;
    (c) Until the CGI session is TERMINATED.

In the draft CGI standard, the error report contains only an *error number* and a *function identifier*. The next draft of the CGI is expected to change the form of the error report to include the error class and to use a unique error number over all parts. The error numbers in Table 4.2 are from DP 9636.

Chapter 4: Control and Error Handling 51

Table 4.2. CGI error detection, reaction and reaction reporting by class

Class	Detection	Reaction	Report
1	Not required, but allowed	not detected	No report!
		detected: Guidelines from CGM document	Error No 101
2	Required	Ignore feature	Error No 201
		Map to supported feature	Error No 202
3	"	"Standardised Reaction"*	Error No 301
4	"	"Standardised Reaction"*	Error No 401
5	"	"Standardised Reaction"*	One error number per state (in range 501-599)
6	"	Described in full in CGI implementation. Since errror is implementation dependent so is error reaction	One per error type
7	"	"	"
* Recommendation is that lists of categories of CGI functions be identified. Reaction then is stated as "Ignore (list of functions)" until "certain state"			

4.5.2 Mechanism for Error Reporting

In DP 9636 errors are reported via a stack mechanism using the POP ERROR STACK and EMPTY ERROR STACK functions. In the revised version errors will be reported via a FIFO queue mechanism, which affects the order of reporting the errors to the client but not the philosophy for recording them. If the queue overflows, the last error report generated replaces the second to last, and a count of lost error reports is incremented. The oldest error report (first detected) was directly accessible via a separate entry in the state list in DP 9636, and will, of course, be the first error reported under the new queue mechanism.

Error detection and reporting can be selectively and independently suppressed class by class via the ERROR HANDLING function. This function is provided on the basis that the CGI is intended for systems programmers implementing graphics support environments. In this role, error detection will be vital during development of the system and in locating bugs reported by clients. In general, however, systems once delivered should not require the extensive error detection and reporting necessary during the development stage and, indeed, would benefit from the speed-up achievable by avoiding unnecessary error checking.

4.6 Interrogation and Inquiry

It is necessary to distinguish between the various mechanisms offered by the CGI for returning information to the client of a CGI. DP9636 recognises five circumstances :

- **Interrogation.** Finds out the capabilities of the virtual device that will be used, concerning which standardised functions are implemented and what argument types are available, as described in the CGI description tables (see also Sect. 2.7.3).

- **Inquiry.** Returns information about the values in the CGI state list which are controlled by the functions in Part 2. Indeed, there are state lists described in each of Parts 2-6, which contain all the values affecting CGI operation set by the client. In some cases, inquiry functions may return values as realised by the CGI implementation from those available, after the client has requested an unattainable value.

- **Input.** Returns operator supplied information (see Chaps. 6 and 9).

- **Retrieval.** Returns items of graphical data from storage areas controlled by the CGI. In the draft standard, there is no segment retrieval function (see Chapter 7), and the only mechanism for retrieving previously defined graphical data is the GET PIXEL ARRAY function–along with the related GET PIXEL ARRAY DIMENSIONS function–included in Part 6 of the CGI (see Chapter 5). These functions are included for compatability with the GKS international standard (IS 7942), but in the context of the raster part they might be used to return the contents of any bitmap. It should be noted that without segment readback the CGI does not provide the functionality to support the GKS WISS workstation concept.

- **GET ESCAPE.** A unique function, which allows the CGI client to obtain non-standardised information from the virtual device. It follows exactly the same pattern as ESCAPE, but allows return parameters.

4.7 Interrogation and Negotiation

Negotiation is the process of establishing the capabilities of the Virtual Device the driver of the CGI will use. This is a two stage process involving interrogation of the facilities provided by the Virtual Device followed by selection of the facilities to be used. Note that selection requires explicit action only where it affects the protocol by which the CGI functions are expressed. For many selections, the action taken by the driver will be to ensure that a particular group of functions is not used.

Clearly negotiation cannot apply to a client working in a one-way output only environment. Negotiation concerns two aspects: interrogation of the device's characteristics (INQUIRE DEVICE...) and interrogation of optional CGI features supported (INQUIRE SUPPORTED...).

A conforming CGI implementation will supply the means to inquire each value in the CGI state list that can be set by other functions, but the specific means by which this ability is supplied is considered to be dependent on the programming language or data stream encoding mechanism in use. No INQUIRY functions are therefore described in the functional description Parts of the proposal, but the contents of the description tables and state lists are defined (see App. D). What is specified is an algorithm for deriving the granularity of information to be handled by a single inquiry function, from the definition of the state lists holding the information. This algorithm then allows those generating the language binding or data encoding to use datatypes suitable to the binding or encoding, to retrieve the granularity of the inquiry function as defined by the standard.

4.8 Miscellaneous Control

All the control functions which didn't fit in elsewhere are classified as "miscellaneous." Obviously, the functions classified here may be restructured to fit elsewhere as the proposal is processed. There are two groups at present:

- Setting functions, for numerical protocol specification other than coordinates, which are handled in Sect. 4.3 above, and for specification of character coding technique. The functions INTEGER PRECISION, REAL PRECISION, INDEX PRECISION, COLOUR PRECISION and COLOUR INDEX PRECISION are discussed in Sect. 13.2 and their importance in the context of the CGI Generator and Interpreter is discussed in Sect.2.6.3.

- Standard ways of addressing non-standard facilities: ESCAPE for communicating device- or system-dependent controls, MESSAGE, for communicating with the virtual device's operator, and APPLICATION DATA for communicating application-specific information to the Virtual Device.

Chapter 5

The Raster Functions in the CGI

5.1 Introduction

The Raster functionality of the CGI provides the facilities to allow the client to create, store, manipulate, and display images defined as sets of pixels. Bitmaps provide the second point in the graphics pipeline (below segmentation) at which a snapshot of the graphics data, at a particular level of refinement, can be kept and manipulated. It represents a level of storage much farther down the pipeline than segmentation, at which stage many more of the indirect references implied in the functions used in the CGI have been converted to a viewable image. For example, by the time the definition of a polyline is stored in a bitmap, the information available at the CGI/client interface about the current settings of line width, etc., have been turned into instructions to set particular pixels in the bitmap.

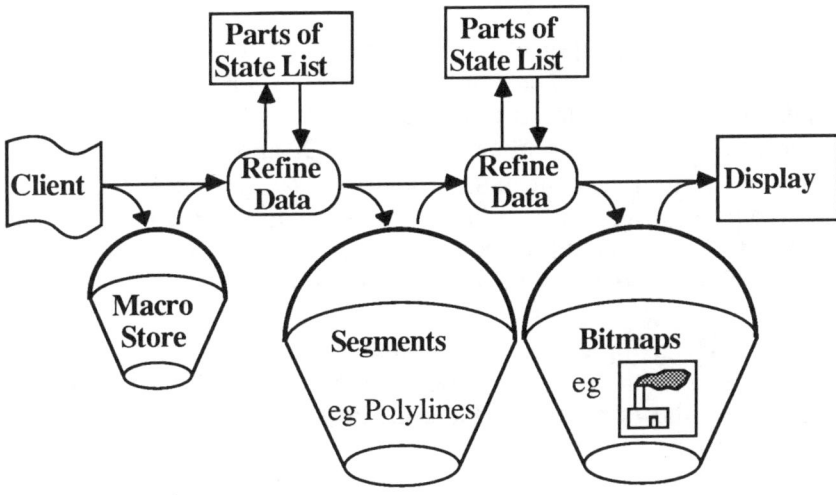

Fig. 5.1. Positions of segment store and bitmaps in the graphics pipeline

In contrast, segmentation (see Chap. 7) can be thought of as a mechanism for the storage and manipulation of non-parameterized or partially parameterized definitions; the raster functions provide a mechanism for storage and manipulation of image portions (Fig. 5.1). At this level of definition, very few aspects of the stored description remain to be elaborated "down-stream" and, thus, there is less need for the concerns, which are relevant in discussing the segmentation facilities, over the changes to system state which may be caused by the manipulation of the stored description.

5.2 Representation and Storage of Bitmaps

The basic units of the raster part are the pixel and rectangular arrangements of pixels known as *bitmaps*. Two types of bitmaps may be defined: *full-depth* bitmaps and *mapped* bitmaps (Fig. 5.2). A full-depth bitmap matches the physical characteristics of the physical device in use, in terms of number of bits per pixel and physical dimensions of each pixel. The mapped bitmap has only one bit per pixel and any pixel can therefore represent only two colours. The MAPPED BITMAP FOREGROUND COLOUR is used to set the colour in which the foreground pixels are rendered (Fig. 5.3).

A client uses the CREATE BITMAP function to define the bitmap. Conversely, to recover the storage associated with a client-defined bitmap, the DELETE BITMAP function is used.

Bitmaps define target portions of image space in raster form. They are created by requesting a bitmap suitable for representing a particular portion of VDC space, under the current VDC ⇒ DC mapping. This defines the position in DC and the number of pixels in X and Y required to hold the contents of the region requested. Any change to the VDC ⇒ DC mapping, which is set up subsequently, will not affect the number of pixels involved in existing bitmaps. It would, of course, affect the area they represent, if their region of DC were to be inversely transformed to VDC.

The VDC ⇒ DC mapping is stored with the bitmap and may be altered at any time when the bitmap has been selected as the current drawing bitmap. This does not alter the number of pixels in the bitmap. No two bitmaps share common memory.

Chapter 5: Raster Functions in the CGI   57

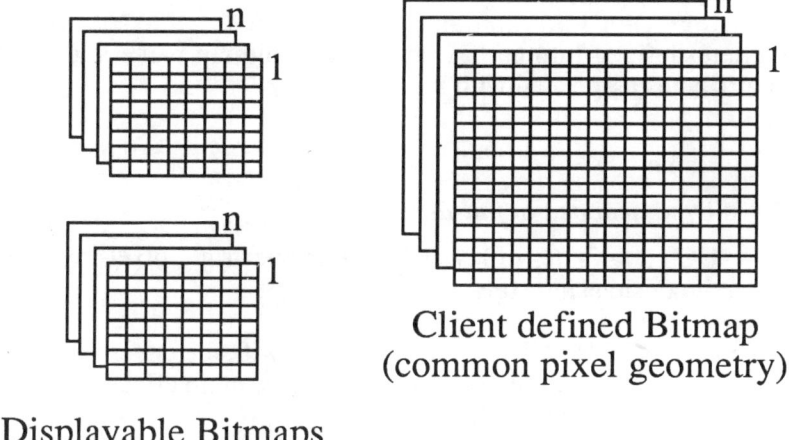

Client defined Bitmap
(common pixel geometry)

Displayable Bitmaps

Fig. 5.2. Types of bitmap

Mapped Bitmaps are one bit deep and mapped:-

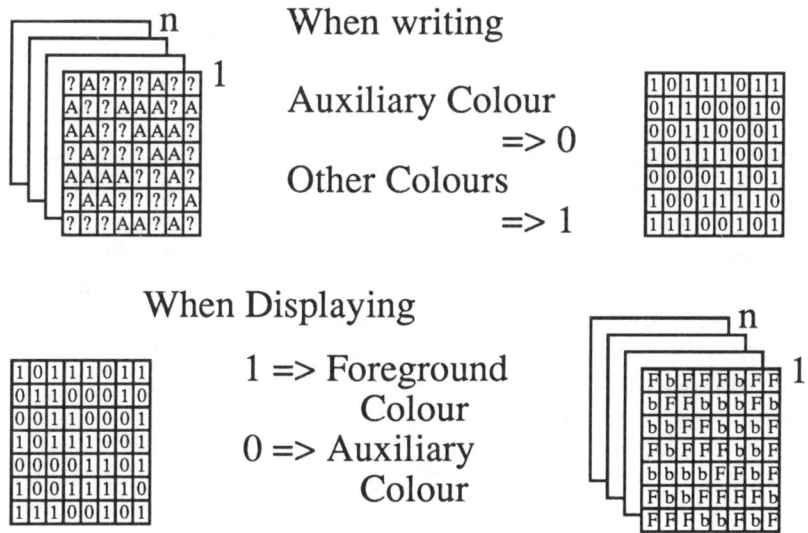

Fig. 5.3. Writing to, and displaying from, mapped bitmaps

58   Part I: The Computer Graphics Interface

5.3 Bitmap Data Structure

Any client-defined bitmap has an index or bitmap name and a number of other attributes associated with it:

- Name
- Type (*mapped* or *full-depth*)
- DC coordinates of lower-left and upper-right pixels, which give the dimensions in pixels
- A VDC Extent/Viewport pair along with the device viewport mapping and specification units that were in effect when the extent and viewport were last set.

Currently, only the last of these may be changed after the bitmap is created.

5.4 Control of Bitmap Manipulations

These functions may be grouped into two sections, those which move blocks of the image data around, and those that control the interpretation and manipulations performed during those moves.

In the first group there are two functions:

- SOURCE DESTINATION BITBLT (Fig. 5.4(a))
- TILE THREE OPERAND BITBLT (Fig. 5.4(b)).

The PIXEL array primitive has also been recently classed as raster control function and should be regarded as a bitblt where the source is a data structure in the user environment. Both of the above functions support the movement and combination of rectangular pieces of bitmaps in memory. For the source destination bitblt, a rectangular area of the source is combined with a region of the same dimensions in the destination bitmap (the currently selected drawing bitmap), according to the logical combination rules specified by the current DRAWING MODE.

The draft standard also specifies a PATTERN SOURCE BITBLT, which specifies a repeating rectangular pattern to be combined with the existing image. This function is duplicated in that the draft CGI also contains a new interior style called BITMAP interior style. It is expected that the PATTERN SOURCE BITBLT will be removed in the next revision of the CGI.

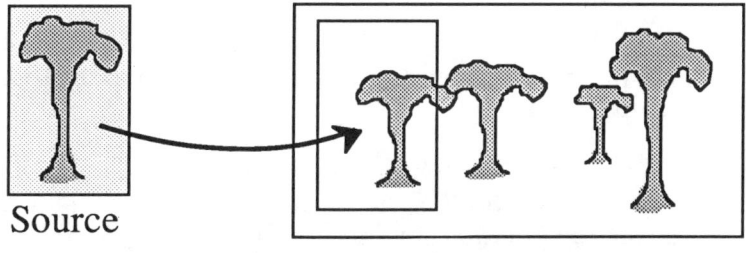

Source

Current Drawing Bitmap = Destination

Transparency On (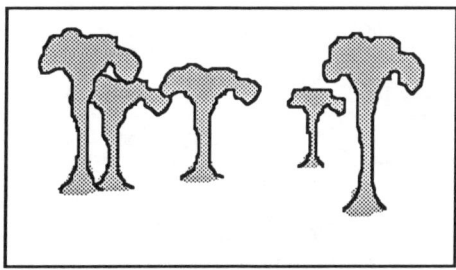 = Auxiliary Colour)

Source Destination Bitblt (Source(Index,Origin), (Destination (Origin),X Offset,Y Offset)

Fig. 5.4(a). The Source Destination Bitblt

For the three operand bitblt the two sources play different roles. The first operand is called the pattern and is repeated as required to cover the whole of the destination region. The second operand matches the destination area in size (number of pixels). Pixel values in this source, which are set to the AUXILIARY COLOUR value, are used in controlling transparency. If transparency is *on* those pixels in the destination bitmap where the equivalent source pixel has the value of auxiliary colour are not affected by the bitblt operation.

The combinations applied in moving the bitmap pieces are controlled by the appropriate DRAWING MODE and may also be affected by the current setting of TRANSPARENCY. Two DRAWING MODE selections are stored–one applying to SOURCE DESTINATION and PATTERN SOURCE bitblts and the second to the three operand bitblt. The drawing modes define a bit by bit logical result between source and destination for two operand bitblt's (16 operations defined–Table 5.1) and between the two sources and the destination for three operand bitblt's (256 combinations–Fig. 5.5). The 256 combinations are arrived at as follows:

(i) There are 8 possible settings of source, pattern, and destination bits before the operation.

(ii) For each of these combinations the destination will take on a value of either 0 or 1. In other words eight bits can be used to specify the final value of the destination bit for each of the possible input combinations.

(iii) The DRAWING MODE 3 selection is made as a number between 0 and 255, the binary representation of which defines the truth table for the result (Fig. 5.5).

Table 5.1

Drawing Mode	Logical Operation
0	d' = 0
1	d' = s AND d
2	d' = s AND (NOT d)
3	d' = s
4	d' = (NOT s) AND d
5	d' = d
6	d' = s XOR d
7	d' = s OR d
8	d' = NOT (s OR d)
9	d' = NOT (s XOR d)
10	d' = NOT d
11	d' = s OR (NOT d)
12	d' = NOT s
13	d' = (NOT s) OR d
14	d' = NOT (s AND d)
15	d' = 1

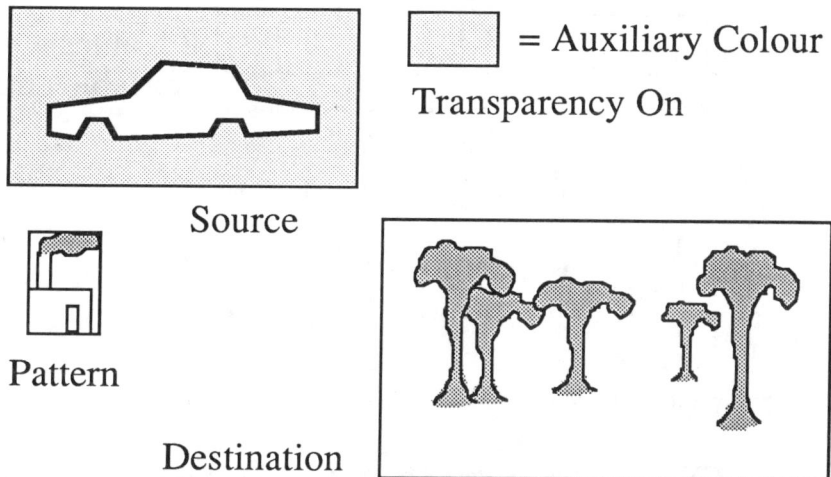

Tile Three Operand Bitblt(Pattern(Index,Region),
   Source(Index,Origin),Destination(Origin),
   X Offset, Y Offset, Drawing Mode 3)

Fig. 5.4(b). The Tile Three Operand Bitblt

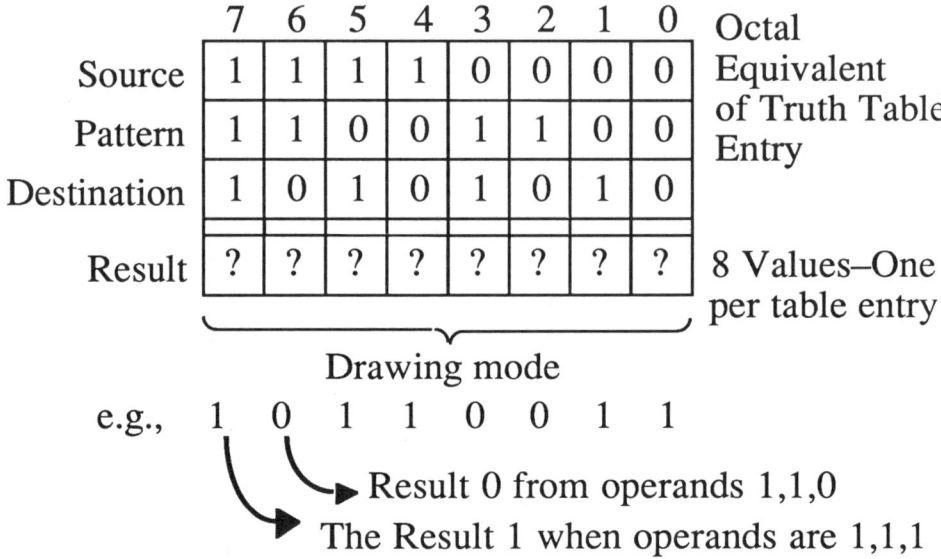

Fig. 5.5. Mapping truth tables to values of Drawing Mode 3

TRANSPARENCY is specified in Part 3 of the CGI. Its effect is that, where the source in the two operand bitblt, or the second source in the three operand bitblt, have the value of the background colour, then, if *transparent* is set, the destination pixel is unaffected. If the setting is *opaque*, all pixels are treated identically.

5.5 Pixel Array

Part 6 also introduces an additional output capability–the PIXEL ARRAY. This function is similar to the CELL ARRAY, with the important proviso that *no mapping of the pixels* takes place. They are real pixels, not virtual. Of course, this also means that their size is device dependent, etc., but has the advantage of guaranteeing that no resampling will take place and, for example, distort the colour balance (Fig. 5.6). Recently graphics experts have attempted to define a unifying framework in an attempt to allow the functionality supported by both cell array and pixel array, but not require two separate functions, in what appears a not-very-integrated fashion. In DP 9636 the PIXEL ARRAY function is treated as an output primitive, but the next version of the standard will redefine PIXEL ARRAY to treat it as a version of the BITBLT function, where a data structure controlled by the client is source for the pixels. This approach overcomes many of the problems associated with having exceptions to the general handling of primitives within the standard.

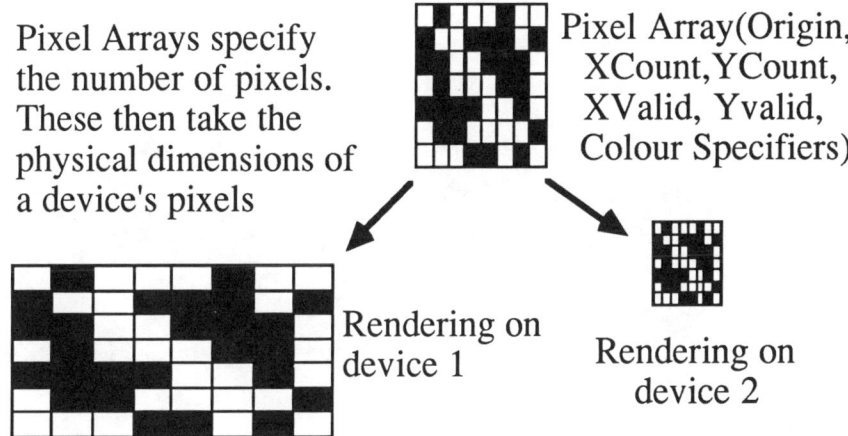

Fig. 5.6. The Pixel Array primitive

5.6 BITMAP Interior Style

The Raster part includes a further interior style (BITMAP) for use with filled areas primitives. This interior style involves filling the interior of a filled area with a repeated pattern from a bitmap (Fig. 3.14). A function is provided to specify the FILL BITMAP.

5.7 Displayable Bitmaps

In a system supporting the raster part of the CGI, a displayable bitmap is a full-depth bitmap, which can be directly tied to the display mechanism. The currently selected displayable bitmap is affected, in the same way as the display surface in any device, by clear screen operations, etc. In addition, if it used as the destination for any bitblt operation, the displayed image is affected. The CGI recognises the possibility of several such bitmaps, providing entries in the description table for details of the capability provided in any implementation. The choice of which displayable bitmap is actually on view is made by using the DISPLAY BITMAP function.

A bitmap can be selected as the destination for graphics primitives, by using the SELECT DRAWING BITMAP function. The area of the bitmap affected by subsequent drawing primitives depends on the current viewing transformation, the CLIP RECTANGLE and CLIP INDICATOR (see Sect. 4.4), and follows the same rules as for any display surface but treating the bitmap as the display surface. The interaction of this approach with the definition of normal viewing will be receiving careful review as the CGI progresses.

Chapter 6

Synchronous Input

6.1 Introduction

The input functionality of the draft CGI standard provides the sort of compatibility and consistency of approach that you would expect of the lowest level of standard in an integrated family of graphics standards. The CGI therefore adopts as a minimum the range of input classes used by the other members of the family of graphics standards (GKS, GKS-3D and PHIGS), operating in any of the modes catered for in those standards.

The CGI includes also input functionality designed to support these other standards and proposals in circumstances where the CGI may, in fact, be controlling only one aspect (workstation/device) of an overall system, which is combining several such CGI devices. Thus the complete system may be capable of providing the full range of graphics input functionality (e.g., all input classes, "local echo," etc.) while an individual CGI-controlled component may perform only a subset of the actions (e.g., Fig. 6.1 which shows a tablet with no locally associated display surface).

6.2 Logical Input Devices and Their Measures

Eight classes of logical input devices (LIDs) are supported and include the six which have become standard in GKS and are proposed (naturally enough) for GKS-3D and PHIGS. An implementation of the CGI may support several logical input devices in any class, each of which, therefore, has a device identifier associated with it. For each LID, an input value (the *measure*) is stored along with a flag giving the value's validity status. The input classes are:

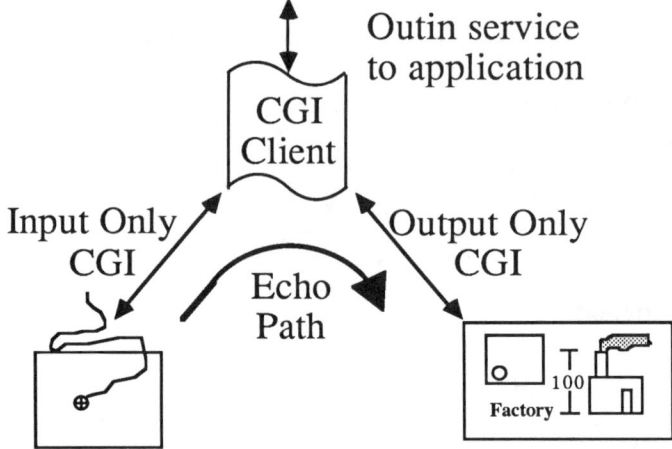

Fig. 6.1. Coordinated use of separate OUTPUT and INPUT CGIs

- CHOICE, returning a value in the range $1...n$, where n is device dependent. If the measure has a value outside this range, the status flag is set to *value invalid*.

- LOCATOR, returning a position in VDC coordinates. This value is generated from the device coordinates by using the inverse of the current VDC extent to device viewport transformation. If the point lies outside the VDC extent (i.e., the DC point was outside the viewport), the status flag is set to *value invalid*).

- PICK, returning values of a segment identifier and the pick identifier (*pickid*) of the primitive picked. The status flag is set to *value OK*, if the following conditions are met :

    - The VDC pick location lies within the VDC extent.

    - The segment exists and is visible and detectable.

    - Some portion of a primitive in the segment overlaps the VDC pick location.

    - If clipping is on, part of the picked primitive lies within the clipping rectangle bound to the primitive.

    - When more than one primitive satisfies these conditions, the pick priority or, if this is the same for both, the display priority is used to define which is returned. If both priorities match, the segment identifier returned is implementation dependent.

- STRING, returning a character string up to a device dependent maximum length. Status flag set according to the length of string typed in.

- STROKE, returning a sequence of positions in VDC, where all of the points must be inside the current viewport for the status flag to be set to *value OK*.

- VALUATOR, returning a numeric value in a device dependent range.

- AREA, returning an array of pixels.

- GENERAL, the input equivalent of a GDP, comprising an identifier and data record.

These classes can be supported in one of four modes, the three included in all the API standards (REQUEST, SAMPLE, and EVENT) and an ECHO REQUEST mode designed to allow support of echoed output on other devices operating in parallel to that being controlled by this CGI INPUT class command sequence. This might, for example, include a tablet controlled by the CGI, providing input data for use on a local screen giving feedback to the operator (see Chap. 9).

Note that the CGI system cannot provide direct support for the GKS concept of several overlapping viewports with input priorities associated. The GKS system allows the particular window/viewport transformation used for LOCATOR input to be chosen from several existing definitions according to the input priority. In GKS these multiple windows are between World Coordinates and VDC and are therefore considered "above" the CGI. Only one GKS transfer is defined below VDC, and this maps to the CGI's sole transformation.

6.3 Coordinate Systems for Stroke and Locator

In DP 9636, mapping from a locator or stroke device to the viewing surface is achieved by:

(i) considering the device's range as the unit square;

(ii) defining an echo window as part of the unit square;

(iii) defining an echo viewport on the viewing surface and mapping the echo window to it;

(iv) an echo extent is defined in VDC and the echo viewport is mapped back to that to generate the position's input.

This scheme is likely to be replaced in the next version of the CGI by one in which the full range of the raw input device's coordinates is used and mapped via a transformation to VDC space. This transformation will be defined by an INPUT VIEWPORT and INPUT EXTENT pair of rectangles. The ECHO will then mapped to the display with a similar pair of rectangles–the ECHO WINDOW and ECHO VIEWPORT.

6.4 CGI Input Model

From the CGI client's perspective, all CGI input functions operate synchronously. Any asynchronous operation is supported via local independent processes that respond synchronously to CGI commands. A logical input device of any class can be considered to be composed of a number of processes depending on the mode of operation with which it is used. INITIALIZE and RELEASE functions allocate Logical Input Devices to the client.

The first of these processes is a measure process, which is the basic component of all input devices. Once a logical input device has been initialised, the measure process associated with it remains active until the logical input device is released. The measure process monitors the state of the logical input device and makes its current measure available on demand. Also associated with the logical input measure is a validity status flag, which may be either *value OK* or *value invalid*, which means that the measure is currently outside the valid range for the logical input device. The client of the CGI can also set the current value of the measure explicitly using the PUT CURRENT xxx MEASURE functions.

The simplest mode of operation is SAMPLE. When the CGI interpreter receives a SAMPLE xxx command, it immediately interrogates the measure process and returns the current value and validity status. No other process is involved (Fig. 6.2).

6.5 Triggers

For modes other than SAMPLE, triggers are used. Each Logical Input Device has an associated list of triggers, which are used to indicate moments of interest, when the trigger is said to "fire." Moments of interest may be simple button pushes but may be more complex, e.g., movement greater than some threshold. The mapping from triggers to logical Input devices is many-to-many (i.e., an input device may be fired by one of many triggers and any trigger may be associated with several input devices). The association of triggers with Logical Input Devices may be performed dynamically and is done using the ASSOCIATE TRIGGERS function.

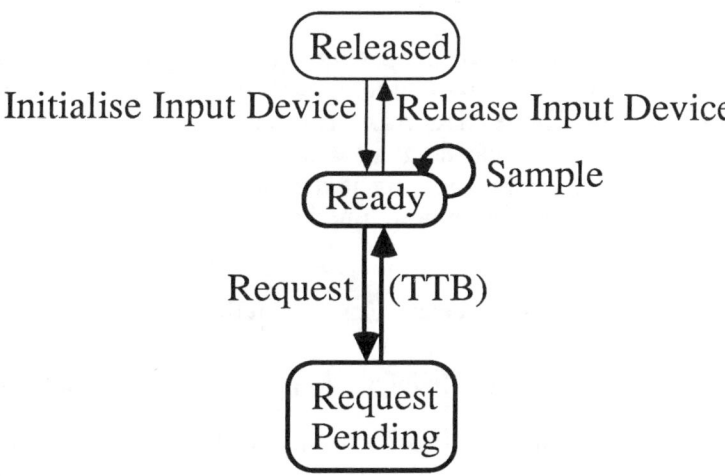

Fig. 6.2. State model for REQUEST and SAMPLE modes

6.6 Request Input

When the CGI interpreter receives a REQUEST xxx function, an event monitor is activated, each of the list of triggers associated with the logical input device is armed, and a timer is started (Fig. 6.3). The triggers interrupt the event monitor if and when they are "fired." The timer performs a similar function to prevent hangup, and there is also a special trigger–the break–which allows the operator to signify abandonment of the input operation. The event monitor then obtains the measure value and status, deactivates the triggers, break, and timer, and returns the value to the client.

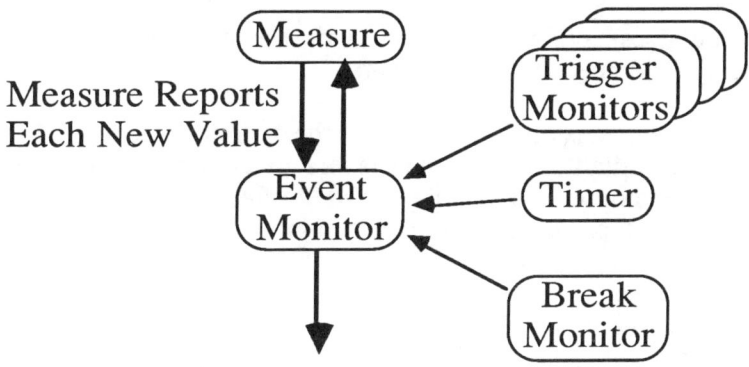

Fig. 6.3. Processes used in REQUEST mode

6.7 Echoing, Prompting, and Acknowledgement

Echoing is the process of supplying immediate feedback to the operator while the operator is using the input devices. Echoing is controlled primarily by the SET ECHO STATE function, which toggles a flag, which determines whether any echo at all will happen. If this flag is set to *echo on,* the current value of the measure is displayed in a form given by the echo type, which is taken from a predefined set, and depends on the class of input device being used.

The following list contains examples of CHOICE echo types:

1. Implementation dependent.

2. Invoke built-in device prompting capability. The echo data record contains a prompt array which indicates, for each device prompting alternative, whether that alternative is to be prompted.

3. Display CHOICE strings. The choice strings are contained in the echo data record and are displayed within the echo area, when selected by the operator "using an appropriate technique" (e.g., light pen). This always seems more like prompt than echo and is, in fact, a mixture where the choice is made by typing alternatives on the keyboard.

4. Variant of CHOICE strings display.

5. Display segment and CHOICE pick identifiers. The echo data record contains a segment identifier for a segment to be displayed within the echo area. The pick identifiers in the echo data record are mapped to the choice numbers.

Other input classes have similar lists of available alternatives, with the first always being implementation dependent.

Prompting is the means used to indicate to the operator that an input device has been made available and that the triggers are armed. It is controlled in a similar way to echoing with a SET PROMPT STATE function and a prompt type. The prompt types do not vary between input classes and are as follows:

1. Implementation dependent.

2. Prompt by sounding a tone. For devices capable of multiple tones, a tone identifier is given in the echo data record.

3. Prompt by displaying one from a set of device prompt outputs, such as LED indicators or icons.

4. Display a prompt message from the echo data record.

Acknowledgement is output that shows the operator that some event has been recorded, without necessarily indicating the exact nature of the interpretation of the event. It is controlled via the SET ACKNOWLEDGEMENT STATE function and an acknowledgement type, which are again the same for all input classes as follows:

1. Implementation dependent.

2. Acknowledge by sounding a tone. For devices capable of multiple tones, a tone identifier is given in the echo data record.

3. Display an acknowledge message from the echo data record.

The various types of action available for the three types of reaction to the user are selected and initialised by the various parameters of SET ECHO DATA commands. These give the class and index of the input device, the echo, prompt, and acknowledgement types, and echo area and echo data record.

The fourth type of reaction to user input, commonly recognised by computer graphics standards and proposals is *feedback*, but because this is concerned with giving the operator information as to the application's interpretation of operator's inputs, it is anticipated that such reaction as is appropriate will be generated as output from the client of the CGI, rather than from the CGI Virtual Device.

6.8 Setting Initial Conditions for Devices

The PUT CURRENT <input class> MEASURE functions are provided to allow the client to initialise a device in a particular state. This has two purposes. The first is to allow the client to control the value of the measure associated with the device. For example, the client may wish to control the value of a locator so as to provide a specific location for the intial echo of the device or to give a starting condition for devices only providing relative measures.

The second purpose of the function is to allow the client to specify that the measure is currently invalid. This is particularly useful in cases where the client wishes to be able to detect whether the operator has used the device. The client first sets the validity flag associated with the measure of the device to be invalid. This value will be retained even if the measure supplied as part of the function invocation is in fact valid. The validity flag will then only be changed if the operator performs an action which provides a valid measure, and by checking the validity status the client is able to tell whether there is valid input awaiting reaction. This is particularly appropriate on devices which cannot be set up with invalid measures (e.g., relative locator devices).

Another set of functions, SET xxx DEVICE DATA, can be used to control certain aspects of the input devices' behavior. For example, the maximum number of STROKE points accepted can be set using SET STROKE DEVICE DATA and the dimension of the pick aperture can be set by SET PICK DEVICE DATA.

PART II

Advanced Features of the CGI

Chapter 7

Segmentation in the CGI

7.1 Introduction

Segmentation is a well understood concept in computer graphics, having been a part of the expected functionality since virtually the start. However, perhaps because of this length of experience in using segments, there are actually many more variations than is generally realized. The basic concept is of a set of functions to control the storage, manipulation, and retrieval of collections of graphics primitives and associated attributes. Figure 7.1 shows a generalized graphics pipeline with three potential areas for the storage of graphical items.

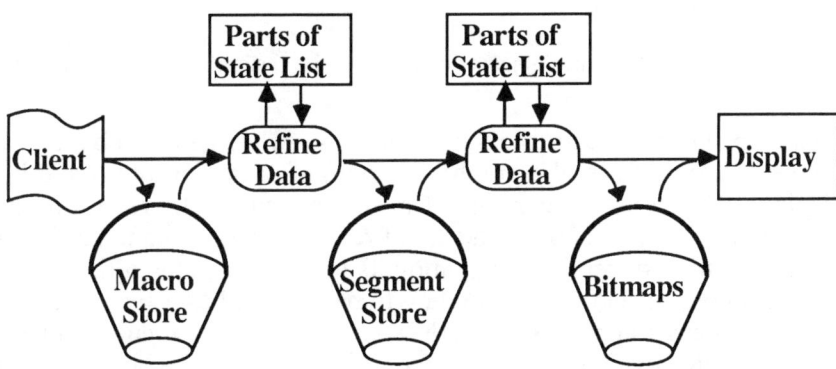

Fig. 7.1. Generic model of data stores in graphics systems

The important characteristics, when it comes to comparing different segmentation systems, potentially including all systems for storage of these partial results from PHIGS-like structure stores to the bitmaps of the CGI proposal (see Chap. 5), are the definitions of what may be changed between segment definition and invocation. This includes three aspects:

- What characteristics are properties of a whole segment and what are properties of other parts of the graphics system (e.g., individual primitives workstations, current view, etc.)?

- What facilities are available to change the content of any segment?

- What are the implications of changing the individual or bundled attribute settings between segment definition and invocation?

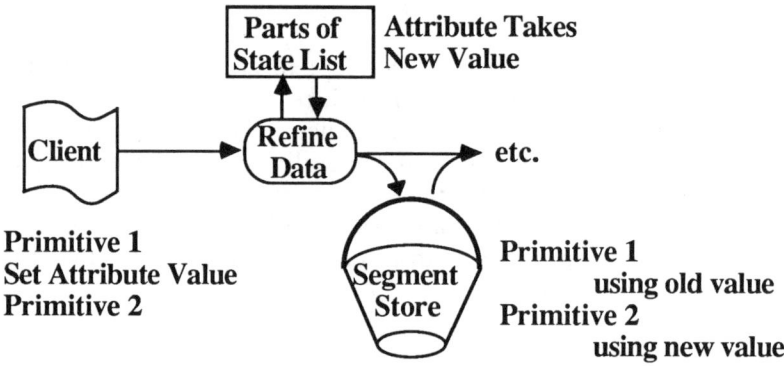

Fig. 7.2 (a). Graphics objects do not affect the system's state when displayed

These are all related to the same question–what can be changed about a segment definition by the graphics system after its definition and before its display? The other concern is: "Can the execution (invocation, etc.) of a segment (as in, for example, the act of redrawing its contents) affect the state of the graphics system?" This amounts to a question as to the nature of the objects stored in segments. Are they to be regarded as a series of commands in some senses comparable to PHIGS structures (i.e., executed in some sense at defined times and with well defined effects) or are the objects descriptions of static entities, as in GKS segments, for example? The differences are illustrated in Fig. 7.2 (a-c). Notice that the visual effects in Fig. 7.2(b) are the same as those in Fig. 7.2(c), but that, in the later case, the state list has been altered by the segment redraw and subsequently displayed primitives are therefore affected.

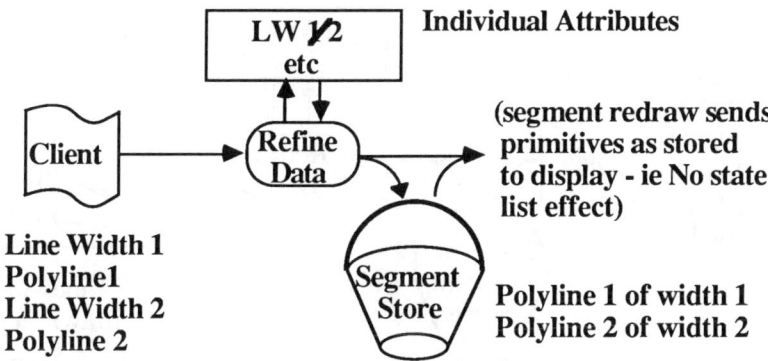

Fig. 7.2(b). Example of segments defining graphics objects

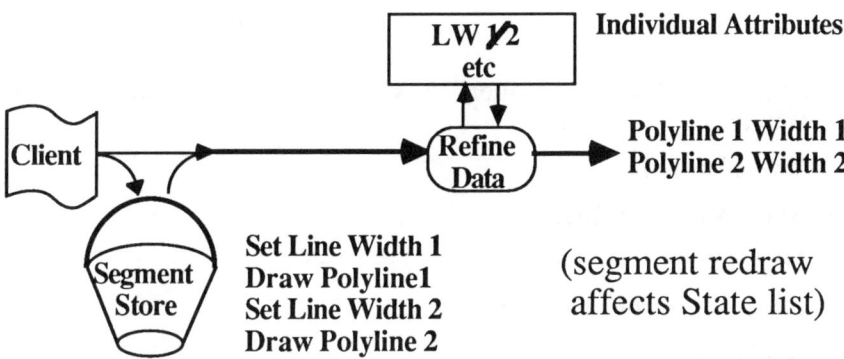

Fig. 7.2(c). Storing executable commands

A third possibility is that incomplete graphics objects are stored, so that the act of redrawing the segment uses whatever state of the attributes is in force at the time of the redraw (Fig. 7.3). The effect of this is that an attribute which is not stored will have the same value for all primitives at the time of the redraw. For example, line width in Fig. 7.3 is the same for all primitives from the segment, even if the attribute has had several values during the segment definition. In this case, line width has effectively become a property of the segment rather than of the individual primitive.

It is concerns like this that make it both important to ensure complete definition as to the place of segments in the graphics pipeline and also difficult to guarantee the completeness of definition. It is this sort of concern that leads to the search for suitable formal specification techniques.

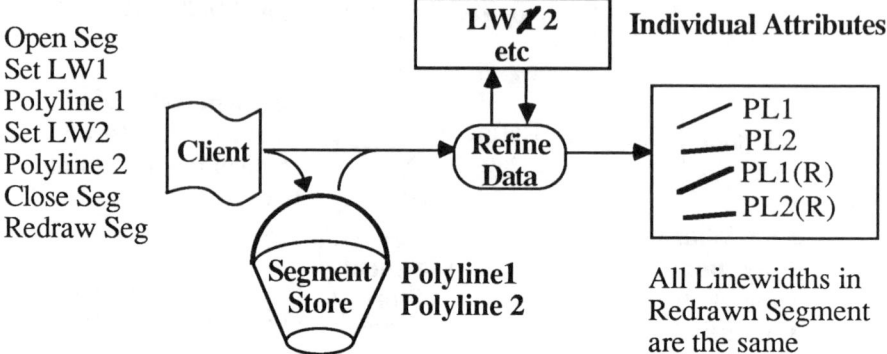

Fig. 7.3. Incomplete objects as segment definitions

7.2 Segments in the CGI

Segments in the CGI have properties which reflect those found in GKS. Segments may be:

- Transformed
- Made Visible or Invisible
- Highlighted
- Ordered from Front to Back
- Made Detectable or Undetectable.

These are the properties that are associated with the whole segment and therefore, for example, individual primitives may be highlighted only if they constitute a whole segment.

The second type of binding of information involves the association of the segment description with the segment name. The CGI currently has limited capabilities to allow this description to be altered. The only selective editing of segment contents is performed using the inheritance filter (see below). In addition, the whole segment can be renamed, deleted, or reopened for appending of extra elements. Finally, a segment may be copied into another segment at which time a copy of the segment body is taken, coordinate data (except for the clip rectangles) are transformed through a copy transformation (allowing shifting, rotating, and scaling of the coordinate system), and then the elements are inserted into the body of the currently open segment. No hierarchical description is maintained, i.e., there is no element stored to refer from one segment to another. The mechanisms for defining the elements' attributes are defined below.

The functions included in Part 4 of the draft CGI standard are explained here in four groups:

- Creation of segments
- Segment attributes
- Segment display
- Segment manipulations.

In addition as with all Parts, the description tables and state lists are included (see App. D) since they constitute the definition of the parts of the system that are inquirable in a binding-specific way.

7.3 Creation of Segments

Segments are created by issuing an OPEN SEGMENT command with a specified identifier. The identifier is supplied by the client but may have been obtained from the CGI implementation via the GET NEW SEGMENT IDENTIFIER function. The definition is completed by a CLOSE SEGMENT function, but additions can be made to previously closed segments following a REOPEN SEGMENT function.

When a segment is open, all primitives are stored as elements in the segment definition, along with their individual attributes, bundle indices, etc., as follows:

- Individual attributes
- ASFs and bundle indices
- AUXILIARY COLOUR
- TRANSPARENCY and DRAWING MODE
- CLIP RECTANGLE and INDICATOR
- Some ESCAPEs.

Remember that a bundle table entry (or bundle index representation) is not an attribute of the primitives and the settings of bundle representations are therefore **not** stored in segments.

In DP 9636, the PIXEL ARRAY from the Raster Part (see Chap. 5) and the PICK IDENTIFIER primitive attribute introduced in this part may be stored in segments. However, decisions about the nature of the PIXEL ARRAY function (which, in the next draft, is expected to be treated as if it were a bitblt operation with the client's data structures as the source of the data) now make it inappropriate for the PIXEL ARRAY to be stored in segments, and the next draft is expected to reflect this change. In addition, in DP 9636, some functions were not allowed to be performed while a segment was open. As a result of the review of the first DP, these recommendations have changed and the list below therefore notes the expected changes in the next version of the CGI. The following functions were prohibited in DP 9636 when a segment was open:

- Raster functions (except PIXEL ARRAY). These are expected to be allowed in future versions, but some consequences will have to be documented.
- CLEAR VIEW SURFACE
- REDRAW ALL SEGMENTS (expected to be allowed)
- REDRAW SEGMENT (expected to be allowed)
- DELETE ALL SEGMENTS (expected to be allowed)
- DELETE SEGMENT (expected to be allowed)
- RESET TO DEFAULTS (expected to be withdrawn from CGI)
- VDC EXTENT
- VDC TYPE
- DEVICE VIEWPORT
- INITIALIZE LID (expected to be allowed in any state)
- Precision and Mode Control.

Other functions are tolerated while the segment is open but not allowed to affect the stored segment description. The effect of application data functions, message functions, and escapes will depend on the individual functions involved, and be registered via the procedures set up recently for the registration of graphical items.

7.4 Segment Attributes

The CGI provides functions to set each of the attributes listed above:
- SEGMENT HIGHLIGHTING (*normal* or *highlighted*)
- SEGMENT VISIBILITY (*visible* or *invisible*)
- SEGMENT DETECTABLILITY (*dectectable* or *undetectable*)
- SEGMENT DISPLAY PRIORITY (larger values closer to the viewer)
- SEGMENT PICK PRIORITY (to distinguish overlapping segments during picking)
- SEGMENT TRANSFORM (a 2x3 matrix).

The segment transform is a transformation matrix associated with each segment, which allows the segment definition to be stored in one coordinate system and be displayed in another. It may contain scales, shifts, and rotations, which are applied to any coordinate data in the primitives comprising the segment. Note that in DP 9636, the transformation was applied to the defining points of the primitive, not to the geometry defined by the untransformed points. For example, a rectangle is defined using opposite corners in VDC space. If the segment containing the rectangle is rotated, the defining points would be tranformed and the new rectangle calculated from the transformed defining points with edges parallel to the axes (Fig. 7.4).

This would, in general, completely alter the aspect ratio of the rectangle. On the other hand, the transformation was explicitly not applied to defining vectors (e.g., character up or character base) because these do not have position, merely length and direction. Thus transformed text in segments would continue to have the same shape and size of character but, in addition, would not be rotated. Cell array would, however, be rotated because it is defined from three points, each of which would be transformed. The only exception to this rule was that any clip rectangle stored in the segment was to be passed unchanged to be used just before mapping the segment to the display via the VDC Extent to Device Viewport mapping (see Chap. 4).

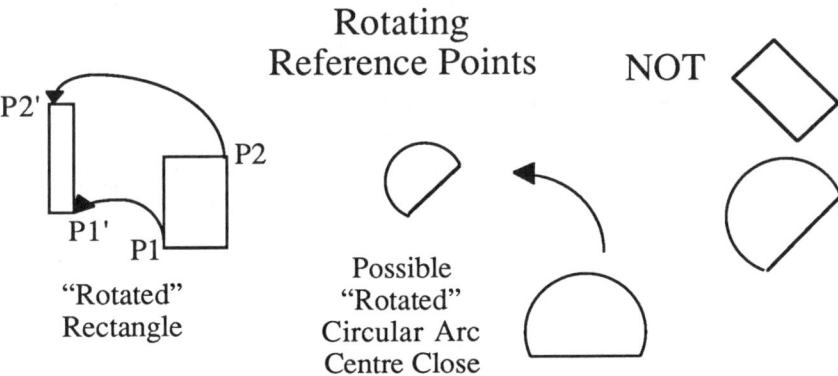

Fig. 7.4. Transforming primitives' reference points only (as in DP 9636)

In addition to the transformation of primitive geometry, parameters and attributes "with significance in VDC" were also to be transformed. For example,

- radius of circle primitives
- pattern size
- character orientation
- line width when specified in VDC
- edge width when specified in VDC
- marker size when specified in VDC
- character height
- fill reference point.

With a parameter like the circle radius, some assumptions had to be made when the transformation was anisotropic. The methods of transformation used were implementation dependent. In the case of the circle, an implementation dependent radius vector was transformed to the new coordinate space and used in the new primitive. Similar problems arose with line widths.

All of these problems arise because of the declaration of the intent of DP 9636 to transform only the reference points used to define the primitive and not the shape itself. This is an unsatisfactory state of affairs in a standard, because the solutions to the problem inevitably mean introductions of "implementation dependent" in the description of the effects to be achieved, thereby undermining the consistency of effect and portability of systems which the standardization process is intended to promote. For these reasons, in the review of DP 9636, a major change was proposed (and has been accepted) that the segment transformations should apply to the loci of points defined by the primitive functions. This statement still has to be interpreted for the rendering of attributes such as scaling factors, but at least there is now a philosophically clean intent to be matched in defining these interpretations.

7.5 Segment Display

Unless a segment is specified as invisible, the primitives that go to make up its definition are automatically routed to the display at the same time as being inserted into the open segment. In addition existing segment definitions may need to be redrawn to keep the picture up-to-date. Segments may be redrawn explicitly using:

- UPDATE (which clears the display surface first)
- REDRAW SEGMENT (for a single named segment) or
- REDRAW ALL SEGMENTS.

Redrawing may also be carried out by the CGI automatically when circumstances which require updating the display are detected, subject to the setting of a flag by the IMPLICIT REGENERATION MODE function. This flag may be set by the client to either *suppressed* or *allowed*. When the flag is set to *suppressed,* the client determines the appropriate time to perform a PREPARE VIEW SURFACE and REDRAW ALL SEGMENTS. When the flag is set to *allowed*, the CGI may embark on a redraw as a result of apparently unconnected function invocations (e.g., a change of bundle table representation). A common usage of the flag would therefore be to toggle between *allowed* and *suppressed* at well defined points in the program where the client required up-to-date display and recognized that the changes from the previously redrawn image were now significant.

In the next version of the CGI a new value of the flag is expected to be added which will allow the client to opt to have a rapid update method used, which may produce a less than perfect result as a result of the update. This new value will be called *uqum* (use quick update method).

Segment display or redisplay introduces the primitives contained in the graphics pipeline back into the pipeline at the stage and in the state at which they were stored. The segments therefore represent the first model of a segment store above (see Fig. 8.2(b)) and contain static objects.

7.6 Segment Manipulations

As stated above, very few segment manipulations are included in the CGI. Segments may be deleted, renamed, or copied into the open segment, using DELETE SEGMENT, RENAME SEGMENT and COPY SEGMENT respectively. The first two of these have obvious effects, but the COPY SEGMENT is more complex and best illustrated by example (Fig. 7.5). In Fig. 7.5(a) a segment is defined that contains Polyline 1 of width 1 and Polyline 2 of width 2.

Figure 7.5(b) shows a continuation of this example where Segment 2 is defined containing Polyline 3 of width 3, a copy of Segment 1, and Polyline 4 of width 3. An INHERITANCE FILTER function is used during the copy process to specify which primitive attributes, if any, should be replaced by the current value of the attribute in the state list. Thus, in Fig. 7.5(b), the inheritance filter for line width is set to *off*, and the lines of Segment 1 are stored, and displayed with the original line width.

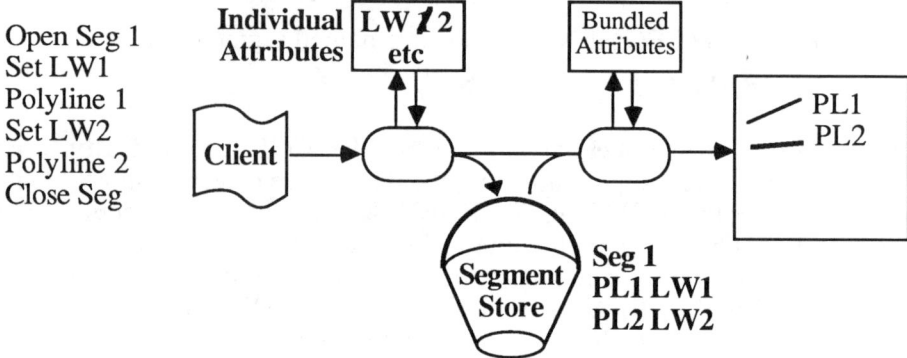

Fig. 7.5(a). Definition of a simple CGI segment

In Fig. 7.5(c), however, the inheritance filter is set to *on* and all of Segment 1's line widths are replaced by Line Width 3, the current setting in the state list. Note that Polyline 1 and Polyline 2 line width attributes are no longer distinguished after the copy. This gives the third model of primitive entities outlined above (Fig. 8.3). To maintain their distinction, the primitives must be stored in separate segments.

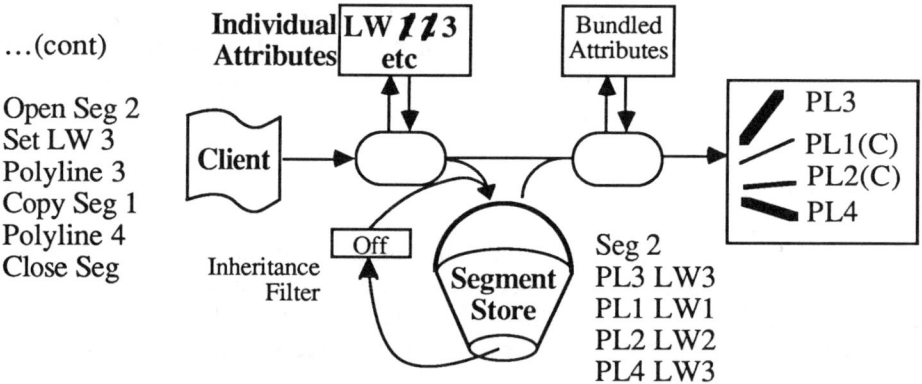

Fig. 7.5(b). Copy without inheritance

The choice of which value of an attribute is used with a primitive may, however, be delayed to display time by using bundled attributes. Recall that primitive attributes include bundle *indices*, and thus any change to the description associated with an index–after segment definition and before display (or redisplay)–will affect the appearance of the primitives associated with that index, even though the primitives *attributes* have remained unchanged (Fig. 7.6). A further level of indirection is introduced by the colour table, if indexed colour is being used.

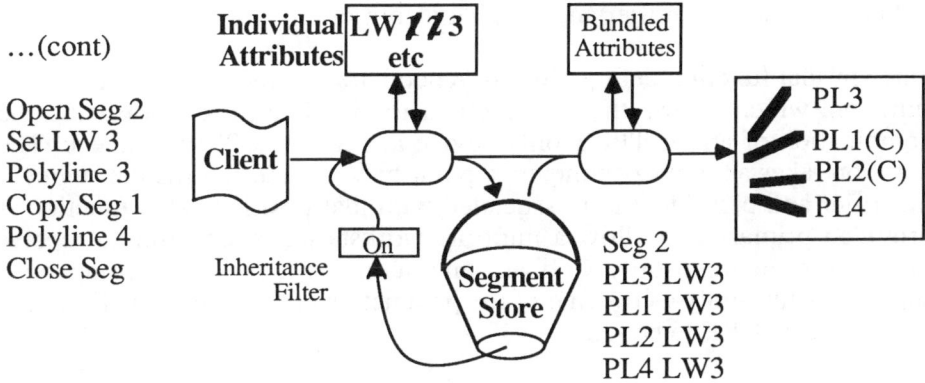

Fig. 7.5(c). Copy with inheritance

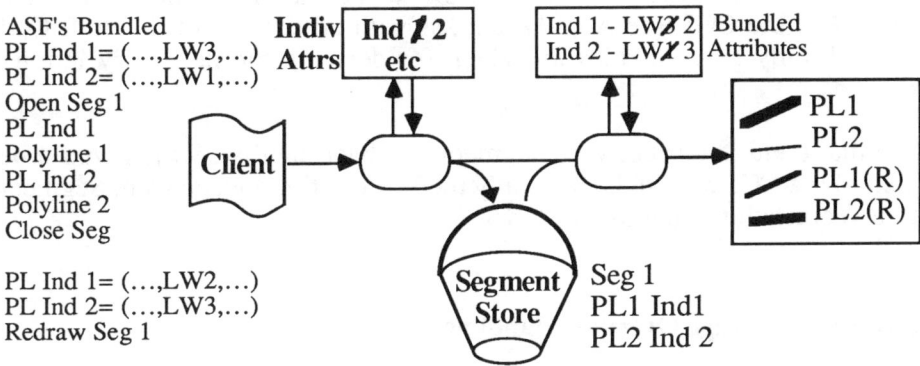

Fig. 7.6. Effect of bundle changes between segment definition and display

The inheritance filter is applied independently to each attribute of a stored primitive at COPY time. Note that, in this context, COPY–when no segment is open–makes sense as a different type of segment redraw, although such usage is currently prohibited. To achieve the effects of the GKS segment model, all entries in the inheritance filter except *clip control* should be set to "segment."

7.7 Pick Input and Segmentation

The Segmentation Part contains the definition of an additional primitive attribute–the PICK IDENTIFIER–which is provided to allow one level of structuring when using the CGI segments with pick input. The attribute is a primitive as opposed to a segment attibute and, therefore, primitives within a segment may have different PICK IDENTIFIERs. Pick input then returns both the segment identifier and the pick identifier.

One unusual function defined in this general area is the SIMULATE PICK function, which allows the CGI's client to simulate pick input using the combination of an OUTPUT-only device and an INPUT-only device. The function takes as input parameters a point in VDC and returns the segment identifier and pick identifier associated with that position. This function is provided primarily to allow a multiple workstation client user to receive input from an input-only CGI and maintain segments for picking on a separate output-only CGI. One of the parameters of this function allows the PICK APERTURE to be set.

7.8 Segment Interrogations and Inquiries

The state lists and description table for the segmentation facilities are defined in Part 4 of the CGI (see App. D) and, as with other Parts of the draft CGI standard, only generic rules are given for deriving the necessary inquiry functions.

Note that there is currently no segment readback facility, which would be required if a CGI were to be to supply the Workstation Independent Segment Store Workstation capability of GKS.

7.9 Segment Storage Overflow Handling

Because segments and their elements are stored in finite amount of space, one error to which–under the current model of error handling–a reaction needs to be specified in the CGI is *segment storage overflow*. The draft CGI standard specifies the actions to be taken if an implementation runs out of segment storage as follows:

(i) Elements up to the one which caused the overflow are stored, and further elements are discarded until the segment is closed.

(ii) If the overflow is caused by an OPEN SEGMENT function, this function is ignored.

(iii) A class six error report is added to the error stack/queue (see Sect. 4.5).

Chapter 8

Further CGI Output and Attribute Functions

8.1 Introduction

In Chap. 3 we saw how the primitives in the CGI are divided into five classes:

- Line functions
- A marker function
- Text functions
- Filled area functions
- A cell array function.

Not all of the CGI primitives in these classes were described in Chap. 3 and, in addition, the description of the Generalized Drawing Primitive was also postponed to this chapter. It is worth emphasizing that the omissions from Chap. 3 were not for reasons of the complexity of the functions, but in order to provide an adequate set for most purposes without overloading the reader with excessive detail and variety. The primitives included here are of rather more specialized interest, in particular circumstances.

The process used to define the attributes of any primitive are identical to those described in Chap. 3–using either bundled or individual attributes (where both are available) and ASFs to distinguish between the alternative sources (Fig. 3.1).

8.2 Additional Line Class Primitives

Three of the six primitives in this class–POLYLINE, CIRCULAR ARC 3 POINT, and CIRCULAR ARC CENTRE–were described in Chap. 3. The remaining three line class primitives are described in the following paragraphs:

8.2.1 DISJOINT POLYLINE

This primitive draws a set of disconnected lines defined by a list of point pairs (Fig. 8.1). The usefulness of this primitive must be seen in the context of the level of refinement of the graphics data at the point in the pipeline corresponding to the device interface. Assuming the CGI is supporting higher level graphics functionality, there may well be occasions when the client wishes to communicate the definition of, for example, a cross-hatched region or a dashed line to a device which does not supply these renderings in the hardware. The DISJOINT POLYLINE will allow the client to define the cross-hatch lines or the set of dashes using a single primitive in a compact fashion.

Disjoint Polyline
(List of Points) (x_2,y_2) (x_3,y_3) (x_4,y_4) (x_5,y_5) etc
(x_1,y_1)

Fig. 8.1. The DISJOINT POLYLINE primitive

8.2.2 CIRCULAR ARC CENTRE BACKWARDS

This line primitive generates an arc in the other sense from CIRCULAR ARC CENTRE (Fig. 8.2). If the two primitives were used with the very same parameters, a complete circle would be generated. This primitive is supplied primarily for use in conjunction with the closed figure functions described below. As stated in Chap. 3, the sense of the arcs is defined such that CIRCULAR ARC CENTRE draws the arc by following the circle in a positive angular direction defined by VDC Extent (see Fig. 4.3) from start ray to end ray. CIRCULAR ARC CENTRE BACKWARDS follows the negative angular direction. The two variations are useful when using the closed figures functions (see Sect. 8.5 below).

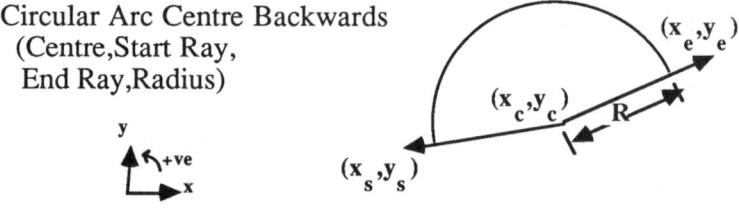

Fig. 8.2. CIRCULAR ARC CENTRE BACKWARDS

8.2.3 ELLIPTICAL ARC

This primitive generates an elliptical arc defined from a conjugate diameter pair (CDP)–see Fig. 8.3. (A conjugate diameter pair is a pair of diameters of the ellipse such that the tangents to the ellipse at the end points of the diameter are parallel to the other diameter).

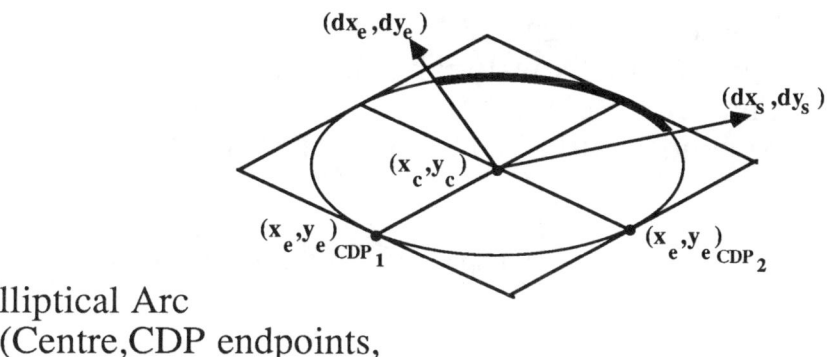

Fig. 8.3. ELLIPTICAL ARC primitive

The attributes used by these line primitives are identical to those for the other primitives in this class, as defined in Chap. 3 (Line Type, Line Width and Line Colour). Each of these attributes may be selected either individually or bundled via an associated ASF and the Line Bundle Index is also an attribute.

8.3 Further Text Primitives

In Chap. 3 only the simplest form of TEXT primitive is described. Two additional primitives complete the text class:

- APPEND TEXT and
- RESTRICTED TEXT.

8.3.1 APPEND TEXT

A text string is defined by either a TEXT primitive or a RESTRICTED TEXT primitive, followed by zero or more APPEND TEXTs. The APPEND TEXT primitive is included to allow a text string to be assembled from several pieces, in between which some of the text attributes (e.g., font) may have been allowed to change. The end of a text string definition is determined by the setting of the final/non-final flag, which is one of the parameters of all text primitives. This is the reason that all the examples in Chap. 3 use only the "Final" setting for this flag. Figure 8.4 shows a simple example of the use of APPEND TEXT.

```
Character Height(1.0)
Text((X,Y),"Non-Final","Sample ")
Character Height(2.0)
Append Text("Final","Append String")
```

(X,Y)

Fig. 8.4. Use of APPEND TEXT primitive

Once the text string has been assembled from its components, it is rendered using the text attributes described in Chap. 3. Only some of these are allowed to change between TEXT and APPEND TEXT, and there is no requirement that every system implement text so as to reflect attribute changes between TEXT and APPEND TEXT accurately. From the complete set of text attributes, only:

    CHARACTER SET INDEX
    ALTERNATE CHARACTER SET INDEX
    TEXT BUNDLE INDEX
    TEXT FONT INDEX
    TEXT PRECISION
    CHARACTER EXPANSION FACTOR
    CHARACTER SPACING
    CHARACTER HEIGHT
    TEXT COLOUR

are allowed to change between TEXT and APPEND TEXT.

8.3.2 The RESTRICTED TEXT Primitive

The RESTRICTED TEXT primitive is subject to the same process of applying the various text attributes, but it is then subject to further restriction in that it must be made to fit within a bounding parallelogram, defined from a width and height given as arguments to the primitive and the directions given by the character base and character up vectors (Fig. 8.5). In order to make the text fit, the CGI implementation is allowed to vary the values of:

CHARACTER HEIGHT,
CHARACTER EXPANSION FACTOR,
CHARACTER SPACING,
TEXT PRECISION
TEXT FONT INDEX.

No attempt is made in the CGI to define algorithms for altering the values used for the various attributes.

Restricted Text(Extent(Width,Height),
    Point,Final/Non-final Flag,String)

eg Restricted Text(DW,DH,(X,Y),"Final",
        "Restricted Text Sample")

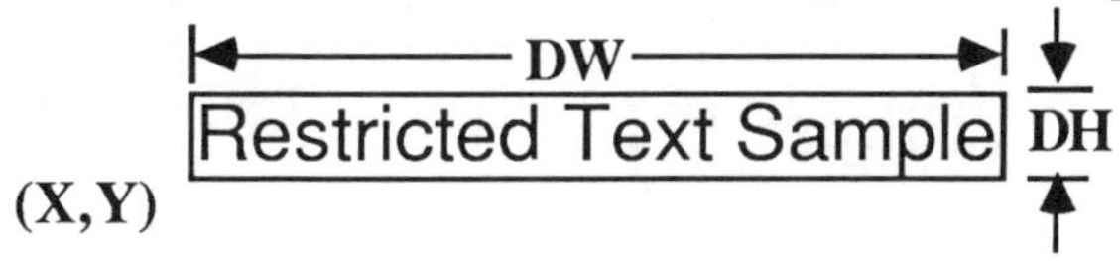

Fig. 8.5. Simple use of RESTRICTED TEXT primitive

RESTRICTED TEXT may be specified with a non-final flag and followed with APPEND TEXT, as shown in Fig. 8.6.

Character Height(1.0)
Restricted Text(DW,DH,(X,Y),"Non-Final",
        "Restricted ")
Character Height(2.0)
Append Text("Final","Append String")

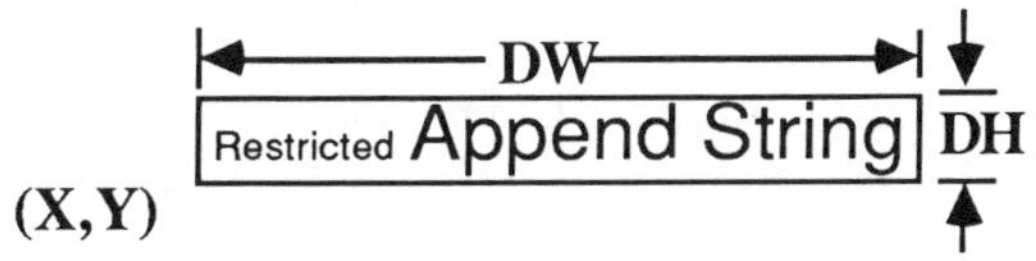

Fig. 8.6. Use of RESTRICTED TEXT and APPEND TEXT together

8.4 Additional Filled Area Primitives

Six of the eight primitives in the Filled Area Class were described in Chap. 3 (POLYGON, POLYGON SET, RECTANGLE, CIRCLE, CIRCULAR ARC 3 POINT CLOSE, CIRCULAR ARC CENTRE CLOSE). There are three other ways that the client can define filled areas:

- ELLIPSE (Fig. 8.7), which uses conjugate diameter pairs to define a complete ellipse. Note that this technique can be used to define any ellipse and not just those with major and minor axes parallel to the coordinate axes.

- ELLIPTICAL ARC CLOSE, in which the area is defined to close in the same way as the closed circular arcs, with the ellipse defined via CDPs (Fig. 8.8).

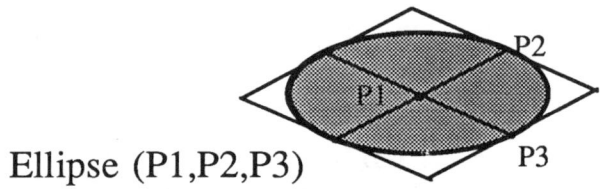

Ellipse (P1,P2,P3)

Fig. 8.7. The ELLIPSE primitive

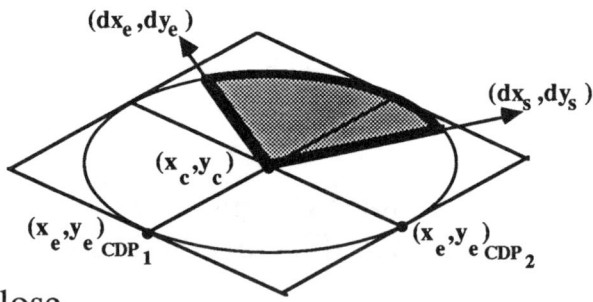

Elliptical Arc Close
 (Centre,CDP endpoints,
  Start Ray,End Ray, Close Type)

Fig. 8.8. ELLIPTICAL ARC CLOSE primitive

- Closed figure definitions, which are a way of composing a boundary from a collection of line primitives and filled areas and having the composite boundary treated in the same way as other filled area primitives (see Sect. 8.5 and Fig. 8.9).

The rendering of the edges of filled area primitives is one area in which compatibility with the other proposed graphics standards has led to a requirement for effects which are counter intuitive. In rendering the filled primitive, the edge is treated as if its rendering takes priority over the display of the interior and, in addition when the interior style is hollow, the interior is rendered using the edge attributes.

8.5 Closed Figures

The closed figure facility allows the client to construct a filled area from a sequence of line primitives and appropriate GDPs, the edges of filled area primitives, edge attributes, and special control functions (Fig. 8.9). A closed figure definition is begun by a BEGIN FIGURE function, following which line elements are used to construct a closed boundary (or set of boundaries). For each line primitive, first and last points are derived from the primitive's parameters. For the first primitive in the figure, its first point becomes the current closure point. For subsequent line primitives, the first point is connected to the last point of the previous line primitive by an implicit edge if necessary (i.e., when they are not coincident). A NEW REGION command is used to complete a boundary, with a further implied edge between the end of the last line primitive and the current closure point if necessary.

Alternatively, including a filled area primitive has the effect of an implied NEW REGION command followed by using the edges of the filled area to define a further complete region. "Invisible" edges in a POLYGON SET primitive are treated as if they had been defined individually with edge visibility flag *off*. If necessary, the closed figure definition may be continued in the same way with more line and filled area primitives until the END FIGURE command is encountered. END FIGURE has the same effect as NEW REGION, but it also terminates the definition and causes the closed figure to be rendered.

The individual edges conceptually use the values of the edge attributes at the time they are included in the figure with the setting of the EDGE VISIBILITY flag being attached to each explicit line primitive and the IMPLICIT EDGE VISIBILITY flag being used for the implicit edges. However, a conforming CGI implementation is allowed to use the EDGE attributes in effect at the time of final closure of the closed figure definition for all the edges in the figure.

Note that, in the example in Fig. 8.9, if all circular arcs in this example are defined using CIRCULAR ARC CENTRE primitives, then either the wheels or the driver's cab of the train will need to use the CIRCULAR ARC CENTRE BACKWARDS primitive, depending on the current definition of VDC Extent.

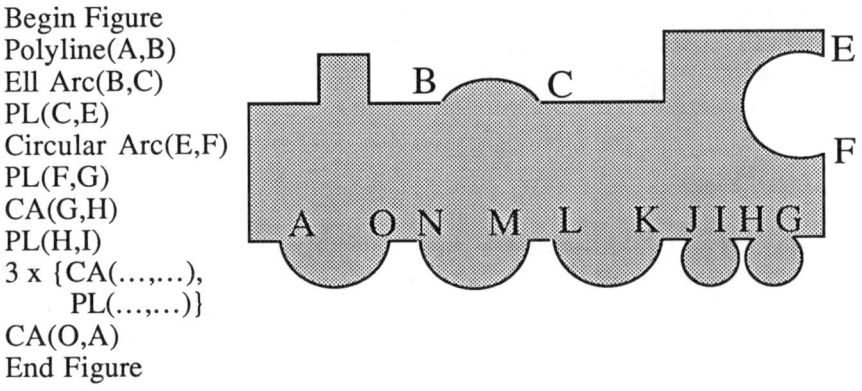

```
Begin Figure
Polyline(A,B)
Ell Arc(B,C)
PL(C,E)
Circular Arc(E,F)
PL(F,G)
CA(G,H)
PL(H,I)
3 x {CA(...,...),
     PL(...,...)}
CA(O,A)
End Figure
```

Fig. 8.9. Closed Figures as a way of constructing Filled Areas

8.6 Controlling Edge Visibility

The POLYGON SET primitive definition contains an additional set of flags that indicate which edges of the boundary should be drawn and which remain invisible (Fig. 3.16). These flags are used only if the edge visibility flag is *on*. A similar set of flags is assembled during the definition of a closed figure either by the explicit value of the EDGE VISIBILITY FLAG at the time an edge is added to the closed figure's definition, or, where implicit edges are added to the boundary, by using the IMPLICIT EDGE VISIBILITY function. These flags are particularly useful when, as with DISJOINT POLYLINE, the CGI is being used to support a client with more advanced graphics facilities, higher up the graphics pipeline. In this case the edge flags are particularly useful in allowing primitives that have been clipped above the CGI to be correctly passed to a device (Fig. 8.10).

8.7 Cell Array Primitive

The CELL ARRAY primitive, taken directly from GKS, is in a class of its own. The Cell Array is defined in the shape of a parallelogram by 3 points and an X and Y count of the number of cells (Fig. 8.11). The positions of each cell are derived by linearly interpolating the correct number of cells in each direction within the parallelogram. Each cell has a colour value interpreted according to the colour selection mode (see Sect. 8.9 below) as either an RGB triplet or an index to the colour table.

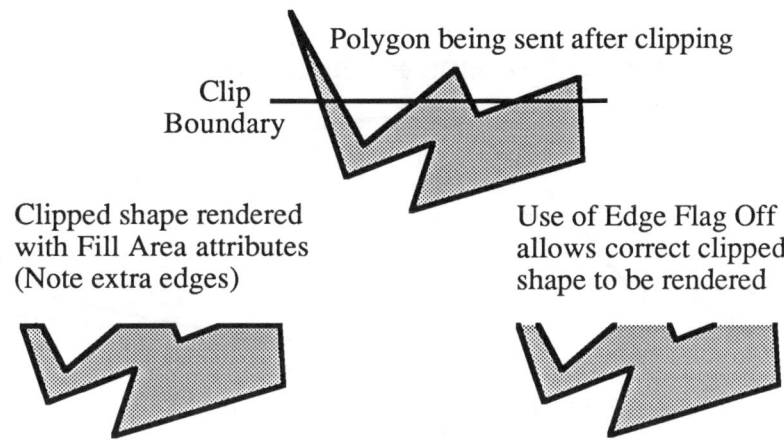

Fig. 8.10. Use of individual edge visibility flags

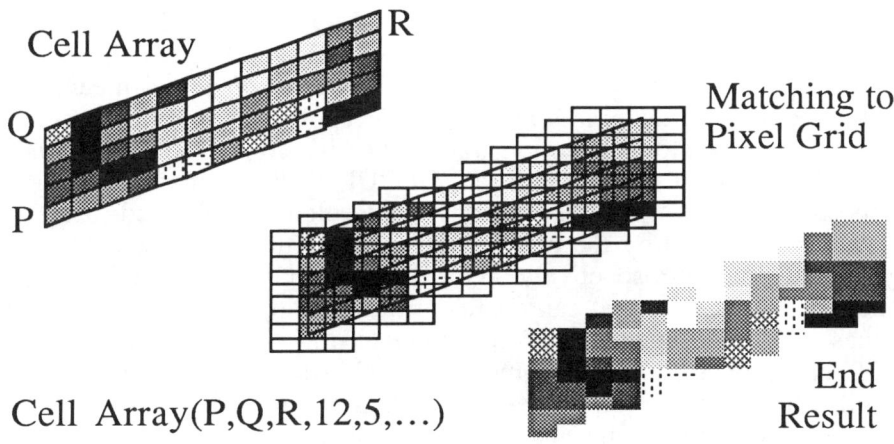

Fig. 8.11. The CELL ARRAY primitive

8.8 Generalized Drawing Primitive

The generalized drawing primitive is a standardized way of accessing non-standard functionality via the CGI (Fig. 8.12). Its parameterization includes a list of VDC coordinates and it is defined as acting in the same way as other primitives, with these coordinates being transformed according to the transformations described in Chaps. 4 and 7.

Generalized Drawing Primitive(Id,Pts,Data Rec)

Fig. 8.12. GENERALIZED DRAWING PRIMITIVE

8.9 Output and Attribute Control Functions

8.9.1 Specification Modes and Colour Definition

In the draft CGI standard, functions in this section include the closed figure set already described above, LINE WIDTH SPECIFICATION MODE, EDGE WIDTH SPECIFICATION MODE, MARKER SIZE SPECIFICATION MODE, and COLOUR SELECTION MODE. Each of the size specification modes may take the values of *absolute* (meaning "in VDC") or *scaled* (meaning that a scaling is applied to a device-dependent nominal size). Colour selection may either be *direct* (RGB triplets) or *indexed* (to a colour table). The SET COLOUR TABLE function is available to specify the RGB triples associated with the colour indices used. The range of values supported by the colour table and whether changes to it appear dynamically and retrospectively on the display can be discovered by inquiry functions. The CGI client can also control the mapping from colour direct values to device specific colour ranges using the COLOUR VALUE EXTENT (see Sect. 13.2 for more details). All parameters subject to a specification or selection mode are stored in the state lists along with the mode used to define them so as to allow correct response to inquiries.

Absolute and scaled modes behave differently under transformation. This is because they are conceptually applied to the geometry of the primitives at different points in the pipeline. Absolute mode specifies the size in VDC units; the size is considered part of the VDC image and transformed according to the VDC to DC transformation. If this transformation is anisotropic, the resulting line widths, for example, are dependent upon the orientation of the lines. The standard provides some guidelines as to the ideal effects expected and defines conforming fall-back behaviour. Where the scaled mode has been selected, it is considered to be applied after the VDC to DC transformation, and the size should therefore be independent of the transformation.

8.9.2 Transparency

In addition to these functions, the CGI Part 3 includes a TRANSPARENCY function which affects the display of gaps in primitives. The circumstances in which this arise vary from primitive to primitive:

- For non-solid lines and edges the gaps between dots or dashes
- For text and markers the portions of the character body or marker which are not solid
- For hatched areas the gaps between hatch lines (Fig. 8.13).

The transparency function controls the status of a transparency flag. If the flag is *off*, the gaps are drawn in a colour specified by the AUXILIARY COLOUR function. If the flag is set to *on*, the existing display is unaffected in the gaps. The transparency flag has no effect when the filled area style is HOLLOW or EMPTY.

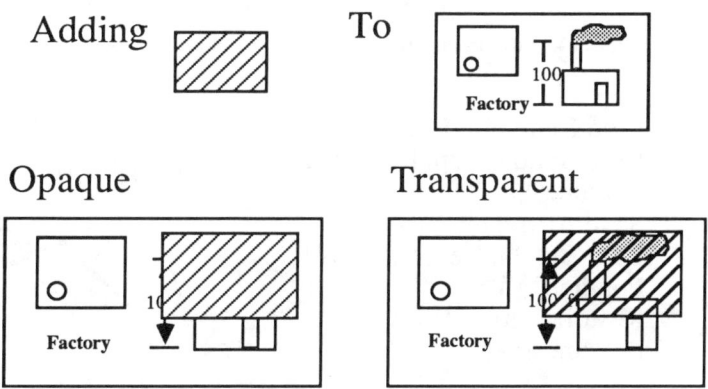

Fig. 8.13. Use of transparency

8.9.3 Setting Bundle Table Contents

To allow the client to set the contents of the bundle tables there is a function for each table of the form <bundle table> REPRESENTATION (for LINE, MARKER, FILL, EDGE, and TEXT) each of which allows the client to set all the attribute values corresponding to one value of a bundle index.

8.10 Save and Restore Primitive Attributes Settings

Two functions are provided to allow the client of the CGI to preserve and reinstate the settings of all primitive attributes–i.e., including bundle indices (Fig. 8.14) but excluding bundle table contents (Fig. 8.15) and similarly for all other indexed attributes–along with the clip rectangle and clip indicator. These functions can be used to control the settings of primitive attributes in force before, during, and after the time when the CGI is in a temporary state, for example, during the definition of a closed figure. The functions use a name parameter allowing several environments to be stored and reused in an arbitrary order.

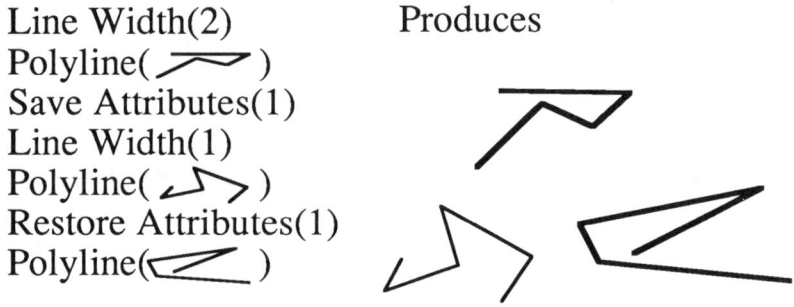

Fig. 8.14. Saving and restoring individual attributes

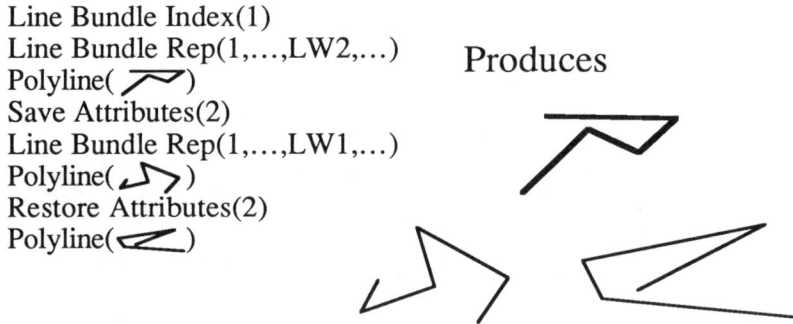

Fig. 8.15. Effect of not saving and restoring bundle representations

8.11 Inquiry and Interrogation

As we pointed out in Chap. 4, a Description Table and State List are defined, and a conforming implementation of the CGI will provide inquiry functions to allow the client to access the current values of the entries in the CGI state list.

A specific function has been provided to allow the GET TEXT EXTENT functionality of GKS to be supported directly.

8.12 New CGI Pipeline Model

As a result of discussions and decisions on the future directions of the draft CGI standard, there has been substantial revision and elaboration of the CGI output pipeline. These revisions have defined the operation of the pipeline by defining the conceptual state of the graphics data at every stage from the interface to the client down to final display (Figs. 8.16 (a-b)). The operation of the pipeline is described in terms of the passage of *graphic objects* from the client to the display. A graphic object is a simple or compound primitive with its associated attribute information, but this definition must be interpreted in the context of whereabouts in the pipeline the definition holds. For example, at some stage a graphic object will have been refined to use the contents of a bundle table representation. However, it is unreasonable to define the graphic object as including the definition of the contents of the bundle, because only the index is, strictly speaking, an attribute of the primitive but, more importantly, because the information about the bundle table contents is not available higher up the pipeline (e.g., when the primitive gets stored in a segment)

At the top end of the pipeline, the graphic objects are undefined. A primitive enters the pipeline without any attributes and potentially without a definition of even the eventual geometry to be associated with it. At this level, the primitive may be held immediately, while a compound primitive (for example, a TEXT string or CLOSED FIGURE composed of several independent parts) is assembled. When the complete shape is defined, the graphic object is formed by combining this with the definitions of the primitive's attributes plus some associated primitive-specific control information (such as DRAWING MODE). The graphic objects are then routed according to the segmentation state: either into the segment store (segment open) or directly to the rendering portion of the pipeline (no segment open).

If a segment is being constructed and is visible, the primitive passes through the segment store and, after having had the segment transformation, etc., associated with it, the primitive is passed down the rendering part of the pipeline. Otherwise, the graphic object is stored without sending the output to the display. With the new pipeline, the concept of giving the client control over whether or not a COPY transformation is associated with the graphic object has been added.

The new pipeline also describes the rendering process in some detail. It defines the order in which the various aspects of the graphic object are associated and applied and intermingles these operations with the "idealized" definition of when clipping and transformations are carried out.

100   Part II: Advanced Features of the CGI

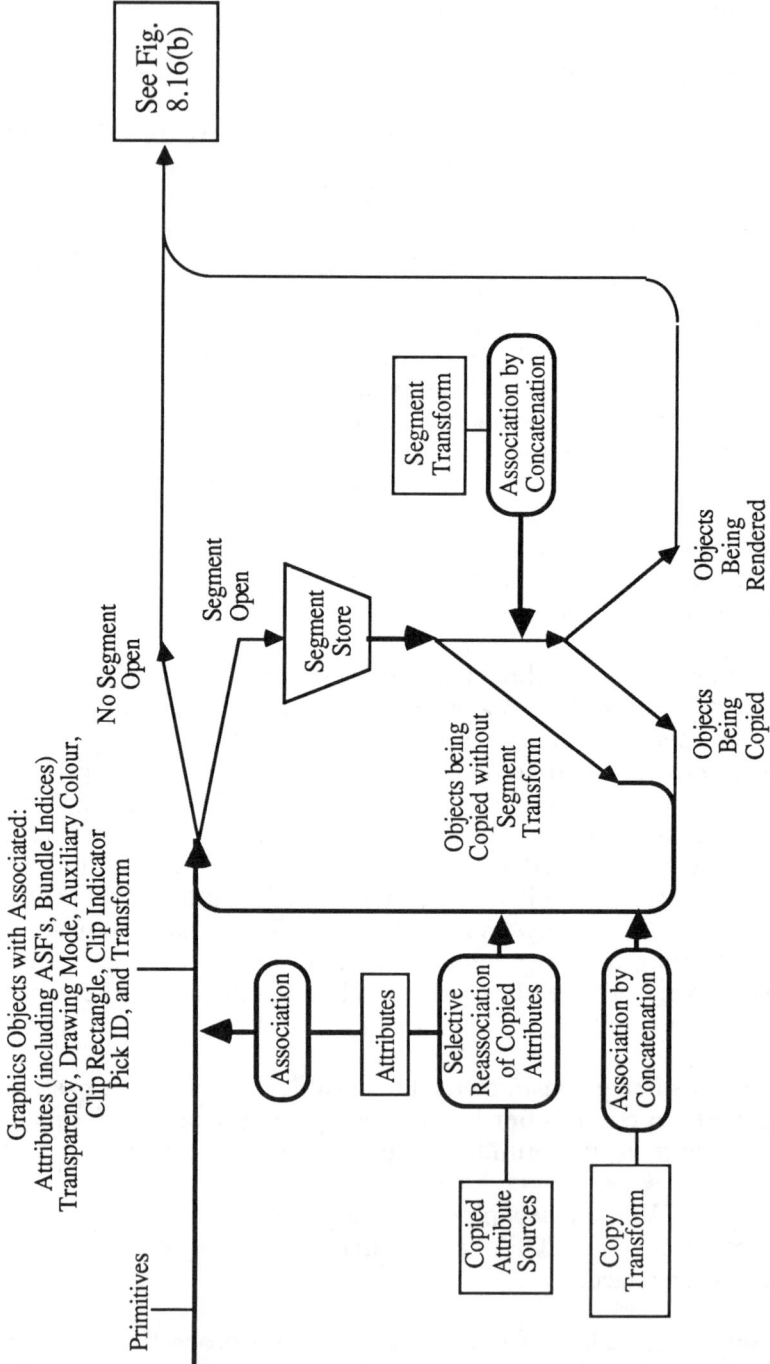

Fig. 8.16(a). The new CGI pipeline model

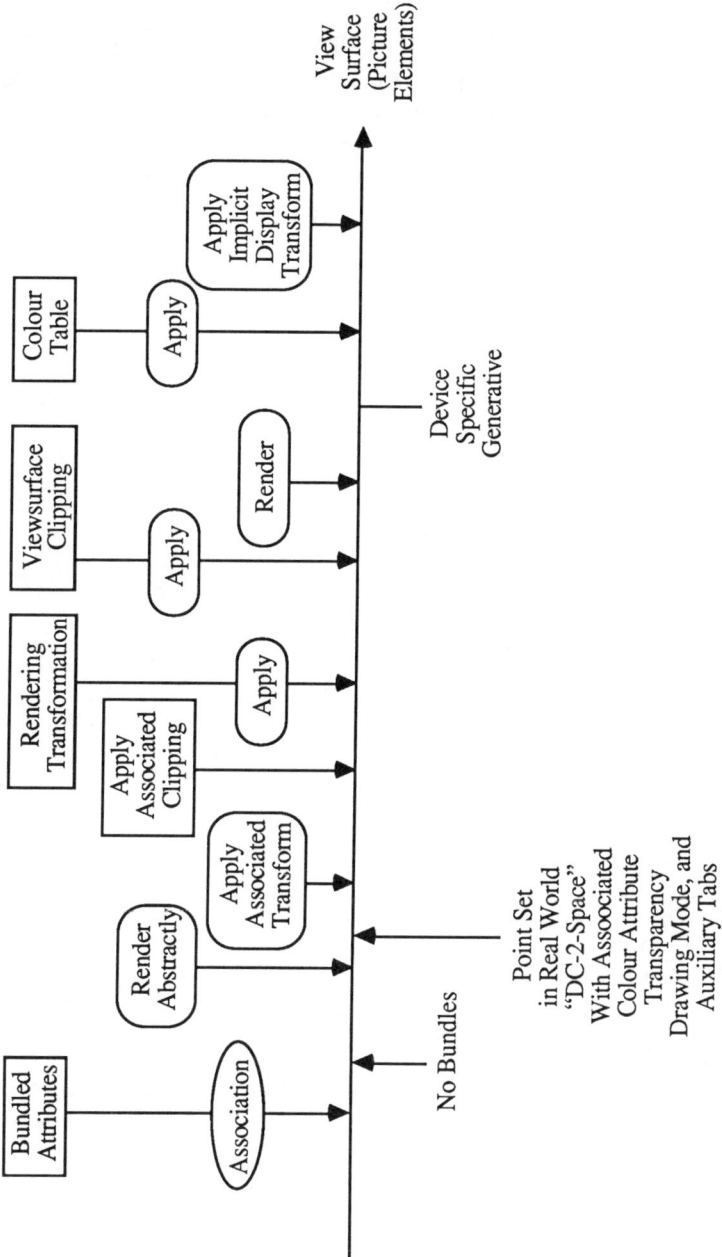

Fig. 8.16(b). The new CGI pipeline model (continued)

8.13 Fonts and Character Sets

Three CGI functions–FONT LIST, CHARACTER SET LIST, and CHARACTER CODING ANNOUNCER–are available to the CGI client to select and specify fonts and character set. These elements are more fully described in the chapter on the CGM (see Sect. 13.2).

Chapter 9

Asynchronous Input

9.1 Introduction

In Chap. 6 we introduced the basic concepts of CGI input. All eight classes of input device were described along with the concepts of triggers, measures, echos, prompts, etc. The control of synchronous modes of operation–REQUEST and SAMPLE–was discussed. These modes are synchronous not only at the interface, which is a level at which all CGI functions are synchronous, but also from the perception of the operator of an interactive system using them.

In this chapter we consider two further modes of operation–EVENT and ECHO REQUEST–which exhibit different levels of asynchronous behaviour. In EVENT mode, the operator of an interactive system is aware of having local control of the input tools with a queue of events being built up (how fast depends on the efficiency of the system and the level of demands placed upon it). In ECHO REQUEST mode, the operator should be only really aware of the same mode of operation as REQUEST mode. However, the client must also be aware of the synchronization problems of controlling more than one device along the lines shown in Fig. 6.1.

As we pointed out in Chap. 6, from the point of view of the CGI client, all CGI input functions operate synchronously. Any asynchronous operation is supported via local independent processes, that respond synchronously to CGI commands. A logical input device of any class was considered to be composed of a number of processes the nature of which depends on the mode of operation with which it is used. In particular the measure process, with its associated validity status, the trigger, timeout, and break processes, and an event monitor process were all described. Those descriptions also apply in the context of this chapter and this chapter assumes that the reader has an understanding of the concepts involved.

9.2 Event Input

EVENT input is handled very similarly to REQUEST input (see Sect. 6.6), but the extra processes (except for the timer) are established by the function ENABLE EVENTS (with arguments indicating a specific device–see Fig. 9.1). After this function is received, every time any of the associated triggers "fires," an event report is placed on the event queue containing the current value and status of the measure process, along with the input device and trigger identification, and a timestamp.

The AWAIT EVENT function interrogates the status of the event queue and, if no event is in the queue, initializes a timer and waits for the first event to occur or the time limit to expire. If there is an event in the queue before the timeout limit expires, then the input class, device identifier, and timestamp of the first report in the queue are returned, along with a queue status of *not empty*.

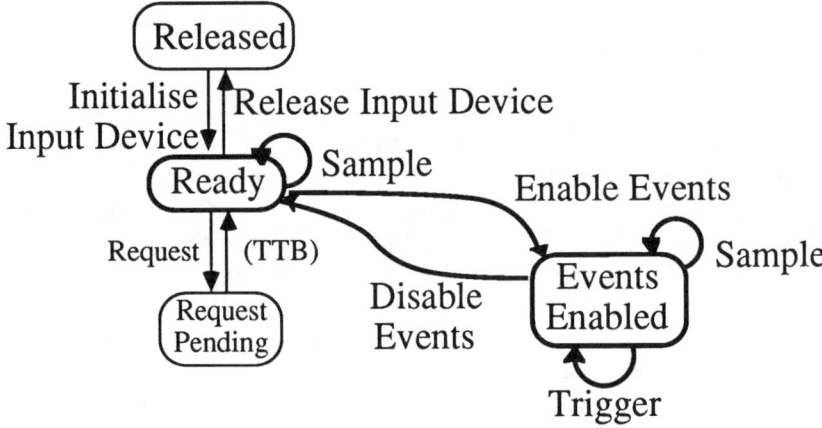

Fig. 9.1(a). State model of Logical Input Device in Event Mode

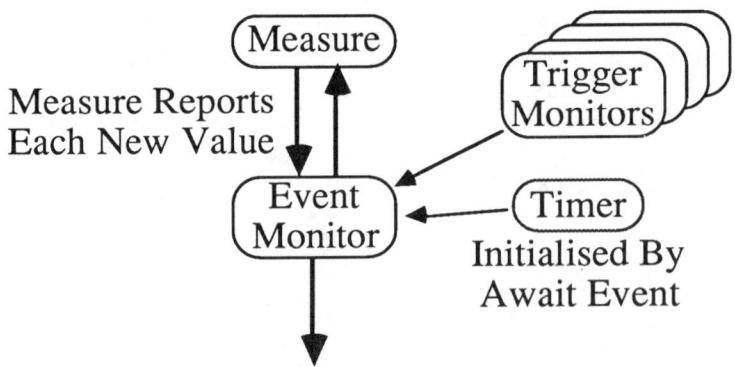

Fig. 9.1(b). Processes active during Event Input

The DEQUEUE xxx EVENT functions are input class specific and used to remove the first event report from the queue, returning the class-specific data types to the client. If these functions are used when the first event in the queue is not of the correct type, an error report is generated and the command is ignored.

The AWAIT EVENT QUEUE TRANSFER function is provided to allow the client to receive the complete event queue in one transfer. A timeout is associated with the function, and the function will return control to the client when either there are event(s) in the queue or the timeout expires, in which case the event queue returned has status *empty*. Note that, if there are events in the queue when the function is received by the interpreter, control (and the contents of the event queue) will be returned immediately.

The DISABLE EVENTS function returns the device to the ready state.

9.3 Event Queue Management

The INITIALIZE and RELEASE EVENT QUEUE functions are provided to allow the CGI's client to set the event queue to an initial empty state and to release resources allocated to the queue, respectively.

The CGI also provides a number of other facilities to allow the client to control the event queue, primarily for circumstances in which the client may be coordinating several CGI devices (e.g., to implement a GKS workstation). In these circumstances, it may be necessary to suspend the operation of the event mechanism on one device because the event queue in another device is full in order to maintain synchronization between the two. Functions are therefore provided to suspend and reinstate the event queue's operation, using BLOCK and UNBLOCK EVENT QUEUE. Blocking prevents the addition of events to the queue, and triggers that fire while the queue is blocked are ignored. However, echoing continues but no acknowledgements are made, because no events are recorded. Blocking the event queue differs from disabling events in that the event queue will persist through a BLOCK/UNBLOCK sequence, whereas, in the normal DISABLE/ENABLE usage, the event queue would be lost.

Because the input devices are made available to the operator for asynchronous use, it is possible that the system may need to suspend the operation of an active input device after the operator has used it to queue an event (e.g., in response to an earlier input action). In the extreme, all the events in the queue may no longer be relevent. The FLUSH <device> EVENTS and FLUSH EVENTS allow selective or complete discarding of events from the queue.

Note that the CGI maintains a record of the event that caused the event queue to overflow. The function, RETRIEVE OVERFLOW EVENT, passes the details of this event to the client. Figure 9.2 shows the states of operation of the event queue.

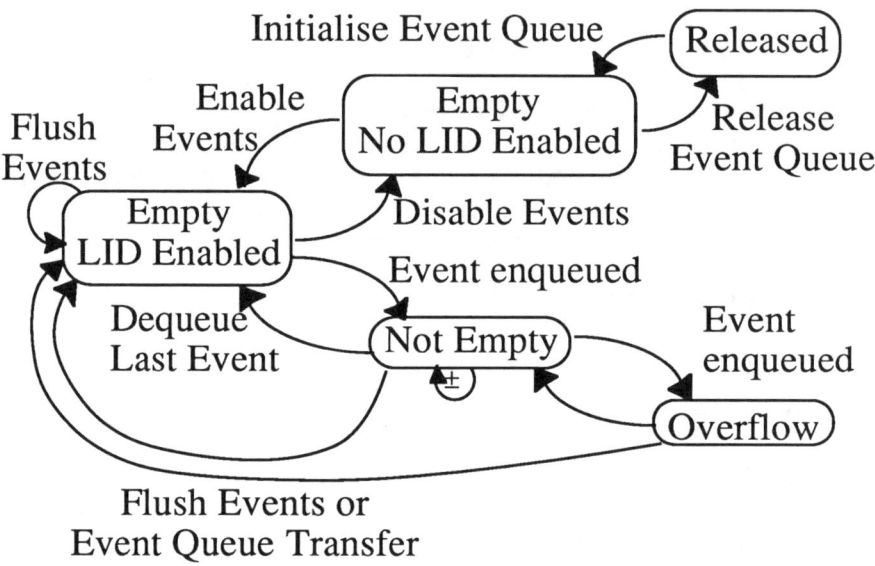

Fig. 9.2. Event Queue states and transitions

9.4 Echo Request Input Mode

ECHO REQUEST mode is designed to allow an INPUT CGI to provide the client with enough information to support the echoing of input on a separate OUTPUT or OUTIN CGI. It operates very similarly to REQUEST input but involves an extra "trigger" (the measure monitor), which fires when the value of the measure has changed. The INITIALIZE ECHO REQUEST command establishes all the same processes as a REQUEST, but it returns control to the client after initializing the various processes and leaving the system in the state where an ECHO REQUEST command may be used.

If REQUEST input has taken place (i.e., the event monitor has completed–see Sect. 6.6), the ECHO REQUEST returns the normal data items associated with a REQUEST input. If the event monitor is still active, the ECHO REQUEST initiates the measure monitor and then waits for either the measure monitor or the event monitor to signal completion of a change of status; finally, it returns the appropriate values to the client. ECHO REQUEST is, therefore, directly comparable to the REQUEST command where control is not returned to the client until the input has been terminated by the firing of one of triggers or the timeout. Figure 9.3 shows the state model of ECHO REQUEST mode operation but differs from the other models in that a new value will act as a trigger and still leave the logical device active, even while control is returned to the client.

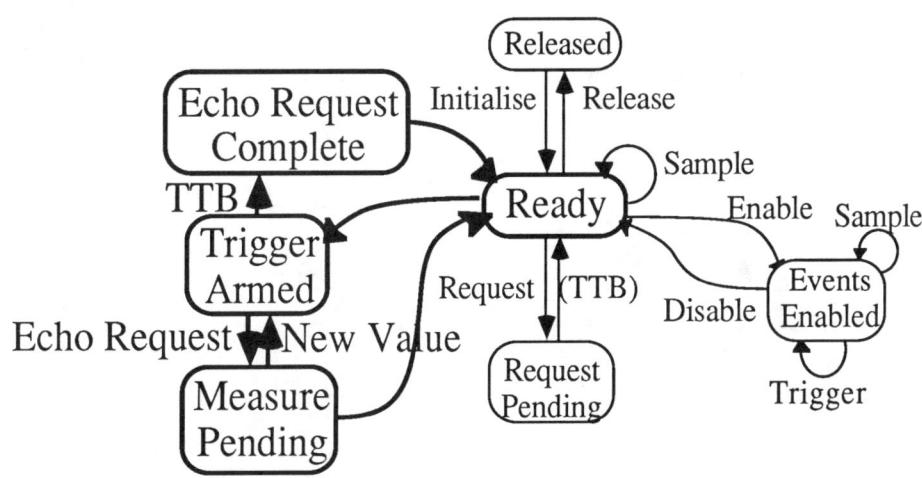

Fig. 9.3. State model of Echo Request Mode operation

The ECHO REQUEST operation provides the input side of the functionality required to support remote echoing from a CGI Logical Input Device to a separate CGI OUTPUT or OUTIN device. The output side of the functionality is provided by the echo output functionality, which allows the CGI client to send a description of the types of echoing, prompting, and acknowledgement to be supported on the output device. The client can then send details of the settings of the input device being echoed, via the two functions INITIALIZE xxx ECHO OUTPUT and UPDATE xxx ECHO OUTPUT. A session of ECHO OUTPUT operation is terminated when the client issues a RELEASE ECHO OUTPUT function.

Figure 9.4 shows the progression of a typical session coordinating OUTPUT and INPUT CGIs to allow the client to provide the effect of REQUEST input with local echoing (i.e., under the client's control).

The ECHO OUTPUT facilities include functions to control the settings of the echo, prompt, and acknowledgement states associated with the echo request mode of operation. The functionality is essentially the same as that provided on an OUTIN device using REQUEST mode and is invoked using the SET <ECHO, ACKNOWLEDGEMENT, or PROMPT> OUTPUT STATE functions.

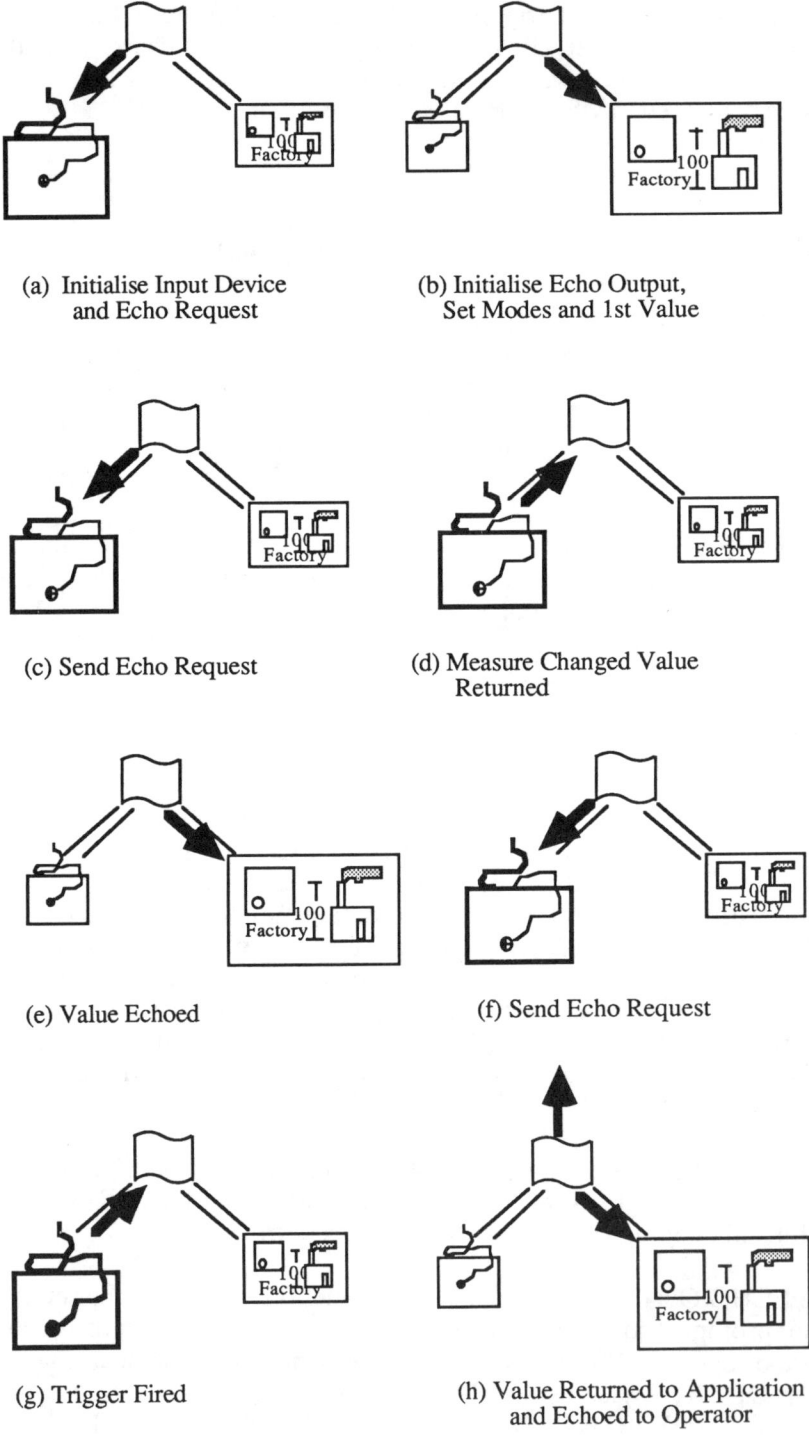

Figs. 9.4(a-h). Stages in remote echoing operations

Chapter 10

CGI Conformance and Constituency Profiles

10.1 Purpose

Constituency profiles are an attempt to recognise that a very large number of "sensible" devices can be configured from various combinations of CGI functions and of different minimum capabilities and default values. Such constituency profiles are expected to be formulated by the constituency itself in most cases similarly to the way in which users in particular areas of CAD are beginning to get together to formulate profiles for CGM interpreters (see Chap. 16 and App. F). The draft CGI standard does contain the first attempt at constituency profiles for the GKS community. The definition of the profiles for GKS are given below.

10.2 Conformance and Constituency Profiles

Part 1 of the CGI draft standard introduces the concepts used in defining conformance to the standard. Two levels of possible conformance are anticipated:

- **Full conformance**, where the CGI functionality contained in a constituency profile is provided in the form specified by one of the language bindings or data stream encodings.

- **Functional conformance**, where private encodings have been used, but the functions incorporated in the implementation perform according to the abstract functionality laid out in Parts 2-6 of the CGI.

With the range of graphics systems and devices to be interfaced, there is a requirement to support a range of different interface configurations. For example, there is a requirement to be able to support output only devices using either two-way or one-way communications (for example, where spoolers support only one-way transfer of information). In addition, input-only and interactive devices must be supported, and the option of coping with one half of an interaction sequence (e.g., input with remote echoing or the echoing of inputs from another device) must be addressed. Even in the context of a system like GKS with relatively few option levels this leads to 16 GKS support configurations (Table 10.1). The functionality required to directly support these levels is detailed in Part 1 of the draft CGI standard, along with a constituency profile for the CGM, which includes 84 CGI functions. There will be some detailed changes following review of DP9636.

Because each of the configurations is defined to address a particular group of users, the term "constituency profile" has been coined to capture the concept of "that grouping of functions required by this group of CGI clients." The method is anticipated as extensible, with new user communities defining groupings to suit their type of work and these new profiles being vetted through a type registration procedure.

Table 10.1. GKS constituency profiles

Profile	Workstation Type	GKS Level
GKS b	IN	b
GKS c	IN	c
GKS 0	OUT	0
GKS 1	OUT	1,2
GKS 0b	OUTIN	0b
GKS 1b	OUTIN	1b,2b
GKS 0c	OUTIN	0c
GKS 1c	OUTIN	1c,2c
GKS bR	IN with Remote Echoing Input	b
GKS cR	IN with Remote Echoing Input	c
GKS 0R	OUT with Echo Output	0
GKS 1R	OUT with Echo Output	1,2
GKS 0bR	OUTIN with Echo Output	0b
GKS 1bR	OUTIN with Echo Output	1b,2b
GKS 0cR	OUTIN with Echo Output	0c
GKS 1cR	OUTIN with Echo Output	1c,2c

The tables that follow show the functions required in the Foundation, GKS, and CGM constituency profiles. The GKS profiles with Remote Echoing are very similar to those without. To conserve space, the two sets of profiles are superimposed in the tables. The following notation is used:

- dot (.) means *not required*; a cross (X) means *required*.

- O indicates that a function is required only for Echo Output;
  I that a function is required only for Remote Echo Input.

	Foundation			GKS						CGM
	Input	2out	1out	0a	12a	0b	12b	0c	12c	

Part 2 Functions

Virtual Device Management

	Input	2out	1out	0a	12a	0b	12b	0c	12c	CGM
INITIALIZE	X	X	X	X	X	X	X	X	X	X
RESET TO DEFAULTS	X	.	X	.	.	.	.	.	.	.
TERMINATE	X	X	X	X	X	X	X	X	X	X
MAKE PICTURE CURRENT	.	X	X	X	X	X	X	X	X	X
SET DEFERRAL MODE	.	.	.	.	X	.	X	.	X	.
PREPARE VIEW SURFACE	.	X	X	X	X	X	X	X	X	X
END PAGE	.	.	X	X	X	X	X	X	X	.
BACKGROUND COLOUR	.	.	.	.	.	.	.	.	.	X

Coordinate Space Control

	Input	2out	1out	0a	12a	0b	12b	0c	12c	CGM
VDC TYPE	.	.	.	.	.	.	.	.	.	X
VDC PRECISION FOR INTEGER POINTS	.	.	.	.	.	.	.	.	.	X
VDC PRECISION FOR REAL POINTS	.	.	.	.	.	.	.	.	.	X
VDC EXTENT	X	X	X	X	X	X	X	X	X	X
DEVICE VIEWPORT	X	X	X	X	X	X	X	X	X	X
DEVICE VIEWPORT SPECIFICATION UNITS	.	.	.	.	.	.	.	.	.	.
DEVICE VIEWPORT MAPPING	.	.	X	.	.	.	.	.	.	.
CLIP RECTANGLE	.	X	X	X	X	X	X	X	X	X
CLIP INDICATOR	.	X	X	X	X	X	X	X	X	X

Error Handling

	Input	2out	1out	0a	12a	0b	12b	0c	12c	CGM
POP ERROR STACK	.	.	.	X	X	X	X	X	X	.
EMPTY ERROR STACK	.	.	.	X	X	X	X	X	X	.
ERROR HANDLING	.	.	.	X	X	X	X	X	X	.

Miscellaneous Control

	Input	2out	1out	0a	12a	0b	12b	0c	12c	CGM
INTEGER PRECISION	.	.	.	.	.	.	.	.	.	X
REAL PRECISION	.	.	.	.	.	.	.	.	.	X
INDEX PRECISION	.	.	.	.	.	.	.	.	.	X
COLOUR PRECISION	.	.	.	.	.	.	.	.	.	X
COLOUR INDEX PRECISION	.	.	.	.	.	.	.	.	.	X
MESSAGE	.	.	.	X	X	X	X	X	X	X
APPLICATION DATA	.	.	.	.	.	.	.	.	.	X
ESCAPE	.	.	.	.	.	.	.	.	.	X
GET ESCAPE	.	.	.	.	.	.	.	.	.	.

Part II: Advanced Features of the CGI

	Foundation			GKS						CGM
	Input	2 Out	1 Out	01a	02a	1b	02b	01c	12c	

Part 3 Functions

Graphical Primitives

	Input	2Out	1Out	01a	02a	1b	02b	01c	12c	CGM
POLYLINE	.	X	X	X	X	X	X	X	X	X
DISJOINT POLYLINE	.	.	X	.	.	.	.	.	.	X
CIRCULAR ARC 3 POINT	.	.	X	.	.	.	.	.	.	X
CIRCULAR ARC CENTRE	.	.	X	.	.	.	.	.	.	X
CIRCULAR ARC CENTRE BACKWARDS	.	.	X	.	.	.	.	.	.	X
ELLIPTICAL ARC	.	.	X	.	.	.	.	.	.	X
POLYMARKER	.	.	X	X	X	X	X	X	X	X
TEXT	.	X	X	X	X	X	X	X	X	X
RESTRICTED TEXT	.	.	X	.	.	.	.	.	.	X
APPEND TEXT	.	.	X	.	.	.	.	.	.	X
POLYGON	.	.	X	X	X	X	X	X	X	X
POLYGON SET	.	.	X	.	.	.	.	.	.	X
RECTANGLE	.	.	X	.	.	.	.	.	.	X
CIRCLE	.	.	X	.	.	.	.	.	.	X
CIRCULAR ARC 3 POINT CLOSE	.	.	X	.	.	.	.	.	.	X
CIRCULAR ARC CENTRE CLOSE	.	.	X	.	.	.	.	.	.	X
ELLIPSE	.	.	X	.	.	.	.	.	.	X
ELLIPTICAL ARC CLOSE	.	.	X	.	.	.	.	.	.	X
CELL ARRAY	.	.	X	X	X	X	X	X	X	X
GENERALIZED DRAWING PRIMITIVE (GDP)	.	.	.	X	X	X	X	X	X	X

Attribute Functions

	Input	2Out	1Out	01a	02a	1b	02b	01c	12c	CGM
LINE BUNDLE INDEX	.	.	X	X	X	X	X	X	X	X
LINE TYPE	.	X	X	X	X	X	X	X	X	X
LINE WIDTH	.	.	.	X	X	X	X	X	X	X
LINE COLOUR	.	.	.	X	X	X	X	X	X	X
LINE REPRESENTATION	.	.	.	.	X	.	X	.	X	.
MARKER BUNDLE INDEX	.	.	X	X	X	X	X	X	X	X
MARKER TYPE	.	X	X	X	X	X	X	X	X	X
MARKER SIZE	.	.	X	X	X	X	X	X	X	X
MARKER COLOUR	.	.	X	X	X	X	X	X	X	X
MARKER REPRESENTATION	.	.	.	.	X	.	X	.	X	.
TEXT BUNDLE INDEX	.	.	X	X	X	X	X	X	X	X
TEXT FONT INDEX	.	.	.	X	X	X	X	X	X	X
TEXT PRECISION	.	.	X	X	X	X	X	X	X	X
TEXT COLOUR	.	.	.	X	X	X	X	X	X	X
TEXT PATH	.	.	X	X	X	X	X	X	X	X
TEXT ALIGNMENT	.	.	X	X	X	b	b	X	X	X
TEXT REPRESENTATION	.	.	.	.	X	.	X	.	X	.
CHARACTER EXPANSION FACTOR	.	.	X	X	X	X	X	X	X	X
CHARACTER SPACING	.	.	X	X	X	X	X	X	X	X
CHARACTER HEIGHT	.	X	X	X	X	X	X	X	X	X
CHARACTER ORIENTATION	.	.	X	X	X	X	X	X	X	X

	Foundation			GKS						CGM
	Input	Out2	Out1	0a	1a	0b	1b	0c	1c	
CHARACTER SET INDEX	.	.	.	.	.	.	.	.	.	X
ALTERNATE CHARACTER SET INDEX	.	.	.	.	.	.	.	.	.	X
FILL BUNDLE INDEX	.	.	X	X	X	X	X	X	X	X
INTERIOR STYLE	.	.	X	X	X	X	X	X	X	X
FILL COLOUR	.	.	.	X	X	X	X	X	X	X
HATCH INDEX	.	.	X	X	X	X	X	X	X	X
PATTERN INDEX	.	.	.	X	X	X	X	X	X	X
FILL REFERENCE POINT	.	.	.	X	X	X	X	X	X	X
PATTERN TABLE	.	.	.	X	X	X	X	X	X	X
PATTERN SIZE	.	.	.	X	X	X	X	X	X	X
FILL REPRESENTATION	.	.	.	.	X	.	X	.	X	.
EDGE BUNDLE INDEX	.	.	X	X	X	X	X	X	X	X
EDGE TYPE	.	.	X	X	X	X	X	X	X	X
EDGE WIDTH	.	.	.	X	X	X	X	X	X	X
EDGE COLOUR	.	.	.	X	X	X	X	X	X	X
EDGE VISIBILITY	.	.	X	X	X	X	X	X	X	X
EDGE REPRESENTATION	.	.	X	.	X	.	X	.	X	.

Output and Attribute Control Functions

	Foundation			GKS						CGM
	Input	Out2	Out1	0a	1a	0b	1b	0c	1c	
COLOUR SELECTION MODE	.	.	.	.	.	.	.	.	.	X
COLOUR VALUE EXTENT	.	.	.	.	.	.	.	.	.	X
AUXILIARY COLOUR	.	.	.	.	.	.	.	.	.	X
TRANSPARENCY	.	.	.	.	.	.	.	.	.	X
COLOUR TABLE	.	.	.	X	X	X	X	X	X	X
LINE WIDTH SPECIFICATION MODE	.	.	.	.	.	.	.	.	.	X
EDGE WIDTH SPECIFICATION MODE	.	.	.	.	.	.	.	.	.	X
MARKER SIZE SPECIFICATION MODE	.	.	X	.	.	.	.	.	.	X
ASPECT SOURCE FLAGS	.	.	X	X	X	X	X	X	X	X
CHARACTER SET LIST	.	.	.	.	.	.	.	.	.	X
BEGIN FIGURE	.	.	X	.	.	.	.	.	.	X
END FIGURE	.	.	X	.	.	.	.	.	.	X
NEW REGION	.	.	X	.	.	.	.	.	.	X
IMPLICIT EDGE VISIBILITY	.	.	X	.	.	.	.	.	.	X
SAVE PRIMITIVE ATTRIBUTES	.	.	.	.	.	.	.	.	.	.
RESTORE PRIMITIVE ATTRIBUTES	.	.	.	.	.	.	.	.	.	.
CHARACTER CODING ANNOUNCER	.	.	.	.	.	.	.	.	.	.
GET TEXT EXTENT	.	.	.	.	.	.	.	.	.	.

	Foundation			GKS						CGM
	Input	2out	1out	01a	102a	0 2b	1 2b	0 2c	1 2c	

Part 4 Functions

Segment Manipulation

GET NEW SEGMENT IDENTIFIER	.	.	.	.	.	.	.	.	.	.
OPEN SEGMENT	.	.	.	.	X	.	X	.	X	.
REOPEN SEGMENT	.	.	.	.	.	.	.	.	.	.
CLOSE SEGMENT	.	.	.	.	X	.	X	.	X	.
COPY SEGMENT	.	.	.	.	X	.	X	.	X	.
DELETE SEGMENT	.	.	.	.	X	.	X	.	X	.
DELETE ALL SEGMENTS	.	.	.	.	X	.	X	.	X	.
RENAME SEGMENT	.	.	.	.	X	.	X	.	X	.
REDRAW SEGMENT	.	.	.	.	.	.	.	.	.	.
REDRAW ALL SEGMENTS	.	.	.	.	X	.	X	.	X	.
IMPLICIT SEGMENT REGENERATION MODE	.	.	.	.	X	.	X	.	X	.
PICK IDENTIFIER	.	.	.	.	X	.	X	.	X	.

Segment Attributes

SEGMENT TRANSFORM	.	.	.	.	X	.	X	.	X	.
SEGMENT VISIBILITY	.	.	.	.	X	.	X	.	X	.
SEGMENT HIGHLIGHTING	.	.	.	.	X	.	X	.	X	.
SEGMENT DISPLAY PRIORITY	.	.	.	.	X	.	X	.	X	.
SEGMENT DETECTABILITY	.	.	.	.	X	.	X	.	X	.
SEGMENT PICK PRIORITY	.	.	.	.	X	.	X	.	X	.

Segment Interrogations

SIMULATE PICK	.	.	.	.	.	.	.	.	.	.
INHERITANCE FILTER	.	.	.	.	X	.	X	.	X	.

	Foundation			GKS				CGM
	Input	2 Output	1 Output	01 a	10 2 b	10 2 c	01 2 c	

Part 5 Functions

Logical Input Device Functions

	Foundation			GKS				CGM
INITIALIZE LOGICAL INPUT DEVICE	X	.	.	.	.	X X X X		.
RELEASE INPUT DEVICE	X	.	.	.	.	X X X X		.
SET ACKNOWLEDGEMENT STATE	.	.	.	.	.	X X X X		.
PUT CURRENT xxx† MEASURE	.	.	.	.	.	X X X X		.
SET ECHO DATA	.	.	.	.	.	X X X X		.
SET ECHO STATE	.	.	.	.	.	X X X X		.
SET xxx† DEVICE DATA	.	.	.	.	.	X X X X		.
SET PROMPT STATE	.	.	.	.	.	X X X X		.
ASSOCIATE TRIGGERS	.	.	.	.	.	. . . .		.
REQUEST xxx†	X	.	.	.	.	X X X X		.
SAMPLE xxx†	.	.	.	.	.	. . X X		.
INITIALIZE ECHO REQUEST	.	.	.	I	I	. . . .		.
ECHO REQUEST xxx†	.	.	.	I	I	. . . .		.
INITIALIZE EVENT QUEUE	.	.	.	.	.	. . X X		.
RELEASE EVENT QUEUE	.	.	.	.	.	. . X X		.
ENABLE EVENTS	.	.	.	.	.	. . X X		.
DISABLE EVENTS	.	.	.	.	.	. . X X		.
BLOCK EVENT QUEUE	.	.	.	.	.	. . X X		.
FLUSH EVENTS	.	.	.	.	.	. . X X		.
FLUSH DEVICE EVENTS	.	.	.	.	.	. . . .		.
AWAIT EVENT	.	.	.	.	.	. . X X		.
DEQUEUE xxx† EVENT	.	.	.	.	.	. . X X		.
AWAIT EVENT QUEUE TRANSFER	.	.	.	.	.	. . . .		.
RETRIEVE OVERFLOW EVENT	.	.	.	.	.	. . . .		.

Echo Output Functions

	Foundation			GKS				CGM
INITIALIZE xxx† ECHO OUTPUT	.	.	.	O O O O O O				.
RELEASE ECHO OUTPUT	.	.	.	O O O O O O				.
SET ACKNOWLEDGEMENT OUTPUT STATE	.	.	.	O O O O O O				.
SET ECHO OUTPUT STATE	.	.	.	O O O O O O				.
SET PROMPT OUTPUT STATE	.	.	.	O O O O O O				.
UPDATE xxx† ECHO OUTPUT	.	.	.	O O O O O O				.

† The "xxx"'s represent functions which exist for each device class (CHOICE, etc.), but the parameterization is obviously different due to the data types used, etc.

	Foundation			GKS						CGM
	Input	2out	1out	01 2a	1 2a	0 2b	1 2b	0 2c	1 2c	

Part 6 Functions

Raster Output and Attributes

PIXEL ARRAY	.	.	.	.	.	.	.	.	.	.
MAPPED BITMAP										
FOREGROUND COLOUR	.	.	.	.	.	.	.	.	.	.
FILL BITMAP (name, region)	.	.	.	.	.	.	.	.	.	.

Raster Control Functions

CREATE BITMAP	.	.	.	.	.	.	.	.	.	.
DELETE BITMAP	.	.	.	.	.	.	.	.	.	.
SELECT DRAWING BITMAP	.	.	.	.	.	.	.	.	.	.
DISPLAY BITMAP	.	.	.	.	.	.	.	.	.	.
DRAWING MODE	.	.	.	.	.	.	.	.	.	.
SOURCE DESTINATION BITBLT	.	.	.	.	.	.	.	.	.	.
TILE THREE OPERAND BITBLT	.	.	.	.	.	.	.	.	.	.
PATTERN SOURCE BITBLT	.	.	.	.	.	.	.	.	.	.

    (note: not expected in next draft)

Raster Inquiry Functions

GET PIXEL ARRAY	.	.	.	X	X	X	X	X	X	.
GET PIXEL ARRAY DIMENSIONS	.	.	.	X	X	X	X	X	X	.

Chapter 11

Implementations of the CGI

11.1 Overview

Strictly speaking, it is premature to discuss implementations of the CGI. The current version of the CGI standard is only at draft proposal stage, within both ANSI and ISO. (See Appendix C for a complete discussion of the stages of standardization and the standardization process.) Nevertheless, the CGI project has been underway within the US since 1981 and within ISO since 1984.

CGI's influence has been felt in software and hardware offered to the commercial marketplace, since IBM offered the Graphics Development Toolkit VDI™ (Virtual Device Interface) for the IBM PC™ in early 1984. The IBM VDI was actually developed by Graphic Software Systems (Beaverton, OR). The VDI is an implementation of a subset of the CGI, as it was specified at the end of 1984. It is oriented around those capabilities needed to support GKS level 0b, augmented by fairly rich raster graphics functionality. Because of GSS's microcomputer market target and early market entry, they concentrated on a lean, fast implementation for the IBM PC. GSS released a second version of this product, known as GSS*CGI™, in the fall of 1985. IBM followed suit with GDT 2.0 in the spring of 1986.

Then in 1986, Digital Research (Monterey, CA) released its Graphics Environment Manager (GEM™). Included with GEM was a graphics subroutine library, known as GEM VDI. Also in 1986, Microsoft (Bellevue, WA) released Microsoft Windows™, with an integrated graphics library, called Microsoft GDI™. All these products were targetted at the IBM Personal Computer, although GSS also has been successful in selling GSS*CGI to UNIX workstation manufacturers.

Obviously, none of these products can implement all the functions of the current version (December 1986) of the CGI, because they were written and released for use long before the current draft was agreed upon. Yet, all were directly influenced by the CGI standard development effort. In fact, several of the current features of the CGI–especially in the raster graphics area–were first suggested or refined by experts from GSS, DRI, and Microsoft.

Towards the end of this period (1986-87), a mainframe and minicomputer GKS software supplier, Nova Graphics International (Austin, TX), actively developed and then marketed a version of the CGI to hardware and workstation suppliers, for embedding in their products. This effort, along with a similar marketing strategy by GSS, has influenced the current generation (1987-88) of graphics chips and boards.

In the rest of this chapter, we will take a closer look at the products and influence of these four companies. The information in this chapter is taken from company documentation and may no longer be completely accurate at the time you read this section. Furthermore, due to limited personal experience with the products, the authors cannot vouch for the performance or correct behaviour of each of the products described. However, all companies seem to be succeeding with their product lines based on CGI, and at least Nova Graphics seems to have a strategy of tracking the development of the CGI standard to influence new versions of its products.

Table 11.1 shows which of the currently specified CGI functions are supported in the products of GSS, DRI, Microsoft, and Nova. We have taken a fairly liberal interpretation of a supported function. In many cases, the function definition or function name has changed since it was included in the commercial product. In other cases, the capability is present (e.g., setting input echo mode on or off) but is provided, not as a separate function, but as a parameter to another function. In still other cases, the function is only partially implemented (e.g., support for upright, non-skewed ellipses, but not arbitrary ellipses). Table 11.1 should not be looked at from a conformance point-of-view. Rather, it indicates, in a very general way, the overlap between the commercial subroutine libraries of four software suppliers and the current version of the CGI draft.

11.2 Traditional Output Primitives and Attributes

GSS, DRI, and Nova provide very similar support for output primitives. Microsoft's GDI provides fewer output primitives. DRI has provided a few new output primitives like rounded rectangle and filled contoured regions.

Nova is the only company to offer nearly the entire CGI attribute model, including settable bundled attributes and the full graphics text model. GSS and DRI lack support for bundles and only partially implement the CGI text model. Microsoft GDI has quite a different attribute model from CGI and finding direct parallels with the CGI attribute model is difficult. Regardless of the similarity with CGI, GSS, DRI, and Microsoft have all found it necessary to offer additional attributes like user-specifiable line types and control over line join and line cap appearance.

11.3 Raster Graphics Capabilities

The CGI is the first graphics standard to contain support for creating and manipulating bitmaps and displaying them on raster output devices. GSS and Microsoft appear to be the strongest in this area, although DRI and Nova can be expected to improve their offerings when the CGI raster functionality becomes stable.

11.4 Control

Nova Graphics is strongest in this area. The other offerings are minimal, but sufficient to support more traditional graphics applications and subroutine libraries like GKS layered on top of the CGI. Nova's leadership here is not surprising, because some of the recent work has involved this aspect of the CGI and because Nova is targetting the use of its CGI as an interpreter of CGMs. Consequently, Nova has followed a development strategy of implementing those functions necessary to support the CGM.

None of the suppliers have yet implemented the CGI error handling philosophy nor have they provided the type and precision functions necessary to specify the data stream protocol for communicating to the CGI device (or metafile). Because of Nova's interest in the metafile, we would expect them to provide these additional functions in a forthcoming release.

Although the CGI is restricted to those functions that control the behaviour of a single virtual graphics device, all the suppliers have empowered their CGI implementations with the ability to address multiple CGI devices concurrently. The ISO experts are still debating how to provide this facility in the CGI standard or, in fact, whether such a specification lies outside the scope of the standard. Current thinking is that concurrent access to multiple CGI devices will be managed outside the standard.

11.5 Segmentation

Only Nova Graphics provides segmentation support in their CGI. GSS, DRI, and Microsoft require the application developer to maintain his own graphical data base.

Nova's implementation is indeed very rich and lacks only the most recently added function–inheritance filter. We would expect that function to be added in a future release.

Despite their lack of attention to the CGI segment model, both DRI (via GEM) and Microsoft (via Windows) offer a collection of user interface management tools–menus, scroll bars, icons, and other objects–that are created and managed by an integrated collection of software in which their CGI resides. This facility can be viewed as a special-purpose segmentation library.

GSS has deliberately chosen to avoid building either a general-purpose segmentation facility or a special-purpose windowing facility. Instead, GSS positions its CGI as a low-level, low-overhead, high-performance tool on which one can easily build segmentation and other such facilities. This marketing and architectural approach is viable as long as GSS targets devices, like the IBM EGA and VGA graphics adapter cards that lack significant high-level firmware and on-board RAM. However, when display lists are kept in the device and the picture may be updated without returning to the application program, CGIs that lack the richer capabilities of segmentation will no longer suffice. DRI and Microsoft are in the same situation, because their windowing objects are built above their internal CGI interface through which they talk to graphics devices.

11.6 Input

Microsoft's input model is not based on the logical input device model that is found in all the interactive graphics standards projects, including GKS, PHIGS, and CGI. Instead, it is based on keyboard and mouse input. All higher level input operations must be constructed out of this physical level of input. This permits fine control over the input dialog, but it places a very large burden on application programmers to build consistent and powerful input tools.

GSS and DRI implement four (*choice*, *locator*, *string*, *valuator*) of the eight logical input devices specified in the current version of the CGI. Nova supports these and adds support for the *pick* and *stroke* logical input devices. The new device classes of *area* and *general* were added so recently that they are not yet implemented by any supplier.

As can be seen from Table 11.1, Nova provides a fairly full implementation of the CGI input model, including most of the functions needed for asynchronous event input. None of the other suppliers follow the CGI model very closely, reflecting the fact that this is the area of the CGI that has changed often and most dramatically in the past two years. GSS and DRI provide the basic facilities needed for GKS level b input; namely, *request* and *sample* input modes. In addition, DRI provides, through GEM, support for asynchronous input via keyboard and mouse.

When the input model is stable, we can expect suppliers targetting the UNIX workstation market to carefully examine the CGI input model for ideas, but the model will be attractive only to those programmers that seek portability across a wide range of interactive graphics devices and that seek to support a wide range of user interfaces. Otherwise, we expect that, as long as the windowed interface popularized by the Apple Macintosh™ remains in vogue, a simpler input model based on low-level access to keyboard and mouse input events will remain the predominant form of input facilities available to graphics systems programmers.

11.7 Hardware Manifestations of the CGI

The development of the CGI has affected three sorts of hardware: graphics chips, graphics boards, and graphics output devices.

The new generation of graphics chips, particularly the Texas Instruments TMS*34010™, the Intel 82786™, and the National Semiconductor RGP™, were profoundly influenced by the CGI. Indeed, the architects of these products had regular access to every draft of the CGI as it evolved and these three companies have participated in a significant manner in the development of the CGI. The result is that, for the first time, what the software wants to be done is closely matched by what the hardware can do. Consequently, it is now possible to build implementations of the CGI that perform at high speed with a minimum of overhead.

At the next level of integration, we are beginning to see a new generation of graphics boards that provide a subset of the CGI as their graphics language. Implemented in firmware either with these new chips or on custom bit-sliced microprocessors, the functionality represented by such boards as the CalComp 3400™ or the Microfield Graphics T4™ and T8™ is impressive as well as easy to interface to higher level graphics subroutine libraries. Because their device command language is based on the CGI, it is easy to adapt existing device drivers to interface to these new boards. Very little emulation software has to be written, because most of the support for the standard graphics output and attribute functions is present in firmware on the board. The bandwidth required to talk to these devices is also reduced compared to earlier versions of the boards, because the new CGI functions supported on the board are generally at a high-level and require less data to generate the desired visual effect.

The moving of CGI functionality down into the hardware is also seen in more elaborate and expensive systems, like vector-to-raster accelerators and printers and plotters. For example, the Precision Image C448™ colour electrostatic plotter has chosen to provide a CGI interface as its only graphics language. To support older graphics applications, CalComp, Versatec, and HPGL filters that map between these older, device-specific graphics formats to the more device-independent CGI are provided by Precision Image. Because so much of a peripheral supplier's success is dependent upon the number of graphics software suppliers that write drivers for his device, Precision Image is hoping that the ease of adapting existing drivers to the CGI will increase the breadth of products that will be able to support their plotter. We would expect other CGI devices to appear on the market over the next several years as the standard becomes frozen and companies become further aware of the advantages of using the CGI as a device interface standard.

Table 11.1. Comparison of CGI functionality by supplier

Part 2 Functions

	GSS	DRI GEM	Microsoft GDI	Nova
Virtual Device Management				
INITIALIZE	X	X	X	X
RESET TO DEFAULTS	X		X	X
TERMINATE	X	X	X	X
MAKE PICTURE CURRENT	X	X	X	X
SET DEFERRAL MODE				X
PREPARE VIEW SURFACE	X	X	X	X
END PAGE				
BACKGROUND COLOUR	X		X	
Coordinate Space Control				
VDC TYPE				
VDC PRECISION FOR INTEGER POINTS				
VDC PRECISION FOR REAL POINTS				
VDC EXTENT			X	X
DEVICE VIEWPORT			X	X
DEVICE VIEWPORT SPECIFICATION UNITS				X
DEVICE VIEWPORT MAPPING				X
CLIP RECTANGLE	X	X	X	X
CLIP INDICATOR				X
Error Handling				
POP ERROR STACK				
EMPTY ERROR STACK				
ERROR HANDLING				

	GSS	GEM	GDI	Nova
	DRI		Microsoft	

Error Handling

POP ERROR STACK
EMPTY ERROR STACK
ERROR HANDLING

Miscellaneous Control

	GSS	GEM	GDI	Nova
INTEGER PRECISION				
REAL PRECISION				
INDEX PRECISION				
COLOUR PRECISION				
COLOUR INDEX PRECISION				
MESSAGE				
APPLICATION DATA				
ESCAPE	X	X	X	
GET ESCAPE				

Part 3 Functions

Graphical Primitives

	GSS	GEM	GDI	Nova
POLYLINE	X	X	X	X
DISJOINT POLYLINE				
CIRCULAR ARC 3 POINT				
CIRCULAR ARC CENTRE	X	X	X	X
CIRCULAR ARC CENTRE BACKWARDS				
ELLIPTICAL ARC	X	X		X
POLYMARKER	X	X		X
TEXT	X	X	X	X
RESTRICTED TEXT				X
APPEND TEXT				
POLYGON	X	X	X	X
POLYGON SET				
RECTANGLE	X	X	X	X
CIRCLE	X	X		X
CIRCULAR ARC 3 POINT CLOSE				
CIRCULAR ARC CENTRE CLOSE	X	X	X	X
ELLIPSE	X	X	X	X
ELLIPTICAL ARC CLOSE	X	X		X
CELL ARRAY	X	X		

	GSS	DRI GEM	Microsoft GDI	Nova
Attribute Functions				
LINE BUNDLE INDEX				X
LINE TYPE	X	X	X	X
LINE WIDTH	X	X	X	X
LINE COLOUR	X	X	X	X
LINE REPRESENTATION			X	X
MARKER BUNDLE INDEX				X
MARKER TYPE	X	X	X	X
MARKER SIZE	X	X		X
MARKER COLOUR	X	X		X
MARKER REPRESENTATION				X
TEXT BUNDLE INDEX				X
TEXT FONT INDEX	X	X	X	X
TEXT PRECISION				X
TEXT COLOUR	X	X	X	X
TEXT PATH				X
TEXT ALIGNMENT	X	X		X
TEXT REPRESENTATION			X	X
CHARACTER EXPANSION FACTOR			X	
CHARACTER SPACING			X	X
CHARACTER HEIGHT	X	X	X	X
CHARACTER ORIENTATION	X	X	X	X
CHARACTER SET INDEX				
ALTERNATE CHARACTER SET INDEX				
FILL BUNDLE INDEX				X
INTERIOR STYLE	X	X	X	X
FILL COLOUR	X	X	X	X
HATCH INDEX	X	X	X	X
PATTERN INDEX	X	X	X	X
FILL REFERENCE POINT				
PATTERN TABLE		X		
PATTERN SIZE				
FILL REPRESENTATION			X	X
EDGE BUNDLE INDEX				X
EDGE TYPE		X		X
EDGE WIDTH		X		X
EDGE COLOUR		X		X
EDGE VISIBILITY		X		X
EDGE REPRESENTATION				X

Chapter 11: Implementations of the CGI   125

	GSS	DRI GEM	Microsoft GDI	Nova

Output and Attribute Control Functions

COLOUR SELECTION MODE				
COLOUR VALUE EXTENT				X
AUXILIARY COLOUR			X	X
TRANSPARENCY			X	X
COLOUR TABLE	X	X	X	X
LINE WIDTH SPECIFICATION MODE				
EDGE WIDTH SPECIFICATION MODE				
MARKER SIZE SPECIFICATION MODE				
ASPECT SOURCE FLAGS				X
CHARACTER SET LIST				
BEGIN FIGURE				
END FIGURE				
NEW REGION				
IMPLICIT EDGE VISIBILITY				
SAVE PRIMITIVE ATTRIBUTES				
RESTORE PRIMITIVE ATTRIBUTES				
CHARACTER CODING ANNOUNCER				
GET TEXT EXTENT	X	X	X	X

Part 4 Functions

Segment Manipulation

GET NEW SEGMENT IDENTIFIER				X
OPEN SEGMENT				X
REOPEN SEGMENT				X
CLOSE SEGMENT				X
COPY SEGMENT				X
DELETE SEGMENT				X
DELETE ALL SEGMENTS				X
RENAME SEGMENT				X
REDRAW SEGMENT				X
REDRAW ALL SEGMENTS				X
IMPLICIT SEGMENT REGENERATION MODE				X
PICK IDENTIFIER				X

Segment Attributes

SEGMENT TRANSFORM				X
SEGMENT VISIBILITY				X
SEGMENT HIGHLIGHTING				X
SEGMENT DISPLAY PRIORITY				X
SEGMENT DETECTABILITY				X
SEGMENT PICK PRIORITY				X

Segment Interrogations

SIMULATE PICK				X
INHERITANCE FILTER				

	GSS	DRI GEM	Microsoft GDI	Nova

Part 5 Functions

Logical Input Device Functions

	GSS	DRI GEM	Microsoft GDI	Nova
INITIALIZE LOGICAL INPUT DEVICE			X	
RELEASE INPUT DEVICE				X
SET ACKNOWLEDGEMENT STATE			X	
PUT CURRENT xxx† MEASURE				X
SET ECHO DATA				
SET ECHO STATE		X		X
SET xxx† DEVICE DATA				
SET PROMPT STATE				X
ASSOCIATE TRIGGERS				
REQUEST xxx†	X	X		X
SAMPLE xxx†	X	X		X
INITIALIZE ECHO REQUEST				
ECHO REQUEST xxx†				
INTIALIZE EVENT QUEUE				X
RELEASE EVENT QUEUE				X
ENABLE EVENTS				X
DISABLE EVENTS				X
BLOCK EVENT QUEUE				X
UNBLOCK EVENT QUEUE				X
FLUSH EVENTS				X
FLUSH DEVICE EVENTS				X
AWAIT EVENT				X
DEQUEUE xxx† EVENT				X
AWAIT EVENT QUEUE TRANSFER				
RETRIEVE OVERFLOW EVENT				X

Echo Output Functions

INITIALIZE xxx† ECHO OUTPUT
RELEASE ECHO OUTPUT
SET ACKNOWLEDGEMENT OUTPUT STATE
SET ECHO OUTPUT STATE
SET PROMPT OUTPUT STATE
UPDATE xxx† ECHO OUTPUT

---

† *The "xxx"'s represent functions that exist for each device class (CHOICE, etc.), but the parameterization is obviously different due to the data types used, etc.*

Chapter 11: Implementations of the CGI 127

	GSS	DRI GEM	Microsoft GDI	Nova
Part 6 Functions				
Raster Output and Attributes				
PIXEL ARRAY	X		X	
MAPPED BITMAP FOREGROUND COLOUR		X		X
FILL BITMAP	X	X	X	
Raster Control Functions				
CREATE BITMAP	X		X	X
DELETE BITMAP	X		X	X
SELECT DRAWING BITMAP	X			X
DISPLAY BITMAP				
DRAWING MODE				
SOURCE DESTINATION BITBLT	X	X	X	X
TILE THREE OPERAND BITBLT				
PATTERN SOURCE BITBLT	X	X	X	X
(note: not expected in next draft; provided by *bitmap* interior style)				
Raster Inquiry Functions				
GET PIXEL ARRAY	X	X	X	
GET PIXEL ARRAY DIMENSIONS	X		X	

PART III

The Computer Graphics Metafile

Chapter 12

CGM Concepts and Purposes

12.1 Metafiles

As we explained in Chap. 1, to exchange pictures among diverse applications and across separate programming environments, information can be captured at an interface and placed in a *graphical metafile*, a formatted disk or magnetic tape file containing graphical commands and data. These files can be transmitted over telephone lines and computer networks to be stored and processed at remote sites or reused locally as a library of predefined pictures.

There are two phases to the use of metafiles (see Fig. 12.1). To create the metafile, a metafile writer, or *generator*, must be available with a graphics package. To read and redisplay metafiles generated on other computers, a metafile reader, or *interpreter*, must be available on the system where the picture is to be used. Two principal kinds of graphical metafiles are being standardized: GKS metafiles and Computer Graphic Metafiles.

12.1.1 GKS Metafiles

A GKS metafile (GKSM) is an audit trail of the GKS commands that were used to generate a particular picture at the level of the GKS workstation. Although GKS metafiles may be interpreted outside the GKS environment, most users will use GKS to both generate and interpret these files. GKS metafiles are not very compact and, if the picture stored in the metafile were designed by the user in an incremental and iterative manner, the metafile may contain a large quantity of superfluous information.

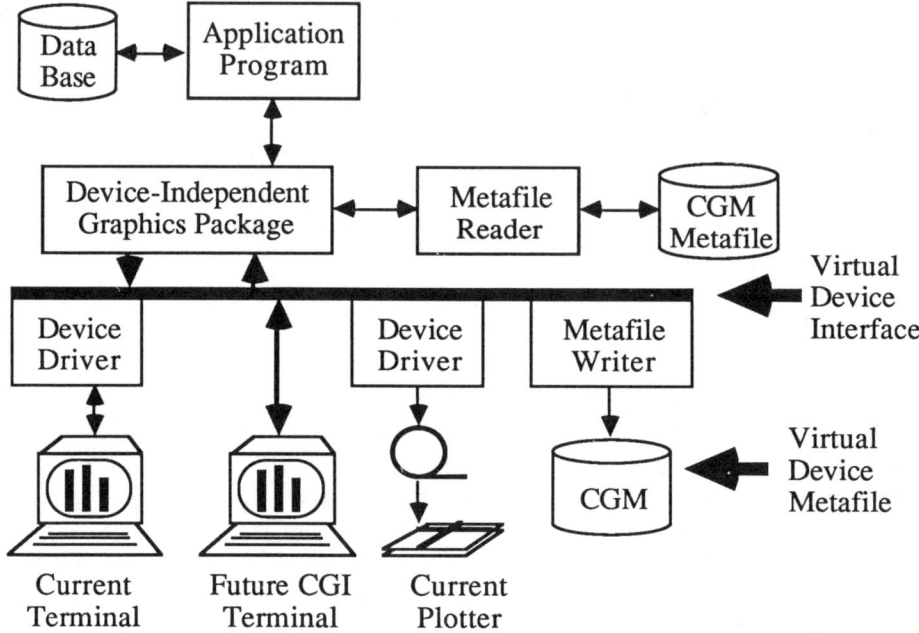

Fig. 12.1. Generating and interpreting metafiles

12.1.2 The Computer Graphics Metafile

The Computer Graphics Metafile (CGM) represents a snapshot of the final image that a program has created. Unlike the GKS metafile, the CGM is not intended to define pictures as an audit trail and, therefore, the definitions may be compressed by storing only the elements that make up the final picture.

The CGM provides a file format suitable for the storage and retrieval of picture description information. The file format consists of an ordered set of elements that can be used to describe pictures in a completely device-independent way (see Fig. 12.2). One or more pictures can be stored in a single metafile, and the metafile is defined in such a way that, in addition to sequential access to the whole metafile, random access to individual pictures is well defined. That is, the pictures are completely independent, one from another: their appearance does not depend upon the order in which they are accessed or displayed.

Metafile

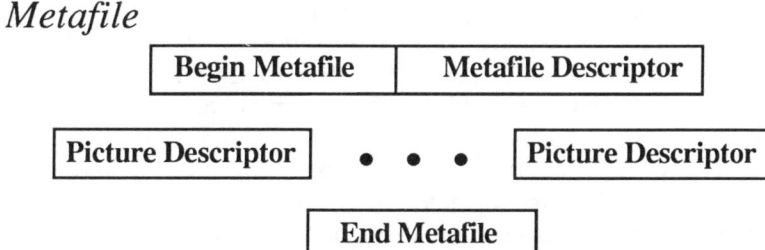

Picture Descriptor

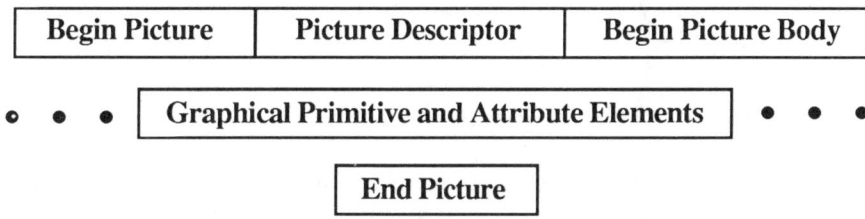

Fig. 12.2. CGM file structure

Two special elements–ESCAPE and APPLICATION DATA–have been provided to support uses of the CGM in ways that go beyond the exchange of pictures. Nongraphical data and graphical elements not yet standardized can be incorporated into CGMs in a regular way. When these extended metafiles are exchanged by cooperating processes, standard commercial products can be used to handle the standard metafile elements, and new code need be written only for the special, non-standardized elements. Large groups of users of extended metafiles can get together and agree upon a set of extensions–just as MAP and TOP users have agreed upon guidelines to the implementation of the OSI standards. For example, the elements of a business chart–like legend entries, tick marks, and axis labels–or the elements of a project schedule–like PERT chart symbols, milestone markers, or project name–could be marked in the metafile. An editing program could be written to read such metafiles and allow modifications to them before rendering the chart on a hardcopy device or including it in a report or manual. All the CGM elements are explained in Chap. 13.

In addition to a functional specification, the CGM standard documents three standard encodings of the metafile semantics. The Character encoding is designed to require minimum metafile size and is suitable for transmission across networks of heterogeneous systems but may be expensive to encode and decode. The Binary encoding requires minimum effort to generate and interpret but is not well suited for exchange between computers of different arithmetic data types. It is nearly as efficiently coded as the Character encoding. The Clear-text encoding provides maximum readability and editability for ease of use by humans (e.g., for debugging purposes) but, generally, pays a heavy penalty in size and performance. The size is much larger because English and other natural languages contain a lot of redundancy. The performance is worse because parsing and recognizing text strings and converting appropriate strings to internal numbers for use by a graphics subsystem is expensive in its use of CPU cycles. The three standardized encodings are all described in more detail in Chap. 14.

If none of the standardized encodings meet the needs of a group of applications that want to exchange pictures, the CGM standard provides guidelines for specifying private encodings. These guidelines are also explained in Chap. 14.

12.2 A Reference Model for Data Interchange

Figure 12.3 shows three levels of data interchange. At the lowest level, simple *files* can be exchanged between systems (path A). The file transfer, access, and management (FTAM) standard–part of the OSI level 7 facilities–is designed to handle this activity, but implementations of FTAM know nothing about the semantics of the contents of the files it transfers. In its full generality, it will automatically convert the format (i.e., syntax) of files as part of the transfer process if the file types have been registered. Indeed, the three encodings of the metafile are being registered for use with FTAM. Although FTAM knows nothing about graphics, it should be possible to use FTAM to transfer graphical metafiles from system to system (paths B and C).

At the next level of exchange, graphical metafiles are used to transfer pictures, drawings, or images between graphical processes (path D). In this case, not only is the syntax known to the cooperating processes, but also the semantics; that is, both processes know about such things as colour tables, bundled attributes, filled areas, and rectangular arrays of colours. However, they don't know about any application-specific information like surfaces and centres of mass, nor relationships between entities like the association between two connected objects. Only extended metafiles that use APPLICATION DATA elements are able to communicate information that goes beyond the elementary picture representation information. Picture files may be sent directly to print spooler tasks (path E) and thence to hardcopy devices (path F), or first they may be manipulated by application-specific programs like desktop publishing applications (path G). Such programs, perhaps written using GKS, will manipulate the pictures, merge the images with other, non-graphical information such as text and document layout commands from a word processing program, and then route the layed-out pages to a print spooler (path H) or directly to a hardcopy device like a laser printer (path I). The spooler and other application programs could use CGI to talk to the graphics hardcopy devices. These application programs may also produce structured, editable output like full drawings that may again be treated as product data bases (path J).

At the highest level of exchange, one needs to transfer product *data bases*. In the CAD/CAM/CIM environment, the product definitions often have a high degree of geometric information; indeed, if the product is a drawing, it may consist principally of information that is pictorial. However, the purpose of a product data base is to support such functions as design, analysis, manufacturing and testing. Furthermore, it is sometimes desirable that cooperating processes not only share a product data base, but also that they share views of the same objects so that, for example, engineers may see the same view and consult with each other concerning the object's design and manufacture. The two principal standards at this level (path K) are the Initial Graphics Exchange Specification (IGES) and the Product Definition Exchange Specification (PDES).

CGM pictures can be derived directly from IGES or PDES formatted data bases (paths L and M) for archiving and for inclusion in technical manuals and reports. Typical CAD/CAM programs, again perhaps written using PHIGS to obtain device independence, will build internal geometric models and data structures by loading data from an external product definition data base (path N). During the processing, CGM picture files may be produced (path O) for later use in such applications as computer-assisted publishing and picture previewing.

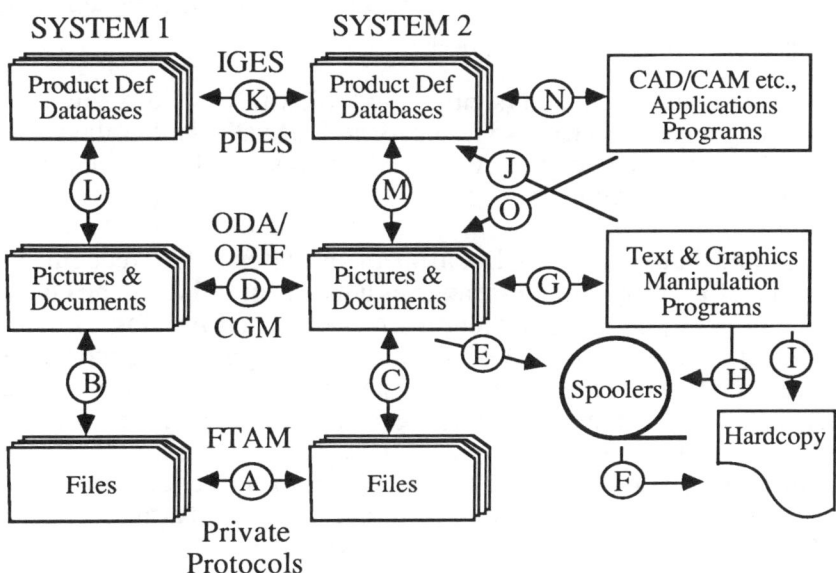

Fig. 12.3. Levels of data interchange

12.3 Purposes of Metafiles

12.3.1 Picture File Transfer and Storage

A graphical metafile, which is used to transfer and store pictures, has great value in a networked environment. For example, PCs are being connected to large mainframe hosts for number-crunching and access to the corporate or engineering data bases. Because the users are trying to exchange information (and not just data) and because pictures convey information much more efficiently than words and numbers, graphical metafiles, especially those extended to handle text and graphics, will play an important role in integrated environments. Because graphical metafiles store pictures in a resolution independent manner, these pictures can be previewed on low-cost displays like those found on today's PCs and still be printed on high-resolution printers, plotters, and camera systems. Metafiles can also be stored for later use–in fact, can be stored for years and then be retrieved for plotting on devices with new capabilities and resolutions not imagined when the metafile was created.

In the text and office systems arena, at this level of interchange, we also find the Office Document Architecture/Office Document Interchange Format (ODA/ODIF) standard (ISO DIS 8613), which is used to exchange so-called "compound documents" that may contain a mixture of pure text, graphics pictures, and facsimile images. The current proposal for a Computer Graphics Content Architecture contains the CGM as its base technology. This proposal is described in more detail in Chap. 15. Thus, the CGM is a very important standard for such applications as technical documentation, maintenance manuals, and project plans.

Another Text and Office Systems standard, the Standard Generalized Markup Language (SGML), also refers to the CGM standard as the means by which externally created pictures and drawings would be imported and merged with a text document.

In the United States, the US Department of Defense has recognized the importance of information interchange as a means of reducing the enormous cost of military system acquisition, maintenance, and training. In 1985, it commenced a Computer-aided Acquisition and Logistical Support (CALS) initiative to encourage the use of formal standards as a mechanism to support interchange of contract deliverables–specifications, documentation, and training materials–between the government and its suppliers. A military standard (MIL-STD-1840A) has been drafted to reference such standards and to provide further particulars concerning conformance to these standards for use by the US Department of Defense. Because technical drawings comprise a significant portion of these deliverables, the CGM has been included (along with IGES and SGML) as major standards for the interchange of information.

Outside the US government, a major industry initiative, called MAP/TOP (Manufacturing Automation Protocols/Technical Office Protocols), was started in the mid-1980s under the leadership of General Motors and the Boeing Company. The MAP portion of the initiative concentrated on getting agreement among commercial suppliers of networking software and hardware so that computers provided by competing manufacturers could be linked together in local area networks on the factory floor and that files could be transferred among them. The TOP portion is concentrating on linking the various tasks with the technical office environment–word processing, presentation graphics, documentation, illustration, and desktop publishing. The most recent release of the TOP specifications (version 3.0) include mention of GKS and CGM as standards to be used in the technical office. Appendix F provides a more detailed explaination of the so-called TOP Application Profile for CGM.

12.3.2 Product Definition Data Base Transfer and Storage

The term *product data* denotes the totality of data elements that completely define the product for all applications over its expected life cycle. Product data includes the geometry, topology, relationships, tolerances, attributes, and features necessary to completely define a component part or an assembly of parts for the purposes of design, analysis, manufacture, test and inspection.

IGES. The Initial Graphics Exchange Specification is a mature mechanism for the digital exchange of database information among present-day CAD systems. Now in its third version, engineering drawings, 3D wireframe and surfaced part models, printed wiring product descriptions, finite element mesh descriptions, and process instrumentation diagrams are addressed by IGES. IGES information, including drawings and 3D wireframe product models, is intended for *human* interpretation at the receiving site.

PDES. Whereas IGES has addressed the need for data exchange where the received product model is interpreted by a human either as a display or as a generated plot, the Product Data Exchange Specification (PDES) project is focussed on exchanging product models with sufficient information content as to be interpretable directly by advanced CAD/CAM application programs. In addition to geometry, PDES will support a wide range of non-geometric data such as manufacturing features, tolerance specifications, material properties, and surface finish specifications.

It must be recognized that IGES and PDES have different technological objectives and are in vastly different stages of development. IGES is mature and in production; PDES is in its early stages of development and will not be ready for use before the late 1980's or early 1990's. IGES is a US standard, while PDES represents the US contribution to the international effort in product data exchange (ISO TC184). Until PDES has been proven, IGES will continue to evolve with upwardly compatible versions to support the commitments already made by industry. Much of the development work on PDES is expected to benefit this continuing IGES work.

Although much of PDES version 1.0 will have little to do directly with graphics, the early work on PDES includes a task to develop a conceptual schema to support the mechanical design of flat plates with circular holes. Wireframe geometry will be used. The schema will support some user-view presentation (viewing) scenarios pertinent to this area of mechanical design. Wireframe geometry entities and the presentation entities have been developed as part of this tasks. These entities use concepts drawn from the graphics standards.

12.3.3 Transaction Recording

Sometimes there is a need to record everything that is passed across an interface. Such transaction files are called *audit trails*. Audit trails can be used for a variety of purposes.

Audit trails provide a simple graphical metafile for the exchange of pictures. The GKS metafile (GKSM) is an example of such a metafile. The GKSM stores all the output transactions at the GKS workstation interface. Consequently, segment contents and segment manipulations are recorded, as well as the usual output primitive and attribute information similar to that recorded in the CGM. Audit trails like the GKSM typically are useful only within a homogeneous graphics system environment, because they are expensive to interpret unless the underlying graphics system is also GKS. Audit trails are also not very compact, because superfluous data may be placed into the metafile–data that records intermediate pictures between those pictures of value to the program.

Audit trails are particularly well suited as a graphical restart/recovery mechanism. The GKSM can be activated concurrently with, say, the graphics display screen. As commands are issued to the GKS workstations to cause picture elements to appear to the operator, they are also captured in the GKSM. If the program were to be aborted unexpectedly, the GKSM could be interpreted at the beginning of the next session to cause the previous picture to be recreated and the GKS system to be placed into the same state that it was in when the program terminated abnormally.

The CGM extensions work described in Chap. 17 is designed to permit the CGM to function as a complete GKSM.

12.3.4 Symbol Libraries

Many graphical applications, especially in the CAD/CAM area, need to start with a collection of graphical symbols that can be used by the operator to build up more complex pictures and drawings. Rather than have the application create these standard symbols from scratch each time a new session starts, it is faster and more convenient to be able to read in the symbol definitions from some external source. Depending upon how these symbols are to be used by the application, a variety of metafiles can be used for this purpose.

In general, the metafile used is a function of the kind of graphical manipulations needed by the application or allowed by the underlying graphics support system. If the system is GKS, a CGM or a GKSM can be used to store symbol instances used to load a symbol library. Each CGM picture or each GKSM segment can correspond to a symbol that can be stored in the Workstation Independent Segment Storage of GKS.

If the underlying system is PHIGS, the application is probably using the PHIGS centralized Structure Store for both viewing and modelling of the graphical elements. The PHIGS Archive File mechanism has been designed to allow the saving and restoring of complete structure networks from the Structure Store. PHIGS defines a complex set of rules for resolving what happens if structures are saved into Archive Files when the networks are not completely defined, and what happens if structures are retrieved from an Archive File when the Structure Store already contains a structure of the same name.

If the application is dealing with product data bases, it may be necessary to load an entire data base prior to allowing the operator to start interacting with the application. But IGES and PDES files can be very large, with complex interrelationships specified within the file; consequently, they are often unsuitable as symbol libraries which would be loaded each time the program is run. Instead, non-standardized, proprietary product data bases may be linked into the application when it is initialized.

In summary, almost any graphical picture or product file format can serve as a symbol library. The appropriate file format to use depends on the application and the underlying graphical system on which the application is built. For portability of symbol libraries, the PHIGS Archive File and CGM offer a general solution, while still demonstrating good performance and size characteristics.

Chapter 13

CGM Elements

Each instance of a Computer Graphics Metafile is a collection of elements drawn from the standardized set of elements listed in Table 13.1. Metafiles have a certain structure as illustrated by the state structure of a hypothetical CGM parser, shown in Fig. 13.1.

Any metafile must contain certain delimiter elements. In addition, a CGM may include control elements to assist in interpretation, picture descriptor elements for declaring parameter modes of attribute elements, graphical primitive elements for specifying visible entities, attribute elements for specifying the appearance of the graphical primitive elements, escape elements for accessing non-standardized features of particular devices, and external elements for communication of information external to the definition of the pictures in the CGM.

The different categories of metafile elements are described in the remainder of this chapter. The Clear Text Encoding of the CGM (see Chap. 14 for more detail) will be used to provide sample CGMs and CGM fragments. If the CGM element has an analogous CGI function, the CGI section reference is given at the right of the line containing the CGM element name and parameter list. If the list of parameters for a CGM element is too long to fit on one line, the parameter list is given in a short paragraph following the CGM element name.

13.1 Delimiter Elements

The five Delimiter Elements listed below give a metafile interpreter sufficient information to permit correct interpretation of the metafile elements and to make informed decisions concerning the resources needed for display.

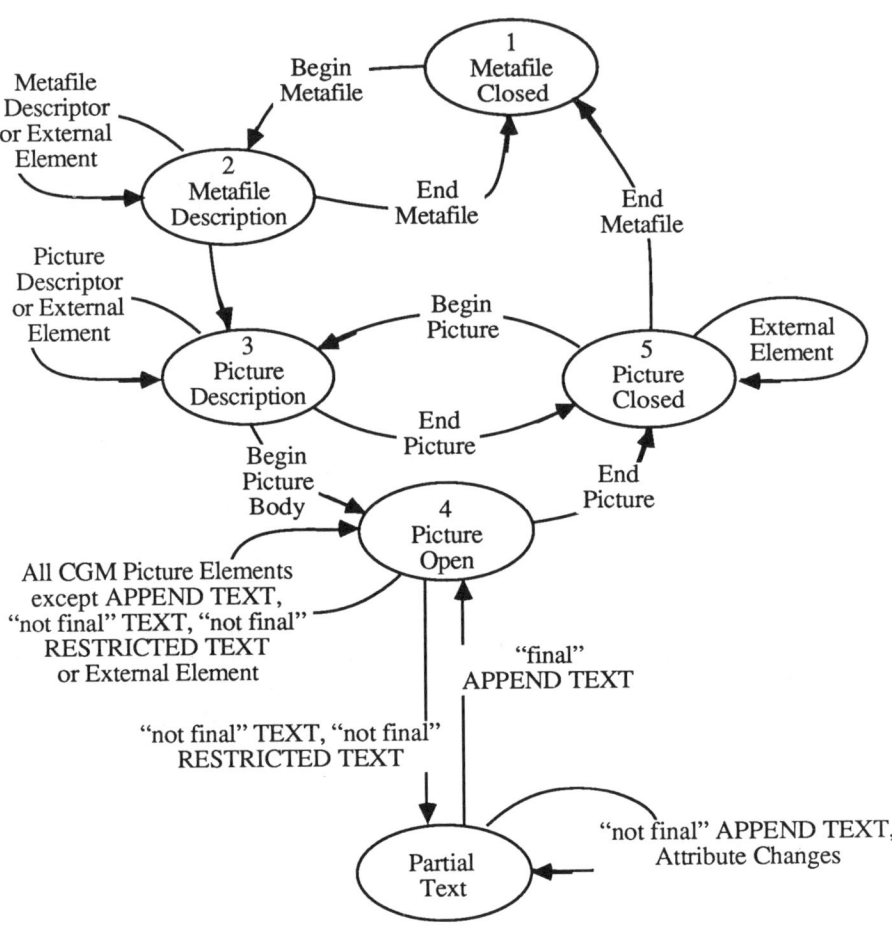

Fig. 13.1. CGM state diagram

Table 13.1(a). CGM elements

Element Class		Elements
Delimiter		BEGIN METAFILE END METAFILE BEGIN PICTURE BEGIN PICTURE BODY END PICTURE
Metafile Descriptor	 * * * * * * * * * * *	METAFILE VERSION METAFILE DESCRIPTION VDC TYPE INTEGER PRECISION REAL PRECISION INDEX PRECISION COLOUR PRECISION COLOUR INDEX PRECISION MAXIMUM COLOUR INDEX COLOUR VALUE EXTENT METAFILE ELEMENT LIST METAFILE DEFAULTS REPLACEMENT FONT LIST CHARACTER SET LIST CHARACTER CODING ANNOUNCER
Picture Descriptor	* * * * 	SCALING MODE COLOUR SELECTION MODE LINE WIDTH SPECIFICATION MODE MARKER SIZE SPECIFICATION MODE EDGE WIDTH SPECIFICATION MODE VDC EXTENT BACKGROUND COLOUR
Control	* * 	VDC INTEGER PRECISION VDC REAL PRECISION AUXILIARY COLOUR TRANSPARENCY CLIP RECTANGLE CLIP INDICATOR
Graphical Primitive		See Table 3.1(b).
Attribute		See Table 3.1(b).
Escape		ESCAPE
External		MESSAGE APPLICATION DATA

Table 13.1(b). CGM elements (cont)

Primitive Type	Primitives		Associated Attributes

Line	POLYLINE
	DISJOINT POLYLINE
	CIRCULAR ARC
	  3 POINT
	CIRCULAR ARC
	  CENTRE
	ELLIPTICAL ARC
			LINE BUNDLE INDEX
			LINE TYPE
			LINE WIDTH
			LINE COLOUR

Marker	POLYMARKER		MARKER BUNDLE INDEX MARKER TYPE MARKER SIZE MARKER COLOUR

Text	TEXT
	RESTRICTED TEXT
	APPEND TEXT
		
		*
		*
			TEXT BUNDLE INDEX
			TEXT FONT INDEX
			TEXT PRECISION
			CHARACTER EXPANSION
			  FACTOR
			CHARACTER SPACING
			TEXT COLOUR
			CHARACTER HEIGHT
			CHARACTER ORIENTATION
			TEXT PATH
			TEXT ALIGNMENT
			CHARACTER SET INDEX
			ALTERNATE CHARACTER
			  SET INDEX

Filled Area	POLYGON
	POLYGON SET
	RECTANGLE
	CIRCLE
	CIRCULAR ARC
	  3 POINT CLOSE
	CIRCULAR ARC
	  CENTRE CLOSE
	ELLIPSE
	ELLIPTICAL ARC
	  CLOSE
			FILL BUNDLE INDEX
			INTERIOR STYLE
			FILL COLOUR
			HATCH INDEX
			PATTERN INDEX
			EDGE BUNDLE INDEX
			EDGE TYPE
			EDGE WIDTH
			EDGE COLOUR
			EDGE VISIBILITY
			FILL REFERENCE POINT
			PATTERN TABLE
			PATTERN SIZE

	GENERALIZED
	  DRAWING
	  PRIMITIVE
			Appropriate standard attributes.

	All above		ASPECT SOURCE FLAGS
	CELL ARRAY		No attributes.
	All colour elements		COLOUR TABLE

BEGIN METAFILE *string.*

END METAFILE.

BEGIN PICTURE *string.*

BEGIN PICTURE BODY.

END PICTURE.

The BEGIN METAFILE and END METAFILE elements each occur exactly once in a complete metafile; the other elements occur as needed to represent one or more pictures. A minimally correct metafile consists of BEGIN METAFILE, a Metafile Descriptor consisting of METAFILE VERSION and METAFILE ELEMENTS LIST (see the next section), and END METAFILE. In the Clear Text encoding, it looks like:

>   BEGMF 'Example 13.1';
>
>   MFVERSION 1;
>
>   MFELEMLIST drawingplus;
>
>   ENDMF;

Of course, when interpreted, this metafile will not produce any visible output on a graphics device.

Other delimiter elements are provided to permit multiple metafiles to be stored on a single tape or disk and, consequently, to be transferred together. Each picture starts with a BEGIN PICTURE element and ends with an END PICTURE element. Between these delimiters, the Picture Descriptor is separated from the description of the picture contents by a BEGIN PICTURE BODY element. A minimal metafile with one picture looks like:

>   BEGMF 'Example 13.2';
>
>   MFVERSION 1;
>
>   MFELEMLIST drawingplus;
>
>   BEGPIC 'Picture 1';
>
>   BEGPICBODY;
>
>   ENDPIC;
>
>   ENDMF;

Once again, when interpreted, this metafile will not produce any visible output on a graphics device. Graphical primitive or escape elements specifying visible output must appear between BEGIN PICTURE BODY and END PICTURE in order for visible output to be produced.

The identifier parameters (of data type string) associated with BEGIN METAFILE and BEGIN PICTURE are not standardized by the CGM.

Every picture in a metafile is totally independent from every other picture in the metafile. This independence is enforced by the semantics of BEGIN PICTURE: the modal values of all metafile elements are returned to their default values at the start of each picture. Therefore, once the Metafile Descriptor has been read, access to individual pictures, on a random as opposed to sequential basis, may be safely accomplished if the encoding, access mechanism, and implementation permit.

13.2 Metafile Descriptor Elements

The Metafile Descriptor (MD) contains a group of elements whose function is to describe the functional capabilities required to interpret the CGM. Of the fifteen MD elements, only two are required to be present in all CGMs: METAFILE VERSION and METAFILE ELEMENT LIST. The metafile descriptor elements are described in the remaining paragraphs of this section.

METAFILE VERSION *version.*

Required element. The current version of the CGM standard is version one (1). Consequently, all CGMs conforming to ISO 8632:1985 must have the version parameter set to 1.

METAFILE DESCRIPTION *string.*

Optional element whose string parameter may used for any purposes such as identifying author, place of origin, and date/time of generation. The contents of the string parameter are not standardized by the CGM.

VDC TYPE *vdc-type.*   4.3

Optional element that declares whether Virtual Device Coordinates are specified as Integer or Real values. Default is INTEGER.

INTEGER PRECISION *precision.* 4.8

Optional element that declares the precision for operands of type *integer* (I) encountered subsequently in the metafile. The precision is defined as the field width measured in units applicable to the specific encoding. See Chap. 14 for the detailed specifications for each encoding.

REAL PRECISION *precision.* 4.8

Optional element that declares the precision for operands of type *real* (R) encountered subsequently in the metafile. The precision is defined as the field width measured in units applicable to the specific encoding. The precision may consist of parameters that define subfields of the base data type. See Chap. 14 for the detailed specifications for each encoding.

INDEX PRECISION *precision.* 4.8

Optional element that declares the precision for operands of type *index* (IX) encountered subsequently in the metafile. The precision is defined as the field width measured in units applicable to the specific encoding. See Chap. 14 for the detailed specifications for each encoding.

COLOUR PRECISION *precision.* 4.8

Optional element that declares the precision for operands of type *colour direct* (CD) encountered subsequently in the metafile. The precision is defined as the field width measured in units applicable to the specific encoding. See Chap. 14 for the detailed specifications for each encoding.

Although the form of the parameter is encoding-dependent, the parameter is a single specification that applies to each or all of the three components (red, green, blue) of parameters of type CD. The precisions of the individual components are not independently and differently specifiable by this element.

COLOUR INDEX PRECISION *precision.* 4.8

Optional element that declares the precision for operands of type *colour index* (CI) encountered subsequently in the metafile. The precision is defined as the field width measured in units applicable to the specific encoding. See Chap. 14 for the detailed specifications for each encoding.

MAXIMUM COLOUR INDEX *index*.

Optional element that specifies an upper bound (not necessarily the least upper bound) on colour index values that will be encountered in the metafile. This element permits a metafile interpreter to know the size of the colour table it is being asked to deal with. Default is 63.

COLOUR VALUE EXTENT *minimum-value, maximum-value*. 8.9

Optional element that specifies lower and upper bounds for the direct colour values that will be encountered in the metafile. These values need not represent the exact extent of the CD values contained in the metafile. The first parameter, known as the *minimum colour value* corresponds to the abstract RGB specification of (0,0,0), which means zero intensity of each of the RGB components and represents black. Similarly, the second parameter, known as the *maximum colour value* corresponds to the abstract RGB specification of (1,1,1), which means full intensity of each of the RGB components and represents white.

METAFILE ELEMENT LIST *list*.

Required element that lists all the elements that may be encountered in the metafile. The four mandatory elements need not be included in the list. The list represents an upper bound of functional capability; it need not be the least upper bound. Every non-mandatory element in the metafile shall be listed, but the list may include elements not found in the metafile. The exact form of the parameter is encoding-dependent and is described in Chap. 14.

The information carried by this element can be used by interpreters to determine the maximum facilities necessary for interpreting the metafile. To encourage support by interpreters for common sets of CGM elements, two shorthand names are provided for use in the metafile elments list. These names–DRAWING SET and DRAWING PLUS CONTROL SET–may be used in conjunction with individual element names in the element list. The DRAWING SET contains most of the CGM elements. The DRAWING PLUS CONTROL SET contains the remaining CGM elements. Note that elements not in the DRAWING SET but in the DRAWING PLUS CONTROL SET are marked with an asterisk (*) in Table 13.1.

METAFILE DEFAULTS REPLACEMENT *list-of-elements*.

This is a complex element, whose parameters are encoding-dependent. The parameters contain instances of other Picture Descriptor, Control, and Attribute elements for which sensible defaults may be specified. The elements that may appear in the parameter list for Metafile Defaults Replacement are the picture descriptor, control, attribute, and escape elements.

The purpose of the list is to change one or more CGM defaults. You will recall that defaults are significant because BEGIN PICTURE causes a metafile interpreter to return the state of the system to the specified default values before interpreting a new picture. For example, the CGM default fill area INTERIOR STYLE is *hollow*. If a metafile generator were preparing to produce a metafile in which most (or all) filled areas in all pictures were to be specified with INTERIOR STYLE *solid*, the generator would have two alternative specification methods available. At the beginning of each picture, it could write an INTERIOR STYLE element, setting the attribute to *solid*, or, in the Metafile Descriptor, it could declare once that the default INTERIOR STYLE for this whole metafile is *solid*, and not *hollow*.

The parameters in the defaults replacement list are order dependent. When an element is encountered in the defaults replacement list, the value replaces the current default value for the element. If an element occurs more than once in the list, then the last value specified is the default value.

When a value has more than one specification mode (e.g., a LINE WIDTH value may be either *scaled* or *absolute*), the METAFILE DEFAULTS REPLACEMENT element may be used to specify its default in either mode. An element that sets a default value in the list shall set the value in the current specification mode. The current specification mode when processing the list is either the default mode defined by the CGM standard (viz., *scaled*) or the mode most recently set by an element in the list.

To change the default line width from its CGM default of scaled 1.0 to a new default of scaled 2.5, the generator would include in the Metafile Descriptor:

> BEGMFDEFAULTS;
>
> LINEWIDTH 2.5;
>
> ENDMFDEFAULTS;

However, if the generator wanted to set line width to an absolute value of 10.0 VDC units, the Metafile Descriptor would need to have:

> BEGMFDEFAULTS;
>
> LINEWIDTHMODE absolute;
>
> LINEWIDTH 10.0;
>
> ENDMFDEFAULTS;

FONT LIST *list-of-font-names*. **8.13**

This optional element permits a set of font names to be provided by the generator to the interpreter. The parameter is a list of strings. Each string is a single font name. The first string in the list is associated with TEXT FONT INDEX 1, the second string with TEXT FONT INDEX 2, and so on.

At present, font names are not standardized, so this information is useful only when prior agreement between generating and interpreting environments has resulted in a known list of names. However, the *ISO Register of Graphical Items*, described in Chap. 2, will register font names. Use of these registered names will increase the likelihood that the metafile will be transportable to interpreting environments, even when prior agreement regarding font names has not taken place.

CHARACTER SET LIST *character-set-type,designation-sequence-tail.* **8.13**

An optional element, which is used to declare the character sets that can be named in subsequent CHARACTER SET INDEX and ALTERNATE CHARACTER SET INDEX attribute elements.

The CGM and CGI standards distinguish between a *character set*, which indicates an alphabet or collection of symbols, and a *font*, which specifies the typeface and weight, or appearance style, of the characters that appear in a character set. That is, German is a character set, while **Times Roman Bold** and ***Helvetica Bold Italic*** are the names of two specific fonts with which the German character set could be rendered. See Figs. 13.2(a) and 13.2(b) to see the difference between varying character set and varying font index.

München   *Munich*

Fig. 13.2(a). Different character set; same font index

München   München

Fig. 13.2(b). Same character set; different font index

The CHARACTER SET LIST element establishes the character set index value that is associated with each of the character sets mentioned in a list of character set declarations, which are provided as parameters of the element. The first character set declaration in the list names the character set whose character set index value is 1, the second declaration names the character set whose index value is 2, etc.

Each character set declaration has two parts: an enumerated parameter, the *character set type,* and a short string parameter, the *designation sequence tail.* There are five types of character sets: 94-character G sets, 96-character G-sets, 94-character multibyte character G sets, 96-character multibyte G-sets, and character sets intended to be designated as "complete codes." The character set type terminology is drawn from ISO 2022, and the designation sequence tails for instances of such character set types are registered in the *International Register Of Coded Character Sets To Be Used With Escape Sequences.*

For example, a Japanese 2-byte character set of 6802 graphic characters has been registered. Its designation sequence tail has the form **<ESC> ... 4/0** to designate it. All such character sets in the register start with <ESC> ..., but each has a unique "tail"–in this case, the **4/0** character. Thus, the following CHARACTER SET LIST element could be used to specify that this 94-character 2-byte Japanese character set is to be referred to by character set index 1:

CHARSETLIST STD94MULTIBYTE '4/0';

Complete information regarding the designation sequence tail parameter can be found in the *International Register Of Coded Character Sets To Be Used With Escape Sequences.* This register is maintained by the Registration Authority for ISO 2375; namely, by the European Computer Manufacturers Association (ECMA), Rue du Rhone 114, CH-1204, Geneva, Switzerland.

The default CHARACTER SET LIST consists of one declaration–for character set index 1. It refers to any character set which includes the nationality-independent subset of ISO 646 coded by the positions specified by ISO 646.

CHARACTER CODING ANNOUNCER *coding-technique.* **8.13**

This optional element informs the metafile interpreter of the code extension capabilities assumed by the metafile generator.

The parameter specifies a *coding technique,* which applies only to the string parameters of TEXT, APPEND TEXT, RESTRICTED TEXT, and possible GENERALIZED DRAWING PRIMITIVE (GDP) elements. The standardized values for the coding technique correspond to the "announcer sequences" of ISO 2022 and are defined below:

BASIC 7-BIT   Character sets are switched by using CHARACTER SET INDEX, which designates a set into code table position G0.

If ALTERNATE CHARACTER SET INDEX appears in the metafile, it is used to access the G1 set by using the control elements SI and SO as described in ISO 2022.

BASIC 8-BIT   Character sets are switched by using CHARACTER SET INDEX and ALTERNATE CHARACTER SET INDEX.

The G1 set may be accessed by characters from columns 10 through 15 of an 8-bit code table. No locking or single shifts are used within the text string.

EXTENDED 7-BIT   Sets G0, G1, G2, and G3 may be invoked using the 7-bit encoding of any of the locking shifts or single shifts, in conformance with ISO 2022. CHARACTER SET INDEX selects G0 while ALTERNATE CHARACTER SET INDEX selects both G1 and G2. Designation of G2 and G3 may be done within text strings, in conformance with ISO 2022. Designation of G0 and G1 may not be done in this fashion.

EXTENDED 8-BIT   Same as EXTENDED 7-BIT, except that 8-bit encodings of the locking shifts or single shifts are used for invocation.

In the following example, the first and third text strings are drawn with character set 1, while the second text string is drawn with character set 2.

```
BEGMF;
... ...
CHARSETLIST  STD94 '4/1' %UK national set%,
             STD94 '6/6' %French national set%;
CHARCODING BASIC7BIT;
... ...
BEGPIC; BEGPICBODY;
TEXT (.3,.7) FINAL 'English';
CHARSETINDEX 2;
TEXT (.3,.5) FINAL 'Français';
CHARSETINDEX 1;
TEXT (.3,.3) FINAL 'English';
ENDPIC; ENDMF;
```

13.3 Picture Descriptor Elements

Picture Descriptor elements provide information that applies to the contents of an entire picture but is not carried over to affect the contents of any other picture in the metafile. If included in a picture, Picture Descriptor elements appear after the BEGIN PICTURE element and before the BEGIN PICTURE BODY element. Escape and external elements are permitted in the Picture Descriptor.

Included among the Picture Descriptor elements are those that declare the parameter modes of other elements, configure the portion of coordinate space that is of interest in the picture, and set the colour to which the view surface is cleared at the start of the picture. These elements are described in detail in the following paragraphs.

SCALING MODE *mode, scale-factor.*

The two-dimensional Cartesian coordinate system used to specify positions and extents of the geometric drawing primitives defines the so-called *VDC Space*. VDC Space may be either an *abstract space*, to be mapped to an arbitrary size on a physical device, or a *metric space*, to be mapped to a particular size. Selection of the mode to be used can be made on a picture-by-picture basis. The SCALING MODE element provides a flag to select abstract space or metric space and a scale factor, which specifies the number of millimeters per VDC unit when metric space is selected. That is, one VDC unit represents one millimeter multiplied by the metric scale factor. For example, to specify a scaled drawing where 1 VDC unit equals one inch, include the following element in the picture descriptor:

SCALEMODE METRIC 25.4;

The default SCALING MODE is *abstract*.

COLOUR SELECTION MODE *mode.*   8.9

Within a single picture, all colour specifications must be either *indexed* or *direct*. This element selects which mode is in effect for the picture. Direct colour values are specified as a triple of red, green, and blue (RGB) colour values.

The default COLOUR SELECTION MODE is indexed; that is, colours are specified indirectly, through integer indices that are mapped through a *colour lookup table* to RGB triples.

The following two fragments of a CGM would give the same effect; the choice of which selection mode to use usually depends upon the mode that the generating process understands.

... BEGPIC;	... BEGPIC;
COLRMODE INDEXED;	COLRMODE DIRECT;
BEGPICBODY;	BEGPICBODY;
COLRTABLE 2	
(0 255 255) (255 255 0);	
LINECOLR 2;	LINECOLR (0 255 255);
LINE (0,0) (1,1);	LINE (0,0) (1,1);
LINECOLR 3;	LINECOLR (255 255 0);
LINE (1,0) (0,1);	LINE (1,0) (0,1);
LINECOLR 2;	LINECOLR (0 255 255);
LINE(0,.5) (1,.5);	LINE (0,.5) (1,.5);
ENDPIC; ...	ENDPIC; ...

If a lot of colour changes are employed, using indexed mode generally results in a more compact CGM.

Specification Modes. Line width, marker size, and edge width may be specified in more than one way. For example, the size of polymarkers may be specified as either an absolute measure in VDC units or as a scale factor to be applied to a device-dependent nominal marker size when the CGM is interpreted. For each attribute element having such multiple modes, an associated Picture Descriptor element defines the mode of the parameter of the attribute element.

LINE WIDTH SPECIFICATION MODE *mode*. 8.9

Only one line width mode may be used within a picture. The mode may be defaulted or set explicitly with the LINE WIDTH SPECIFICATION MODE element. All occurrences of line width elements shall have parameters specified in the current mode.

The default LINE WIDTH SPECIFICATION MODE is scaled.

MARKER SIZE SPECIFICATION MODE *mode*. 8.9

Only one marker size mode may be used within a picture. The mode may be defaulted or set explicitly with the MARKER SIZE SPECIFICATION MODE element. All occurrences of marker size elements shall have parameters specified in the current mode.

The default MARKER SIZE SPECIFICATION MODE is scaled.

EDGE WIDTH SPECIFICATION MODE *mode.*   **8.9**

Only one edge width mode may be used within a picture. The mode may be defaulted or set explicitly with the EDGE WIDTH SPECIFICATION MODE element. All occurrences of edge width elements shall have parameters specified in the current mode.

The default EDGE WIDTH SPECIFICATION MODE is scaled.

VDC EXTENT *first-corner, second-corner.*   **4.3**

The Virtual Device Coordinate system of the CGM is the same as that of the CGI (see Chap. 4 for more details). The VDC extent provides a rectangular frame for the region of interest in a picture. It is intended that the visible portion of an image be contained within the VDC extent, but specification of values outside the VDC extent is permitted in CGM elements.

The extent is set with the VDC EXTENT element by specifying the locations of the lower-left corner and the upper-right corner of this extent as seen by the viewer of the picture. As explained in Chap. 4, the values of the coordinates for either dimension may be either increasing or decreasing from lower-left to upper-right. For example, where an application has an image stored in a coordinate system with an upper-left origin, a CGM can be efficiently generated without recalculating all coordinate positions by simply specifying an appropriate VDC EXTENT element.

The VDC extent thus establishes the sense and orientation of VDC space. Furthermore, positive angles are specified as being measured in the direction from the positive x-axis to the positive y-axis. These definitions affect some attributes, including CHARACTER ORIENTATION and CHARACTER PATH.

The default VDC EXTENT is (0,0) to (32767,32767) if VDC TYPE is integer and (0.0,0.0) to (1.0,1.0) if VDC TYPE is real.

BACKGROUND COLOUR *red-value, green-value, blue-value.*   **4.1**

Each picture defines a graphical image independent of the other images in a metafile. The background colour of the image may be explicitly specified by the BACKGROUND COLOUR element. If this element is missing from the Picture Descriptor, the default background colour, which is device-dependent, is used.

The single parameter of BACKGROUND COLOUR is always specified as an RGB triple, regardless of the current value of colour selection mode. If the colour selection mode is indexed, the BACKGOUND COLOUR ELEMENT defines the initial representation of colour index 0 for the picture.

13.4 Control Elements

Control Elements specify address space, clipping boundaries, and format descriptions of the CGM elements. Control of some of these format descriptions may be accomplished by Metafile Descriptor elements (e.g., VDC TYPE), while control of others is accomplished by the control elements described in the following paragraphs.

Control elements may appear only in the picture body, after the BEGIN PICTURE BODY element and before the END PICTURE element. Consequently, control element values may take on several different values as the picture is defined.

VDC Space and Range. The graphical primitive elements of a metafile define virtual images. The coordinates of these elements are absolute 2-D VDC. VDC space is a 2-D Cartesian space of *infinite precision* and *infinite extent*. Only a subset of VDC space, the *VDC Range*, is realizable on any physical graphics device. The VDC range comprises all coordinates representable in the format specified by the declared VDC TYPE (a Metafile Descriptor element) and one of the VDC precision elements–VDC INTEGER PRECISION or VDC REAL PRECISION–described below.

The VDC range thus defined (a rectangular subregion of the VDC Space) does not enclose a continuum of values but has a distinct granularity set by the current precision element in effect. Regardless of the aspect ratio of the VDC Range and the granularity within the range, it is implicit that one VDC unit in the x-direction represents the same distance as one VDC unit in the y-direction in VDC Space. It is the responsibility of the metafile interpreter to enforce this requirement.

Precision Parameter Encoding. The form of the precision parameter depends on the specific encoding; the value of the parameter indicates the precision for operands of data type *point* and data type *VDC value*. The precision is defined as the field width measured in units applicable to the specific encoding.

These elements enable metafiles to change the form of parameters in other metafile elements in the middle of a picture definition so that more efficient storage and transmission of data can be used when less precision is required to represent the image. The following example shows how 2 digits of precision might be used to specify the positioning of labels, while 5 digits of precision might be used for drawing lines.

```
       ... ...
       BEGPICBODY;
       VDCREALPREC 0.0 1.0 2;
       TEXT (0.50,0.90) final 'Drawing Title';
       VDCREALPREC 0.0 1.0 5;
       LINE  (0.32455,0.55120) (0.43674,0.55120)
           ... ...
             (0.87694,0.98965) (0.78688,0.98965);
       VDCREALPREC 0.0 1.0 2;
       TEXT (0.85,0.05) final 'Drafted by John Jones';
       ENDPIC; ... ...
```

VDC INTEGER PRECISION *precision.* 4.3

Normally, this element is used only when VDC TYPE is *integer*, but it may also be used to specify the precision of subfields of data types **point** and **VDC**, when VDC TYPE is *real*.

The default VDC INTEGER PRECISION is encoding dependent.

VDC REAL PRECISION *precision.* 4.3

Normally, this element is used only when VDC TYPE is *real*, and it may also be used to specify the precision of subfields of data types **point** and **VDC**.

The default VDC REAL PRECISION is encoding dependent.

AUXILIARY COLOUR *colour-specifier.* 8.9

The auxiliary colour index or direct colour value (depending upon COLOUR SELECTION MODE) is set as specified by the parameter.

The auxiliary colour is applied to drawing of primitives as described under the TRANSPARENCY element below.

The default AUXILIARY COLOUR is 0, if the colour selection mode is indexed, and is a device-dependent background colour, if the colour selection mode is direct. **Note that this statement about the default AUXILIARY COLOUR corrects an error in the standard as originally published.**

Because many devices would have difficulty implementing transparency without direct hardware support, interpretation of this element is implementation-dependent.

TRANSPARENCY *indicator.* 8.9

The transparency indicator is set to *on* or *off*, as indicated by the parameter. TRANSPARENCY controls the application of AUXILIARY COLOUR to the drawing of subsequent primitives.

When TRANSPARENCY is *off*, the following graphical primitives are affected as described:

line elements	When LINE TYPE is non-solid, the dashes and dots are drawn in the current LINE COLOUR as usual, and the spaces between are drawn in the AUXILIARY COLOUR.
polymarker	For devices that display markers within raster cells, pixels that are within the cell but not part of the marker definition are displayed in the AUXILIARY COLOUR.
text elements	For devices that display text characters within raster cells, pixels that are within the cell but not part of the character definition are displayed in the AUXILIARY COLOUR.
filled-area elements	When interior style is *hatch*, pixels in the interior of the filled-area element that are not on a hatch line are displayed in the AUXILIARY COLOUR; when EDGE TYPE is non-solid, the dashes and dots are drawn in the current EDGE COLOUR as usual, and the spaces between are drawn in the AUXILIARY COLOUR.

When TRANSPARENCY is *on*, the portions of the above primitives that would be drawn in AUXILIARY COLOUR when TRANSPARENCY is *off* are rendered transparently; that is, nothing is drawn in that portion of the primitive when the primitive is drawn.

The default TRANSPARENCY is *on*. Because many devices would have difficulty implementing transparency without direct hardware support, interpretation of this element is implementation-dependent.

CLIP RECTANGLE *first-corner, second-corner.* 4.4

Two corner points, passed as parameters, define the clip rectangle in VDC space. When the CLIP INDICATOR is *on*, only the portions of graphics elements inside or on the boundary of the clip rectangle are drawn. For CGI processes, the clip rectangle will be the intersection of the CGI clip rectangle, the effective viewport, and the default viewport (if the CGI clip indicator is set to *clip rectangle*) or will be the intersection of the image of the VDC extent and the default viewport (if the CGI clip indicator is set to *effective viewport*).

The default CLIP RECTANGLE is the entire VDC extent.

CLIP INDICATOR *indicator.* 4.4

The state of the clip indicator is set to *on* or *off*, as specified by the parameter.

When the CLIP INDICATOR is *on*, only the portions of graphics elements inside or on the boundary of the clip rectangle are drawn.

When CLIP INDICATOR is *off*, clipping of graphical primitives is not required. However, it is implementation and interpreter dependent whether or not clipping is performed to some limit such as the VDC EXTENT or to the display surface boundaries even when CLIP INDICATOR is *off*. Such an action may be initiated by the interpreter in accordance with the needs of the implementation and the devices supported by the implementation.

The CGM generator should set CLIP INDICATOR *off*, if it knows that the data being placed into the metafile are already clipped. This permits the interpreting processing from having to check all coordinates against the clipping rectangle.

The default CLIP INDICATOR is *on*.

13.5 CGM Tailoring

The ability to specify the VDC Range (via the VDC precision elements) and the VDC Extent provides a CGM client with the flexibility to configure the addressability of generated metafiles in any way possible. The metafile may be configured as an abstract, normalized address range for maximum device independence. It can also be configured to mimic the addressability of a particular target device in order to take advantage of particular device characteristics. The address range of such a device-specific metafile is just another normalized address range with the normalization limits inherent in the VDC-customizing element; therefore, device independence is maintained. Such tailoring of the coordinates in a metafile can eliminate the need for transformation of coordinates at metafile interpretation time for the target device. The ability to specify the VDC Extent thus allows for the exact registration of the coordinates in a metafile with the addressable points on the target graphics device.

For example, consider targetting a CGM picture at a display with 1024 by 1280 resolution. The following CGM fragment would permit VDC coordinates to be mapped one-to-one with the addressable points of the target output device. An intelligent CGM interpreter could use this knowledge and avoid extra processing mapping from VDC to device coordinates and could also avoid introducing extra aliasing effects, if the stored image in the CGM had already be subjected to anti-aliasing algorithms.

```
           BEGMF;
      ... ...; VDCTYPE INTEGER; ......;
      BEGPIC;
      VDCEXT (0,0) (1023,1279);
      BEGPICBODY;
      VDCINTEGERPREC 0 1279;
      POLYGON (2,2) (1021,2) (1021,1277) (2,1277);
           ... ...; ENDPIC; ENDMF;
```

The use of VDC EXTENT to directly encode world coordinates of large dynamic range and very small granularity will often result in performance penalties at metafile interpretation time and may result in decreased portability if such VDC extents exceed those compatible with less capable metafile interpreters.

In addition to VDC tailoring, a metafile generator can limit or tailor the functional content of a metafile to accomodate particular device capabilities or the needs of certain applications. The metafile generator process can announce such a functional tailoring to the metafile interpreter by including a precisely correct METAFILE ELEMENT LIST element. For example, if a CGM were produced as a result of converting a CalComp plot file, the only graphical primitive element used might be POLYLINE. If the metafile element list showed that only the POLYLINE element were present in the CGM, relatively limited interpreters would be able to determine that they would be able to interpret successfully at least this CGM.

13.6 Graphical Primitive Elements

Nineteen graphical primitives are specified for use in describing CGM pictures. All primitives are also available in the CGI and have been explained extensively in Parts I and II of this book. In the paragraphs that follow, all graphical primitives are listed (for the reader's convenience), but, in general, only aspects of the primitive unique to the CGM are discussed.

POLYLINE *point-list*. 3.2

DISJOINT POLYLINE *point-list.* 8.2

This element allows significant data compression for applications required to perform line pattern generation or vector polygon fill prior to metafile generation in a graphics system. It may also be used productively in representing such presentation aids as grids.

POLYMARKER *point-list.* 3.2

TEXT *point, flag, string.* 3.4

RESTRICTED TEXT *extent, point, flag, string.* 8.3

APPEND TEXT *flag, string.* 8.3

POLYGON *point-list.* 3.5

POLYGON SET *list-of-{point, edge-out-flag}.* 3.5

The ability to intermix visible and invisible edges is provided to accomodate clipping of polygons *before* they are placed in the CGM; a clipped polygon edge is typically invisible.

CELL ARRAY. 8.7

> *3 corner-points*
> *number-of-columns, number-of-rows*
> *local-colour-precision*
> *cell-colour-specifiers*

The *local colour precision* parameter declares the precision of the *cell colour specifiers*. The precision is interpreted for either indexed or direct colour, according to the COLOUR SELECTION MODE of the picture. The form of the parameter is encoding dependent. If the picture uses indexed colour selection, the form of the parameter is the same as that for COLOUR INDEX PRECISION; if the picture uses direct colour selection, the form of the parameter is the same as that for COLOUR PRECISION.

Legal values of the *local colour precision* include all the legal values of COLOUR (INDEX) PRECISION. In addition, each encoding specifies a special value, the *default colour precision indicator*, which indicates that the colour specifiers of the element are to be encoded in the COLOUR (INDEX) PRECISION of the metafile; that is, to indicate that the *local colour precision* defaults to COLOUR (INDEX) PRECISION.

Where knowledge of a specific target device is available to the metafile generator, VDC EXTENT, VDC TYPE, and VDC precision elements can be set in such a way that pixel arrays can be represented by CELL ARRAY elements in an efficient and compact fashion. When displayed by a metafile interpreter on the target devices, cells comprising the image can be mapped one-to-one with device coordinate units, avoiding aliasing effects that occur when the resolution of the picture description does not match the resolution of the display device.

GENERALIZED DRAWING PRIMITIVE–GDP. 8.8

> *identifier, point-list*
> *data-record*

The parameters of a GDP are interpreted and utilized in an interpreter dependent manner. However, the *ISO Register of Graphical Items* will be used to register extensions to the CGM drawing set.

When registration of GDPs occurs, some registered GDPs may correspond to some of the standardized metafile graphical primitive elements like CIRCLE and ELLIPSE.

RECTANGLE *corner-1, corner-2*. 3.5

CIRCLE *centre, radius* 3.5

CIRCULAR ARC 3 POINT. 3.2

> *starting-point, intermediate-point, ending-point.*

If the three specified coordinates are collinear, the specification is mathematically degenerate and the interpretation of this element is implementation dependent.

CIRCULAR ARC 3 POINT CLOSE. 3.5

> *starting-point, intermediate-point, ending-point*
> *close-type*

If the three specified coordinates are collinear, the specification is mathematically degenerate and the interpretation of this element is implementation dependent.

CIRCULAR ARC CENTRE. 3.2

> *centrepoint, start-vector, end-vector, radius*

If the start ray and end ray coincide, it is implementation dependent whether the defined arc subtends zero degrees or 360 degrees of central angle.

CIRCULAR ARC CENTRE CLOSE. 3.5

> *centrepoint, start-vector, end-vector, radius*
> *close-type*

If the start ray and end ray coincide, it is implementation dependent whether the defined arc subtends zero degrees or 360 degrees of central angle.

ELLIPSE *centrepoint, first-CDP-endpoint, second-CDP-endpoint.* 8.4

The specified ellipse is mathematically non-degenerate if and only if the three specifying points are non-collinear. It is implementation dependent how degenerate ellipses are rendered.

ELLIPTICAL ARC. 8.2

> *centrepoint, first-CDP-endpoint, second-CDP-endpoint*
> *start-vector, end-cector*

The specified portion of an ellipse is mathematically degenerate if the three specifying points are collinear. It is implementation dependent how portions of degenerate ellipses are rendered. If the start ray and end ray are coincident, it is implementation dependent whether the defined arc subtends zero degrees or 360 degrees of central angle.

ELLIPTICAL ARC CLOSE. 8.4

> *centrepoint, first-CDP-endpoint, second-CDP-endpoint*
> *start-vector, end-vector*
> *close-type*

The specified portion of an ellipse is mathematically degenerate if the three specifying points are collinear. It is implementation dependent how portions of degenerate ellipses are rendered. If the start ray and end ray coincide, it is implementation dependent whether the defined arc subtends zero degrees or 360 degrees of central angle.

13.7 Attribute Elements

Thirty-five graphical primitive attributes are specified for use in describing CGM pictures. As with the graphical primitives, all primitive attributes are also available in the CGI and, as before, all attribute elements are listed, only aspects of the attribute unique to the CGM are discussed, and the default value for each attribute element is given even if the CGI default value is identical.

LINE BUNDLE INDEX *index*.   3.2

The default LINE BUNDLE INDEX is 1.

LINE TYPE *indicator*.   3.2

Ideally, line type is maintained continuously between adjacent spans of a single POLYLINE element. This consideration does not apply to other line elements, as they do not have interior defining vertices. The CGM standard does not require continuity between separate, but graphically connected, polyline elements, nor does it require continuity across sections of a single polyline element that may have been clipped away.

The CGM provides no means of specifying whether or not line type is maintained continuously across the segments of POLYLINE and DISJOINT POLYLINE elements.

The default LINE TYPE is solid.

LINE WIDTH *specifier*.   3.2

Line width is measured perpendicular to the defining line (that is, it is independent of the orientation of the defining line). A wide line is aligned with its ideal zero-width defining line such that the distance between the defining line and either edge is half the line width.

The appearance of lines at endpoints (*line caps*) and at interior vertices or corners (*line joins*) cannot be specified by CGM elements. However, new elements to control these aspects of line primitives are being considered for future extensions to the CGM (see Chap. 17).

If the LINE WIDTH SPECIFICATION MODE is *scaled*, the default LINE WIDTH is 1.0; if *absolute*, the default is 1/1000 of the longest side of the rectangle defined by the default VDC EXTENT.

LINE COLOUR *specifier*.   3.2

If the COLOUR SELECTION MODE is *indexed*, the default LINE COLOUR is 1; if *direct*, the default colour is the foreground colour, which itself is device-dependent.

MARKER BUNDLE INDEX *index*.   3.3

The default MARKER BUNDLE INDEX is 1.

MARKER TYPE *indicator.* 3.3

As with the CGI, marker type *dot* is intended to be displayed always as the smallest visible point on the display surface at metafile interpretation time. Thus, POLYMARKER with MARKER TYPE *dot* can function as a "polypoint" primitive element.

The default MARKER TYPE is the asterisk (*).

MARKER SIZE *specifier.* 3.3

If the MARKER SIZE SPECIFICATION MODE is *scaled*, the default MARKER SIZE is 1.0; if *absolute*, the default is 1/100 of the longest side of the rectangle defined by the default VDC EXTENT.

MARKER COLOUR *specifier.* 3.3

If the COLOUR SELECTION MODE is *indexed*, the default MARKER COLOUR is 1; if *direct*, the default colour is the foreground colour, which itself is device-dependent.

TEXT BUNDLE INDEX *index.* 3.4

The default TEXT BUNDLE INDEX is 1.

TEXT FONT INDEX *index.* 3.4

Metafile generators should insure that the selected character set and the text font are compatible. However, if an interpreter encounters a situation where they are incompatible, the text font will be temporarily changed to render the requested character set, if such a font is available on the target device.

The default TEXT FONT INDEX is 1; that is, an implementation dependent font that can represent the character set specified in ISO 646.

TEXT PRECISION *indicator.* 3.4

The default TEXT PRECISION is *string*; that is, use the device's hardware text facilities, ignoring many of the text attributes, if they are not supported in the device.

CHARACTER EXPANSION FACTOR *value.* 3.4

The default CHARACTER EXPANSION FACTOR is 1.0; that is, use the aspect ratio specified by the font designer.

CHARACTER SPACING *value.* 3.4

The default CHARACTER SPACING is 0.0; that is, use the character spacing built into the text font character definitions by the font designer.

TEXT COLOUR *specifier.* 3.4

If the COLOUR SELECTION MODE is *indexed*, the default TEXT COLOUR is 1; if *direct*, the default colour is the foreground colour, which itself is device-dependent.

CHARACTER HEIGHT *value.* 3.4

The default CHARACTER HEIGHT is 1/100 of the length of the longest side of the rectangle defined by the default VDC extent.

CHARACTER ORIENTATION 3.4

> *up-vector-x-component, up-vector-y-component*
> *base-vector-x-component, base-vector-y-component*

The way in which the application above the metafile generator or the metafile generator itself might use this element is described in the following. (This explanation is compatible with the way this function is described in the CGI; see Chap. 4 for more details.)

A vector whose length is the character height (baseline-to-capline distance) and whose direction is the desired character up vector is created. A second vector is also created with the same length, whose direction is negative 90-degrees from the up vector. This pair of vectors may be transformed before being given to the metafile generator as the parameters to CHARACTER ORIENTATION.

If the resultant vectors are not orthogonal, the text extent rectangle becomes a parallelogram, and the characters are skewed. If the vectors have different lengths, the aspect ratio derived from the font design and the character expansion attribute will be altered. If the positive angle from the up vector to the base vector is less than 180-degrees, the following effects occur: characters are mirror imaged and the "intuitive" notions of right and left (as applied to TEXT PATH and TEXT ALIGNMENT) are reversed.

The default CHARACTER ORIENTATION is (0,1,1,0); that is, the up vector is parallel to and has the direction of the positive VDC y-axis, and the base vector is parallel to and has the direction of the positive VDC x-axis. With the default VDC EXTENT, text will be upright and run to the right as expected.

TEXT PATH *indicator.* 3.4

The default TEXT PATH is *right*, as appropriate for most Western languages, including English.

TEXT ALIGNMENT. 3.4

> *horizontal-alignment-indicator, vertical-alignment-indicator*
> *continuous-horizontal-alignment-value*
> *continuous-vertical-alignment-value*

The default TEXT ALIGNMENT is *normal horizontal, normal vertical*. For default text, the lower left corner of the first character comprising the text string will be aligned with the text position.

CHARACTER SET INDEX *index.* 3.4

One use of this element is to switch among character sets for different languages.
The default CHARACTER SET INDEX is 1; that is, the character set corresponding to ISO 646.

ALTERNATE CHARACTER SET INDEX *index.* 3.4

The default ALTERNATE CHARACTER SET INDEX is 1; that is, character sets will not be changed even if an alternate character set is invoked by using ISO 2022 controls within a string parameter of the TEXT, RESTRICTED TEXT, and APPEND TEXT primitives.

FILL BUNDLE INDEX *index.* 3.5

The default FILL BUNDLE INDEX is 1.

INTERIOR STYLE *indicator.* 3.5

The default fill INTERIOR STYLE is *hollow*.

FILL COLOUR *specifier.* 3.5

If the COLOUR SELECTION MODE is *indexed*, the default FILL COLOUR is 1; if *direct*, the default colour is the foreground colour, which itself is device-dependent.

HATCH INDEX *index.* 3.5

The default HATCH INDEX is 1, which selects a pattern of *horizontal, equally spaced parallel lines*.

PATTERN INDEX *index.* 3.5

The default PATTERN INDEX is 1.

EDGE BUNDLE INDEX *index.* 3.5

The default EDGE BUNDLE INDEX is 1.

EDGE TYPE *indicator.* 3.5

The remarks relating to line type continuity also apply to edge type.

The default EDGE TYPE is *solid*.

EDGE WIDTH *specifier.* 3.5

The remarks relating to measuring line width also apply to edge width. However, the CGM standard does not require any particular alignment of the finite-width displayed edge with the zero-width defining line.

If the EDGE WIDTH SPECIFICATION MODE is *scaled*, the default EDGE WIDTH is 1.0; if *absolute*, the default is 1/1000 of the longest side of the rectangle defined by the default VDC EXTENT.

EDGE COLOUR *specifier.* 3.5

If the COLOUR SELECTION MODE is *indexed*, the default EDGE COLOUR is 1; if *direct*, the default colour is the foreground colour, which itself is device-dependent.

EDGE VISIBILITY *flag.* 3.5

The default EDGE VISIBILITY is *off*; that is, fill areas will be rendered without edges.

FILL REFERENCE POINT *point.* 3.5

The default FILL REFERENCE POINT is the lower-left corner point of the default VDC extent.

PATTERN TABLE. 3.5

> *pattern-table-index*
> *number-of-columns, number-of-rows*
> *local-colour-precision*
> *pattern-colour-specifiers*

The *local colour precision* parameter declares the precision of the *pattern colour specifiers*. The precision is interpreted for either indexed or direct colour, according to the COLOUR SELECTION MODE of the picture. The form of the parameter is encoding dependent. If the picture uses indexed colour selection, the form of the parameter is the same as that for COLOUR INDEX PRECISION; if the picture uses direct colour selection, the form of the parameter is the same as that for COLOUR PRECISION.

Legal values of the *local colour precision* include all the legal values of COLOUR (INDEX) PRECISION. In addition, each encoding specifies a special value, the *default colour precision indicator*, which indicates that the colour specifiers of the element are to be encoded in the COLOUR (INDEX) PRECISION of the metafile; that is, to indicate that the *local colour precision* defaults to COLOUR (INDEX) PRECISION.

This element may appear throughout the picture body. However, the effect of changes in the pattern table on any existing graphical primitive elements that use the affected indices is not addressed by the CGM standard.

The default PATTERN TABLE has one entry. The entry consists of one solid coloured cell. If the COLOUR SELECTION MODE is *indexed*, the default colour specification of that single cell is 1; if *direct*, the default colour specification is the foreground colour, which itself is device-dependent. The colour specification is specified with local colour precision equal to the *default colour precision indicator*, which itself is encoding-dependent.

PATTERN SIZE. 3.5

height-vector-x-component, height-vector-y-component
width-vector-x-component, width-vector-y-component

The default PATTERN SIZE is (0, dy, dx, 0), where dy and dx are, respectively, the height and width of the default VDC extent. That is, any fill area primitive, which is specified with interior style *pattern* and which uses the default pattern table, pattern index, and pattern size, will be filled solid with a device-dependent foreground colour.

COLOUR TABLE *starting-index, list-of-colour-specifiers.* 8.9

Just as with the pattern table, this element may appear throughout the picture body and the effect of changes in the colour table on any existing graphical primitive elements that use the affected indices is not addressed by the CGM standard.

By default, colour index zero (0) is set to a device-dependent background colour; all other indices are set to a device-dependent foreground colour.

ASPECT SOURCE FLAGS *list-of-{ASF-type, ASF-value}.* 3.1

By default, all ASPECT SOURCE FLAGS are set to *individual*.

13.8 Escape and External Elements

ESCAPE *function-identifier, data-record.* 4.8

Just as with the CGI, the ESCAPE element provides access to device capabilities not specified explicitly by the CGM standard. A function identifier parameter specifies the particular escape function. Non-negative values of this identifier are reserved for registration in the ISO Register of Graphical Items and for future standardization; negative values of the identifier are available for implementation dependent (that is, private) use.

The second parameter to this element contains all the function-specific data necessary to fully define the desired function.

This element has been deliberately underspecified. Software and applications making use of the ESCAPE element is inherently less portable than applications avoiding use of ESCAPE.

MESSAGE *flag, string.* 4.8

The MESSAGE element specifies a string of characters used to communicate information to operators at metafile interpretation time through a path separate from normal graphical output.

If the action required flag parameter is *action*, the metafile interpreter may need to pause to wait for an operator response. Because the message and an associated pause may be directed at a particular device, only the interpreter is in a position to decide if a pause is appropriate. Character set selection for the MESSAGE element string parameter is independent of any character set selection specified by CGM elements and is not otherwise standardized.

APPLICATION DATA *identifier, data-record.* 4.8

This element supplements the information in the metafile in an application-dependent way. It has no effect on the picture generated by interpreting the metafile, nor any effect on the states of the metafile generator or metafile interpreter.

The content of the identifier and data record parameters is not standardized.

The contents of the data record may include, for example, such information as history data associated with each picture, a description of algorithms used to generate the picture, structural information and connectivity data.

13.9 Metafile Defaults

The CGM standard proscribes default values for those values not explicitly set in a METAFILE DEFAULTS REPLACEMENTS element.

The default values of some elements are dependent upon the values of other elements. However, the value of the dependent element does not automatically change with the value of the element upon which it depends is changed explicitly by appearing in a METAFILE DEFAULTS REPLACEMENTS element. Rather, it too must be changed explicitly by also appearing in the METAFILE DEFAULTS REPLACEMENTS element.

For example, the default clip rectangle is equal to the VDC EXTENT. When VDC TYPE is *real*, the default VDC EXTENT is (0,0) (1.0,1.0). Suppose we wanted a default VDC EXTENT of (-1.0,-1.0)(1.0,1.0). If we used the CGM fragment below on the left, only VDCs in the positive quadrant would be visible, because the default clipping rectangle would still be (0,0) (1.0,1.0). Only if we also change the default clipping rectangle, as shown by the CGM fragment below on the right, will we get the desired effect.

BEGMF; ... ...;	BEGMF; ... ...;
VDCTYPE REAL;	VDCTYPE REAL;
BEGMFDEFAULTS;	BEGMFDEFAULTS;
VDCEXT (-1.,-1.,1.0,1.0);	VDCEXT(-1.,-1.,1.0,1.0);
	CLIPRECT (-1.,-1.,1.0,1.0);
ENDMFDEFAULTS; ... ...;	ENDMFDEFAULTS; ... ...;
BEGPIC; ...; BEGPICBODY;	BEGPIC; ... ...; BEGPICBODY;
RECT (-0.9,-0.9) (0.9,0.9); ...;	RECT (-0.9,-0.9) (0.9,0.9); ...;

Some elements have defaults that are encoding dependent. These values are specified in the next chapter, where each of the standardized encodings are described.

Chapter 14

CGM Encodings

The CGM standard consists of four parts: a Functional Description (Part 1), which describes the semantics of the CGM as explained in the previous chapter, and three standardized *encodings* of the CGM, which contain syntactic information only. These encodings are:

- the Character Encoding (Part 2), which uses ASCII bytes, including control characters, to represent the element codes and parameters;

- the Binary Encoding (Part 3), which uses internally formatted binary numbers to represent the data; and

- the Clear Text Encoding (Part 4), which uses only the 94 printing characters from the ISO 646 7-bit code table to represent the data.

Neither the Character encoding nor the Binary encoding is very readable by humans, while the Clear Text encoding is. But the Clear Text encoding is not very compact, while the other two encodings are. The Binary encoding is the fastest to read and write, but it is least suitable for transmission over communication lines, because all 8-bits in a byte are meaningful.

In this chapter, we discuss some of the details of each standardized CGM encoding scheme. We also present guidelines for private encodings of the CGM, if none of the standardized encodings are suitable for a specific application. The encodings are presented in order of frequency of availability in commercial implementations in the United States.

14.1 Binary Encoding

14.1.1 Overview

The Binary encoding of the CGM provides a representation of the CGM syntax that can be optimized for speed of generation and interpretation. The encoding uses binary data formats that are much more similar to the data representations used within computer systems than the data formats of the other encodings.

The principal features of the Binary encoding are:

1. **Partitioning of parameter lists.** Metafile elements are coded in one or more partitions; the first partition of an element always contains the operation code (*opcode*), which consists of an Element Class code and an Element Identifier.

2. **Alignment of elements.** Every element begins on a word boundary. Alignment of partitions that require an odd number of octets is effected by padding with an octet with all bits zero. A no-op element is available. It may be used to align data on machine-dependent record boundaries for speed of processing.

3. **Uniformity of format.** All elements have an associated parameter length value, specified as an octet count. Therefore, it is possible to scan the metafile rapidly, without interpreting it.

4. **Alignment of Coordinate Data.** At default precisions, coordinate data always start on 16-bit boundaries. Similarly, rows within CELL ARRAY colour lists must also begin on 16-bit boundaries. Consequently, on a wide class of computing systems, single coordinates do not have to be assembled from pieces of multiple computer words.

5. **Extensibility.** The arrangement of Element Class and Element Id values has been designed to allow future growth, such as the new graphical elements that are being planned for the Addenda to the CGM (see Chap. 17).

The binary encoding is relatively simple to generate and parse. All elements have one of two command header formats: *short* and *long*. Both formats have a first 16-bit word with three fields–a 4-bit opcode class, a 7-bit opcode identifier (*id*), and a 5-bit operand length (*len*) field. In the short form of the command, the number of bytes of operand data is contained in the *len* field (see Fig. 14.1(a)). The short form can accomodate up to 30 bytes of data: the value *31* in this field is a special flag indicating that the element is in long format (see Fig. 14.1(b)).

Bit Position	15 14 13 12	11 10 9 8 7 6 5	4 3 2 1 0	
Use	Element Class	Element Identifier	Parameter List Length	Word 1

Fig. 14.1(a). Format of a short-form command header

Bit Position	15 14 13 12	11 10 9 8 7 6 5	4 3 2 1 0	
Use	Element Class	Element Identifier	1 1 1 1 1	Word 1
	P	Parameter List Length		Word 2

Fig. 14.1(b). Format of a long-form command header

In long form, the second 16-bit word contains the data length in the least significant 15 bits. If the first (most significant) bit is 0, the count is the complete count. If 1, the element is to be continued with another so-called *data partition*. Following the data for the first data partition will be another 16-bit control word containing the 1-bit flag and the 15-bit data count followed by the data itself (for an example, see Fig. 14.2).

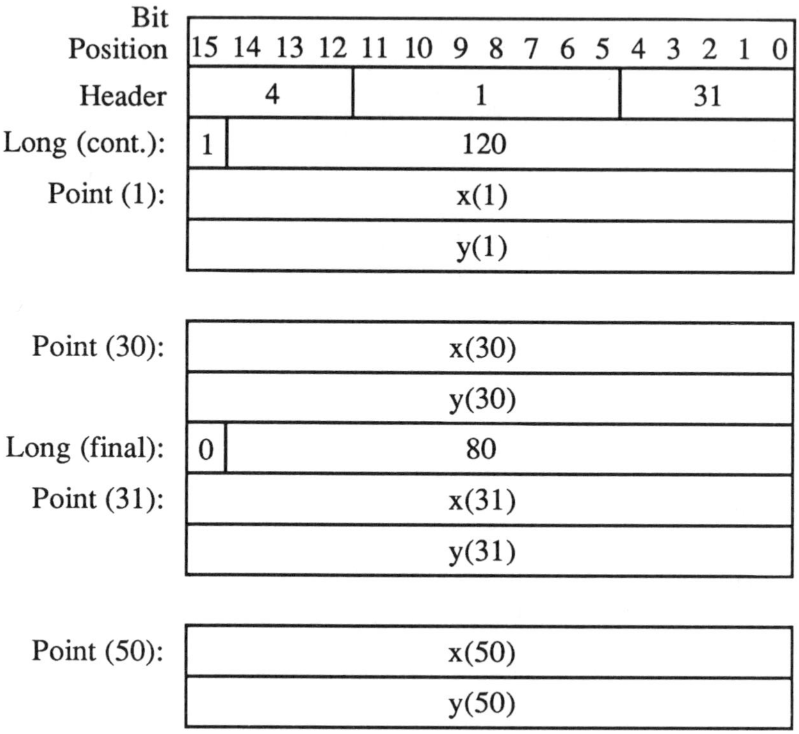

Bit Position	15 14 13 12	11 10 9 8 7 6 5	4 3 2 1 0
Header	4	1	31

Long (cont.):	1	120
Point (1):		x(1)
		y(1)

Point (30):		x(30)
		y(30)
Long (final):	0	80
Point (31):		x(31)
		y(31)

Point (50):	x(50)
	y(50)

Fig. 14.2. Partitioned POLYLINE with 50 points

Integers and indices are stored alike; negative values are represented as 2's complement integers.

Real numbers may be represented either as ANSI/IEEE floating point numbers or as fixed point values.

Strings are similar to elements themselves in that they can be represented in short or long form. Short strings may contain up to 254 characters: the character count is stored in the first byte of the string. If the character count is 255, the second two bytes contain a (high order) flag bit and a 15-bit character count. If the flag bit contains a 0, this partial string completes the string parameter. If 1, this partial string is followed by another partial string (preceded by its own 16-bit continuation flag and count field), and so on. See Fig. 14.3 for an example.

Bit Position	15 14 13 12	11 10 9 8 7 6 5	4 3 2 1 0
Header	4	1	16

Point 0,2:	0
	2
Point 1,3:	1
	3
Point 2,1:	2
	1
Point 0,2:	0
	2

Fig. 14.3. Example of a short-form string

14.1.2 List of Binary Encoding Metafile Element Codes

The following list indicates the class and element codes associated with each metafile element. These are the codes used in the METAFILE ELEMENTS LIST element.

Class	*Element Code*	*Element Name*
0	1	BEGIN METAFILE
0	2	END METAFILE
0	3	BEGIN PICTURE
0	4	BEGIN PICTURE BODY
0	5	END PICTURE
1	1	METAFILE VERSION
1	2	METAFILE DESCRIPTION
1	3	VDC TYPE
1	4	INTEGER PRECISION
1	5	REAL PRECISION
1	6	INDEX PRECISION
1	7	COLOUR PRECISION
1	8	COLOUR INDEX PRECISION
1	9	MAXIMUM COLOUR INDEX
1	10	COLOUR VALUE EXTENT
1	11	METAFILE ELEMENT LIST

Class	Element Code	Element Name
1	12	METAFILE DEFAULTS REPLACEMENT
1	13	FONT LIST
1	14	CHARACTER SET LIST
1	15	CHARACTER CODING ANNOUNCER
2	1	SCALING MODE
2	2	COLOUR SELECTION MODE
2	3	LINE WIDTH SPECIFICATION MODE
2	4	MARKER SIZE SPECIFICATION MODE
2	5	EDGE WIDTH SPECIFICATION MODE
2	6	VDC EXTENT
2	7	BACKGROUND COLOUR
3	1	VDC INTEGER PRECISION
3	2	VDC REAL PRECISION
3	3	AUXILIARY COLOUR
3	4	TRANSPARENCY
3	5	CLIP RECTANGLE
3	6	CLIP INDICATOR
4	1	POLYLINE
4	2	DISJOINT POLYLINE
4	3	POLYMARKER
4	4	TEXT
4	5	RESTRICTED TEXT
4	6	APPEND TEXT
4	7	POLYGON
4	8	POLYGON SET
4	9	CELL ARRAY
4	10	GENERALIZED DRAWING PRIMITIVE
4	11	RECTANGLE
4	12	CIRCLE
4	13	CIRCULAR ARC 3 POINT
4	14	CIRCULAR ARC 3 POINT CLOSE
4	15	CIRCULAR ARC CENTRE
4	16	CIRCULAR ARC CENTRE CLOSE
4	17	ELLIPSE
4	18	ELLIPTICAL ARC
4	19	ELLIPTICAL ARC CLOSE
5	1	LINE BUNDLE INDEX
5	2	LINE TYPE
5	3	LINE WIDTH
5	4	LINE COLOUR

Class	Element Code	Element Name
5	5	MARKER BUNDLE INDEX
5	6	MARKER TYPE
5	7	MARKER SIZE
5	8	MARKER COLOUR
5	9	TEXT BUNDLE INDEX
5	10	TEXT FONT INDEX
5	11	TEXT PRECISION
5	12	CHARACTER EXPANSION FACTOR
5	13	CHARACTER SPACING
5	14	TEXT COLOUR
5	15	CHARACTER HEIGHT
5	16	CHARACTER ORIENTATION
5	17	TEXT PATH
5	18	TEXT ALIGNMENT
5	19	CHARACTER SET INDEX
5	20	ALTERNATE CHARACTER SET INDEX
5	21	FILL BUNDLE INDEX
5	22	INTERIOR STYLE
5	23	FILL COLOUR
5	24	HATCH INDEX
5	25	PATTERN INDEX
5	26	EDGE BUNDLE INDEX
5	27	EDGE TYPE
5	28	EDGE WIDTH
5	29	EDGE COLOUR
5	30	EDGE VISIBILITY
5	31	FILL REFERENCE POINT
5	32	PATTERN TABLE
5	33	PATTERN SIZE
5	34	COLOUR TABLE
5	35	ASPECT SOURCE FLAGS
6	1	ESCAPE
7	1	MESSAGE
7	2	APPLICATION DATA

14.1.3 Binary Encoding Defaults

The following settings represent the default values for the Binary encoding.

REAL PRECISION	Fixed point; whole part 16 bits; fractional part 16 bits.
INTEGER PRECISION	16 bits.
COLOUR PRECISION	1 octet (per colour component).
COLOUR INDEX PRECISION	1 octet.
INDEX PRECISION	16 bits.
VDC REAL PRECISION	Fixed point; whole part 16 bits; fractional part 16 bits.
VDC INTEGER PRECISION	16 bits.
VDC EXTENT	If VDC TYPE is REAL, default VDC EXTENT is (0.0,0.0) , (0.999...,0.999...).
	If VDC TYPE is INTEGER, default VDC EXTENT is (0,0), (32767,32767).
COLOUR VALUE EXTENT	Minimum is (0,0,0); maximum is (255,255,255).

14.2 Clear Text Encoding

14.2.1 Overview

The Clear Text encoding is more complex than the Binary encoding to decode. The basic syntax is:

OPCODE <*sep*> OPERAND < *sep* > OPERAND ... <*term*>

OPCODE is a word like MARKER. *Term* can be either *slash* or *semicolon*–consequently, clear text elements are self-delimiting, unlike the binary encoding where the elements have a leading data count. *Sep* can be one of several characters, such as *blank*, *tab*, and *comma*. Some operands, like points, may be placed in parentheses for increased readability; e.g.,

MARKER (100., 150.);

All "poly" elements, like POLYLINE, can be encoded either with absolute coordinates or incremental coordinates.

Any word can have embedded "null" characters (i.e., either a *national currency symbol*–like $ or £–or a *hyphen*), which have no meaning and can be discarded during parsing. Numbers can be represented in any radix (base) from 2 to 16. Integers may have a decimal point, but no fractional part. Reals may be represented in a format resembling either the Fn.m or the En.m format of FORTRAN. Enumerative types are keywords like *LEFT*, *RIGHT*, *UP*, and *DOWN*.

Strings are delimited by matching single quotes (') or matching double quotes ("). Single or double quotes can be included in a string by doubling the character within the string. For example, the phrase *He said, "Won't anyone help me!"*, would be represented in the CGM as the string:

"He said, ""Won't anyone help me!"""

Strings can be contiguous with other operands without a separator.

Comments are delimited by surrounding percentage signs (%). They can extend across multiple lines and be placed anywhere in a Clear Text CGM.

The richness of syntax leads to a very friendly and easy-to-use encoding of the CGM, excellent for debugging and quick test picture generation (e.g., by using a text editor). However, parsing and decoding the CGM is considerably slower and more complex than processing a binary encoding.

14.2.2 List of Clear Text Encoding Derived Element Names

The following list indicates the Clear Text derived element names associated with each metafile element.

Derived Name	Element Name
BEGMF	BEGIN METAFILE
ENDMF	END METAFILE
BEGPIC	BEGIN PICTURE
BEGPICBODY	BEGIN PICTURE BODY
ENDPIC	END PICTURE

Derived Name	Element Name
MFVERSION	METAFILE VERSION
MFDESC	METAFILE DESCRIPTION
VDCTYPE	VDC TYPE
INTEGERPREC	INTEGER PRECISION
REALPREC	REAL PRECISION
INDEXPREC	INDEX PRECISION
COLRPREC	COLOUR PRECISION
COLRINDEXPREC	COLOUR INDEX PRECISION
MAXCOLRINDEX	MAXIMUM COLOUR INDEX
COLRVALUEEXT	COLOUR VALUE EXTENT
MFELEMLIST	METAFILE ELEMENT LIST
	METAFILE DEFAULTS REPLACEMENT
BEGMFDEFAULTS	Begin-metafile-defaults
ENDMFDEFAULTS	End-metafile-defaults
FONTLIST	FONT LIST
CHARSETLIST	CHARACTER SET LIST
CHARCODING	CHARACTER CODING ANNOUNCER
SCALEMODE	SCALING MODE
COLRMODE	COLOUR SELECTION MODE
LINEWIDTHMODE	LINE WIDTH SPECIFICATION MODE
MARKERSIZEMODE	MARKER SIZE SPECIFICATION MODE
EDGEWIDTHMODE	EDGE WIDTH SPECIFICATION MODE
VDCEXT	VDC EXTENT
BACKCOLR	BACKGROUND COLOUR
VDCINTEGERPREC	VDC INTEGER PRECISION
VDCREALPREC	VDC REAL PRECISION
AUXCOLR	AUXILIARY COLOUR
TRANSPARENCY	TRANSPARENCY
CLIPRECT	CLIP RECTANGLE
CLIP	CLIP INDICATOR
LINE	POLYLINE
INCRLINE	
DISJTLINE	DISJOINT POLYLINE
INCRDISJTLINE	
MARKER	POLYMARKER
INCRMARKER	
TEXT	TEXT
RESTRTEXT	RESTRICTED TEXT
APNDTEXT	APPEND TEXT
POLYGON	POLYGON
INCRPOLYGON	
POLYGONSET	POLYGON SET

Derived Name	Element Name
INCRPOLYGONSET	
CELLARRAY	CELL ARRAY
GDP	GENERALIZED DRAWING PRIMITIVE
RECT	RECTANGLE
CIRCLE	CIRCLE
ARC3PT	CIRCULAR ARC 3 POINT
ARC3PTCLOSE	CIRCULAR ARC 3 POINT CLOSE
ARCCTR	CIRCULAR ARC CENTRE
ARCCTRCLOSE	CIRCULAR ARC CENTRE CLOSE
ELLIPSE	ELLIPSE
ELLIPARC	ELLIPTICAL ARC
ELLIPARCCLOSE	ELLIPTICAL ARC CLOSE
LINEINDEX	LINE BUNDLE INDEX
LINETYPE	LINE TYPE
LINEWIDTH	LINE WIDTH
LINECOLR	LINE COLOUR
MARKERINDEX	MARKER BUNDLE INDEX
MARKERTYPE	MARKER TYPE
MARKERSIZE	MARKER SIZE
MARKERCOLR	MARKER COLOUR
TEXTINDEX	TEXT BUNDLE INDEX
TEXTFONTINDEX	TEXT FONT INDEX
TEXTPREC	TEXT PRECISION
CHAREXPAN	CHARACTER EXPANSION FACTOR
CHARSPACE	CHARACTER SPACING
TEXTCOLR	TEXT COLOUR
CHARHEIGHT	CHARACTER HEIGHT
CHARORI	CHARACTER ORIENTATION
TEXTPATH	TEXT PATH
TEXTALIGN	TEXT ALIGNMENT
CHARSETINDEX	CHARACTER SET INDEX
ALTCHARSETINDEX	ALTERNATE CHARACTER SET INDEX
FILLINDEX	FILL BUNDLE INDEX
INTSTYLE	INTERIOR STYLE
FILLCOLR	FILL COLOUR
HATCHINDEX	HATCH INDEX
PATINDEX	PATTERN INDEX
EDGEINDEX	EDGE BUNDLE INDEX
EDGETYPE	EDGE TYPE
EDGEWIDTH	EDGE WIDTH
EDGECOLR	EDGE COLOUR
EDGEVIS	EDGE VISIBILITY

Derived Name	Element Name
FILLREFPT	FILL REFERENCE POINT
PATTABLE	PATTERN TABLE
PATSIZE	PATTERN SIZE
COLRTABLE	COLOUR TABLE
ASF	ASPECT SOURCE FLAGS
ESCAPE	ESCAPE
MESSAGE	MESSAGE
APPLDATA	APPLICATION DATA

14.2.3. Clear Text Encoding Defaults

The following settings represent the default values for the Clear Text encoding.

REAL PRECISION	Minimum real = -32767; Maximum real = 32767; Digits = 4.
INTEGER PRECISION	Minimum integer = -32767; Maximum integer = 32767.
COLOUR PRECISION	Maximum component = 255.
COLOUR INDEX PRECISION	Maximum integer = 127.
INDEX PRECISION	Minimum integer = 0; Maximum integer = 127;
VDC REAL PRECISION	Minimum real = 0.0; Maximum real = 1.0; Digits = 4.
VDC INTEGER PRECISION	Minimum integer = -32767; Maximum integer = 32767.
COLOUR VALUE EXTENT	BLACK is (0,0,0); WHITE is (255,255,255).

14.3 Character Encoding

14.3.1 Overview

The Character encoding is self-delimiting like the Clear Text encoding, and it is also more complex to code and decode than the Binary.

Opcodes are one or two characters from columns 2 and 3 of the ISO 646 7-bit or 8-bit code table. All parameter data come from columns 4 through 7 of the table. For the remainder of this section, we restrict our discussion to coding with the 7-bit code table. The same principles apply to coding with the 8-bit table.

Two fundamental encoding formats are used for parameter data: *basic format* and *bitstream format*. In basic format, each byte of each operand has bits reserved to flag whether it is the final byte of data or not. In basic format, only enough bytes are used to held the given piece of data, thus compressing the data for small numbers. For example, integers with absolute value less than 16 would require only 1 byte; integers with absolute value less than 512 only 2 bytes; and so on. Most parameters are encoded using basic format.

Bitstream format is generally more efficient, but is not self-delimiting: some piece of information like a data count is needed to indicate how much data must be processed and where the bitstream ends. Colour lists, colour direct values, and incremental mode points are encoded in this format. High data compression for the point data is achieved by a Differential Chain Code (DCC) method. A Huffman code is used to further compress the DCC data, which are designators for points on a DCC ring.

The Character encoding has seven ways to encode colour lists: the lists can be basic or bitstream format, run-length or full-list encoded, and the colour selection mode can be indexed or direct.

Strings in the encoding are delimited by Start-of-String (SOS) and String Terminator (ST) pairs. SOS is coded as ESC-X and ST as ESC-[, where ESC- denotes the control character ESCAPE. The Character encoding permits *character substitution* of certain sensitive characters like all the control characters (columns 0 and 1 of the code table), *space*, *tilde*, and *del*, which may cause problems in some operating system and communications environments. These sensitive characters can be replaced in the metafile by 2-character code sequences starting with the character 7/14. The use of character substitution is declared in the parameters of the BEGIN METAFILE element.

14.3.2 List of Character Encoding Metafile Element Codes

The following list indicates the ISO 646 7-bit code table characters used to encode each metafile element. A few of the more common primitive elements are coded with only one character; all others take two.

Element Code 1	Element Code 2	Element Name
3/0	2/0	BEGIN METAFILE
3/0	2/1	END METAFILE
3/0	2/2	BEGIN PICTURE
3/0	2/3	BEGIN PICTURE BODY
3/0	2/4	END PICTURE
3/1	2/0	METAFILE VERSION
3/1	2/1	METAFILE DESCRIPTION
3/1	2/2	VDC TYPE
3/1	2/3	INTEGER PRECISION
3/1	2/4	REAL PRECISION
3/1	2/5	INDEX PRECISION
3/1	2/6	COLOUR PRECISION
3/1	2/7	COLOUR INDEX PRECISION
3/1	2/8	MAXIMUM COLOUR INDEX
3/1	2/9	COLOUR VALUE EXTENT
3/1	2/10	METAFILE ELEMENT LIST
		METAFILE DEFAULTS REPLACEMENT
3/1	2/11	Begin-metafile-defaults
3/1	2/12	End-metafile-defaults
3/1	2/13	FONT LIST
3/1	2/14	CHARACTER SET LIST
3/1	2/15	CHARACTER CODING ANNOUNCER
3/2	2/0	SCALING MODE
3/2	2/1	COLOUR SELECTION MODE
3/2	2/2	LINE WIDTH SPECIFICATION MODE
3/2	2/3	MARKER SIZE SPECIFICATION MODE
3/2	2/4	EDGE WIDTH SPECIFICATION MODE
3/2	2/5	VDC EXTENT
3/2	2/6	BACKGROUND COLOUR
3/3	2/0	VDC INTEGER PRECISION
3/3	2/1	VDC REAL PRECISION
3/3	2/2	AUXILIARY COLOUR
3/3	2/3	TRANSPARENCY
3/3	2/4	CLIP RECTANGLE
3/3	2/5	CLIP INDICATOR

Element Code 1	Element Code 2	Element Name
2/0		POLYLINE
2/1		DISJOINT POLYLINE
2/2		POLYMARKER
2/3		TEXT
2/4		RESTRICTED TEXT
2/5		APPEND TEXT
2/6		POLYGON
2/7		POLYGON SET
2/8		CELL ARRAY
2/9		GENERALIZED DRAWING PRIMITIVE
2/10		RECTANGLE
3/4	2/0	CIRCLE
3/4	2/1	CIRCULAR ARC 3 POINT
3/4	2/2	CIRCULAR ARC 3 POINT CLOSE
3/4	2/3	CIRCULAR ARC CENTRE
3/4	2/4	CIRCULAR ARC CENTRE CLOSE
3/4	2/5	ELLIPSE
3/4	2/6	ELLIPTICAL ARC
3/4	2/7	ELLIPTICAL ARC CLOSE
3/5	2/0	LINE BUNDLE INDEX
3/5	2/1	LINE TYPE
3/5	2/2	LINE WIDTH
3/5	2/3	LINE COLOUR
3/5	2/4	MARKER BUNDLE INDEX
3/5	2/5	MARKER TYPE
3/5	2/6	MARKER SIZE
3/5	2/7	MARKER COLOUR
3/5	3/0	TEXT BUNDLE INDEX
3/5	3/1	TEXT FONT INDEX
3/5	3/2	TEXT PRECISION
3/5	3/3	CHARACTER EXPANSION FACTOR
3/5	3/4	CHARACTER SPACING
3/5	3/5	TEXT COLOUR
3/5	3/6	CHARACTER HEIGHT
3/5	3/7	CHARACTER ORIENTATION
3/5	3/8	TEXT PATH
3/5	3/9	TEXT ALIGNMENT
3/5	3/10	CHARACTER SET INDEX
3/5	3/11	ALTERNATE CHARACTER SET INDEX
3/6	2/0	FILL BUNDLE INDEX
3/6	2/1	INTERIOR STYLE
3/6	2/2	FILL COLOUR
3/6	2/3	HATCH INDEX
3/6	2/4	PATTERN INDEX

Element Code 1	Element Code 2	Element Name
3/6	2/5	EDGE BUNDLE INDEX
3/6	2/6	EDGE TYPE
3/6	2/7	EDGE WIDTH
3/6	2/8	EDGE COLOUR
3/6	2/9	EDGE VISIBILITY
3/6	2/10	FILL REFERENCE POINT
3/6	2/11	PATTERN TABLE
3/6	2/12	PATTERN SIZE
3/6	3/0	COLOUR TABLE
3/6	3/1	ASPECT SOURCE FLAGS
3/7	2/0	ESCAPE
3/7	3/0	DOMAIN RING
3/7	2/1	MESSAGE
3/7	2/2	APPLICATION DATA

14.3.3. Character Encoding Defaults

The following settings represent the default values for the Character encoding.

REAL PRECISION	Largest-real-code = 10; Smallest-real-code = -10; Default-exponent-for-reals = -10; Exponents-allowed = 1 (*forbidden*)
INTEGER PRECISION	10
COLOUR PRECISION	6
COLOUR INDEX PRECISION	10
INDEX PRECISION	10
VDC REAL PRECISION	Largest-real-code = 10; Smallest-real-code = -10; Default-exponent-for-reals = -10; Exponents-allowed = 1 (*forbidden*)
VDC INTEGER PRECISION	20

DOMAIN RING	Angular resolution factor = 0;
	Ring size for VDC type integer = 1;
	Ring size for VDC type real,
	   if smallest-real-code < -8 = 2 exp(-8-*src*)
	Ring size for VDC type real,
	   if smallest-real-code ≥ -8 = 1.

COLOUR VALUE EXTENT	Minimum is (0,0,0); maximum is (63,63,63).

14.4 Private Encodings

In addition to the standard encodings, a functionally conforming metafile may also use a non-standardized–that is, *private*–encoding. While the CGM standard itself does not prescribe rules for private encodings, it does suggest minimum criteria that private encodings should meet.

These criteria include:

1. All CGM elements shall have a specified encoding, with the exception of the precision commands–some of which may not be applicable to the private encoding. Furthermore, an element that sets an interpretation mode for other elements may be implicit in the commands that it affects, instead of being coded explicitly as a separate element. For example, a procedural encoding might include separate calls for ABSOLUTE LINE WIDTH(VDC) and SCALED LINE WIDTH(R), while omitting LINE WIDTH SPECIFICATION MODE.

2. All CGM functionality shall be realizable (for example, both integer and real Virtual Device Coordinates), except where noted above under criterion 1.

3. The private encoding shall utilize sufficient precision to accommodate the Minimum Suggested Capability List (see Table 14.1). For example, all standardized precisions of bundle indices shall be able to represent the range [1...5], inclusive.

Furthermore, in accordance with design guidelines used for developing the standardized encodings, designers of private encodings should insure that:

- it is possible to translate a metafile encoded in one of the standardized encodings into the private encoding without loss of information;

- it is possible to translate a metafile encoded in the private encoding to one of the standardized encodings without loss of information.

Finally, private encodings should support at least the range of coordinate data precisions standardized in the Binary Encoding of the CGM.

Table 14.1. Suggested minimum capabilities for a CGM interpreter

Capability	Minimum Suggested Interpreter Support
CHARACTER CODING ANNOUNCER	Basic 7-bit
FONT LIST	at least one font capable of displaying the character set described below, see CHARACTER SET LIST
CHARACTER SET LIST	at least one character set which includes the nationality-independent subset of ISO 646 in the positions specified in ISO 646
BACKGROUND COLOUR	1, interpreter dependent
AUXILIARY COLOUR	transparent
TRANSPARENCY	on
TEXT string size for alignment	80 characters
Vertices for POLYGON and POLYGON SET	128
LINE BUNDLE INDEX	5
LINE TYPE	solid,dash,dot,dash-dot,dash-dot-dot
LINE WIDTH	1, interpreter dependent
LINE COLOUR	1, interpreter dependent
MARKER BUNDLE INDEX	5
MARKER TYPE	dot,plus,asterisk,circle,cross
MARKER SIZE	1, interpreter dependent
MARKER COLOUR	1, interpreter dependent
TEXT BUNDLE INDEX	2
TEXT FONT INDEX	1
TEXT PRECISION	string,character
CHARACTER EXPANSION FACTOR	1, interpreter dependent
CHARACTER SPACING	1, interpreter dependent
TEXT COLOUR	1, interpreter dependent
CHARACTER HEIGHT	1, interpreter dependent
CHARACTER ORIENTATION	along the axes of VDC space
TEXT PATH	right,left,up,down
TEXT ALIGNMENT	normal vertical,top,bottom,baseline, normal horizontal,left,centre,right
CHARACTER SET INDEX	1
ALTERNATE CHARACTER SET INDEX	1
FILL BUNDLE INDEX	5
INTERIOR STYLE	hollow,solid,pattern,hatch,empty
FILL COLOUR	1, interpreter dependent
HATCH INDEX	1, interpreter dependent
PATTERN INDEX	1, interpreter dependent
EDGE BUNDLE INDEX	5
EDGE COLOUR	Same as LINE COLOUR
EDGE TYPE	Same as LINETYPE
EDGE WIDTH	Same as LINE WIDTH
PATTERN SIZE	1, interpreter dependent

Chapter 15

Relationship of the CGM to Other Standards

15.1 CGI

CGI draws extensively for its model of a graphics picture on the CGM. It should be possible to generate a CGM through the CGI in a straightforward way. Consequently, all the CGM graphical primitive and attribute elements are present in the CGI. However, since the CGM was technically frozen, new primitive and attribute functions have been added to the CGI. Consequently, these functions need to be added as elements of the CGM. The CGM Addendum 1 project assigned to ISO/IEC JTC1/SC24 will add all those CGI functions, not yet in the CGM, that were considered to be technically frozen as of June, 1987.

The data stream encodings of CGI will be based on the encoding principles of the corresponding encodings of the CGM. Furthermore, where functions are identical in parameterization and equivalent in semantics in the two standards, the encodings will be identical. This will permit firmware and hardware to be developed that could serve as interpreters for both CGI data streams and CGM files.

15.2 GKS

The CGM standard borrows its model of a graphics system from GKS (ISO 7942:1985). All of the GKS primitives and attributes can be represented as CGM elements.

The GKS standard includes the concepts of metafile input and output workstations, as well as functions providing access to and interpretation of metafiles. It does not, however, contain a metafile definition as part of the standard. Instead, Annex E of GKS contains the definition of a GKS metafile (GKSM). The suggested GKSM is an audit trail at the workstation interface of the GKS functions, containing all the dynamic information originally available in the output stream of an entire interactive graphics session.

The CGM standard defines a metafile for the capture of static picture definitions. Specifically, it contains adequate functionality to serve as a picture capture mechanism in the GKS environment. Because use of the CGM was not intended to be restricted to GKS environments, there is not a one-to-one mapping between all the functions of the two standards—CGM lacks some GKS facilities while offering others not available in GKS. This raises some questions about generation and interpretation of CGM in a GKS environment.

While the CGM can capture static picture definitions from any level of GKS, the relationship of CGM elements to GKS functions is most straightforward at output level 0 of GKS. When the dynamic functions from levels 1 and 2 of GKS are used by applications, the strategies for generating proper picture definitions are both more numerous and more complex. Implementation and application requirements will dictate the best strategy to use.

The principal differences between GKS and CGM that impact the generation of CGMs that could serve as GKSMs are described in the following.

1. There are no CGM counterparts for the GKS elements that set and change the workstation transformation.

2. The SET XXX REPRESENTATION functions for setting workstation attributes in the coresponding bundle tables are not present in CGM.

3. All functions referring to segments are missing from CGM.

Because of these differences, the CGM in its current form can serve as a GKSM only for GKS programs operating at output level 0. The current work on CGM Addendum 1, described in Chap. 17, when completed, will augment CGM with elements that will permit the CGM to be used as a GKSM for all levels of GKS.

The fact that CGM contains functionality not present in GKS causes no special problems when a CGM is being output from GKS, because such elements would simply not be generated. Thus, the interpretation by GKS of a CGM generated by GKS is well defined. Annex E of the CGM standard details the mapping between GKS functions and CGM elements, when the CGM is used for static picture capture.

The interpretation by GKS of a CGM generated outside GKS is less well defined. Generally speaking, support for such elements as DISJOINT POLYLINE, POLYGON SET, CIRCLE, and APPEND TEXT will have to be emulated on top of the more primitive GKS drawing set. This is not a particularly unusual situation. Most device drivers for printers and plotters must provide software emulation of this nature. Indeed, one of the more successful CGM interpreter library implementations (developed by Lofton Henderson, the CGM Document Editor) is designed to be layered on top of a GKS implementation.

Notwithstanding the above, there is substantial interest within the ISO graphics standards community to upgrade the capabilities of GKS during the next revision of the standard. The CGI/CGM primitives and attributes will be very high priority items considered for inclusion in the next version of GKS.

15.3 Registration of Graphical Items

For certain elements, the CGM defines value ranges of parameters as being reserved for registration. The meanings of these values will be defined using the established procedures of the ISO *International Registration Authority for Graphical Items*. These procedures do not apply to values and value ranges specified as being reserved for implementation-dependent or private use; these values and ranges are not standardized.

Applications, therefore, shall not use parameter values in the reserved ranges for implementation-dependent or private use. Those metafile elements that will be affected by registration of graphical items are:

> LINE TYPE
>
> MARKER TYPE
>
> HATCH STYLE
>
> EDGE TYPE
>
> FONT LIST
>
> GENERALIZED DRAWING PRIMITIVE
>
> ESCAPE

Registration of character sets for use with the CHARACTER SET LIST element is according to the procedures established by ISO 2375.

15.4 Office Document Architecture

ISO 8613–Office Document Architecture (ODA) and Interchange Format (ODIF)–is an international standard, whose purpose is to facilitate the interchange of documents. ODA allows the interchange of documents either:

- to allow presentation as intended by the originator;

- to allow processing such as editing and reformatting.

The composition of a document in interchange can take various forms:

- *formatted* form, allowing presentation of the document;

- *processable* form, allowing processing of the document;

- *formatted processable* form, allowing both presentation and processing.

Furthermore, ISO 8613 allows for the interchange of documents containing one or more different types of content such as text, raster images, graphics, and sound. Documents are considered to be items such as memoranda, letters, invoices, forms, and reports, which may include pictures and tabular material. The content elements used within the documents may include graphic characters, geometric graphics elements, and photographic elements–all potentially within one document.

Part 8 of ISO 8613 is known as the Geometric Graphics Content Architecture. Part 8:

- defines a graphics content architecture to be used in conjunction with the rest of ODA/ODIF;

- defines an interface that allows the use of graphics content structured according to the CGM standard within ODA documents;

- defines those aspects of positioning and imaging applicable to the presentation of CGM pictures in a basic layout object;

- defines the presentation attributes available when including CGM pictures in documents;

- describes a content layout process, which together with the document layout process for text-only documents, determines the layout of CGM pictures in basic layout objects and the dimensions of these basic layout objects.

In the current version of ODA Part 8, a picture to be imported can be obtained from a single CGM containing only a single picture. The CGM must be encoded according to the Binary Encoding principles (ISO 8632-3).

When the picture is imported, a *region of interest*–a rectangular subset with VDC space–may be designated for imaging within the ODA document. In addition, *picture orientation* may be specified as a layout directive. By varying the specification of these two presentation attributes, the picture contained in the CGM may be clipped, rotated, scaled and mirrored to fit the space available in the document. You may also control the horizontal and vertical alignment of the picture as it is placed inside the area set aside for it in the document and whether the aspect ratio of the stored CGM picture is changed as it is imaged with the document.

Additional presentation attributes are provided in ODA to:

- Specify the default bundle representations of the line, marker, text, fill area and edge bundles.

- Specify a default pattern representation.

- Specify a default colour table and background colour.

- Announce a set of CGM types and precisions.

- Specify default individual attributes for line, marker, text, fill area, and edge renditions.

- Specify a default transparency and auxiliary colour.

- Specify a default VDC Extent, Clip Rectangle, and Clip Indicator.

The purpose of all these attributes is to permit interchange of documents containing pictures in such a fashion that the originator of the document may specify the document with sufficient precision that the appearance, when imaged by the recipient, is guaranteed to be what the originator intended.

The default settings of these attributes are consistent with the TOP 3.0 Application Profile for the CGM, which is described in more detail in Appendix F.

15.5 Standard Generalized Markup Language

SGML is an ISO standard (ISO 8879) that contains syntactic facilities to indicate the logical structure of a document. Using SGML, one can create and register document formatting languages similar to *nroff* and *troff*, so familiar to users of Unix™ systems. The SGML standard permits graphics images to imported into its documents from external files. The CGM is referenced as the standard to be used in representing these graphical images.

Annex A of the Geometric Graphics Content Architecture (ISO 8613-8) described in the previous section contains a representation of the geometric graphics presentation attributes according to the rules present in SGML.

Chapter 16

Implementations of the CGM

Although CGM was published in late 1986, already by the end of 1987 nearly two dozen companies in the United States had released products or announced plans for products incorporating support for the CGM.

Support for the CGM generally manifests itself in three principal ways. First, an application like CAD or business presentation graphics may offer the ability to write out (*export*) a CGM file that captures one or more of the pictures or drawings created during a design session. Second, an application like a desktop publishing system or a print spooler for a special piece of hardware may provide the ability to read in (*import*) a CGM file for imaging purposes. Third, a few applications (*graphics editors*) have the ability to import CGM files, make modifications to the picture descriptions contained therein, and write them back out again as CGM files.

Support for the CGM is also packaged differently by the various commercial suppliers. First, CGM interpreters and generators may be supplied as independent graphics subroutine libraries, to be linked into any application that needs a CGM importing or exporting capability. Second, CGM implementations may be stand-alone programs, with a user-interface module, that permits operator specification of which files are to be used and which devices are to be selected for display. Third, CGM importing or exporting may be tightly coupled to a specific application, without being offered for sale in any general way. This, in fact, is the most prevalent form of CGM implementation. That is, software and hardware suppliers view the CGM as an interchange standard to be supported, rather than a product to be sold. Only suppliers that target the OEM and system software markets have created products that embody the CGM technology for resale to application and system developers.

In this chapter, we will briefly describe the commercial products that incorporate support for the CGM–as exporters, importers, and editors. The product descriptions are based on available documentation and represent those products known to the authors as of December 1987. The authors cannot vouch for the correctness or quality of any of these implementations. This survey is not exhaustive; rather, it is meant to give a good picture of the range of uses for the CGM. No doubt, some supplier's products have been omitted–but not deliberately!

You will note that CGM implementations are available on a wide range of hardware platforms (mainframes and minicomputers, workstations and personal computers) and operating systems (MS-DOS™ and UNIX™, VAX/VMS™ and PRIMOS™, etc.). Implementations of the CGM can be built that are completely machine-, operating system-, programming language-, and device-independent. Later in this chapter, we briefly describe an industry demonstration event, **GraphNet'88**, sponsored by the National Computer Graphics Association and planned for their annual conference, *Computer Graphics'88*, in late March, 1988, in Anaheim, California. The demonstration will illustrate the benefits of System Integration, using CGM as the formal vehicle for obtaining interchange of graphics pictures– drawings, graphs and charts, and images.

Some suppliers have chosen to support only one encoding of the CGM–usually the Binary Encoding. Others support all three encodings. Because the CGM standard does not specify the behaviour of conforming CGM generators and interpreters, there is a wide-range of support (and lack of support!) for particular CGM elements. At the end of this chapter, we will discuss some of the current barriers to CGM interchange and recommend some actions to alleviate the problem. You may also wish to read App. F, where we explain the TOP CGM Application Profile– an approach to achieving predictable CGM interchange that is worthy of broad industry support.

16.1 CGM Exporters

16.1.1 On Mainframes, Minicomputers, and Workstations

Several mainframe and minicomputer companies have chosen to provide CGM drivers with their general-purpose graphics subroutine libraries. Sometimes, these libraries are GKS implementations; other times they represent their own proprietary software products. Computer companies that have adopted this approach include Digital Equipment Corporation (Maynard, MA), Hewlett-Packard Corporation (Sunnyvale, CA), and Wang Laboratories (Lowell, MA). Independent software companies following this strategy include Advanced Technology Center (Culver City, CA), Computer Associates (Garden City, Long Island, NY), Pansophic Systems (Oak Brook, IL), Precision Visuals (Boulder, CO), Nova Graphics (Austin, TX), Template Graphics Software (San Diego, CA), and UNIRAS (Denmark).

The effect of this strategy is that any application layered on top of the graphics library automatically gains a CGM exporting capability. For example, the Pansophic D-PICT/INTELLICHART interactive presentation graphics application gained CGM output capability when it was written on top of their GKS, supplied by ATC.

This strategy has also been followed to a great degree in the UNIX™ workstation market. In addition to Digital, HP, and Wang, Masscomp (Cambridge, MA), Prime (Framingham, MA) and Sun (Mountain View, CA) plan on offering CGM exporting capability embedded into their graphics libraries. In addition, the implementations of some of the independent software companies give CGM capabilities to Apollo, IBM, and Silicon Graphics platforms, as well as to many of the other workstations already mentioned.

To encourage the use of CGMs, McDonnell-Douglas Corporation (St. Louis, MO) has placed a Fortran implementation of CGM in the public domain. This implementation conforms to an early draft of the TOP CGM Application Profile.

16.1.2 On Personal Computers and in Hardware

For the personal computer market, the strategy has been the same, but the marketing result different. One company–Graphic Software Systems (Beaverton, OR)–has written a CGM driver at the level of their CGI. Called GSS*CGM, this product has been sold to over 200 OEMs, large and small, including IBM, AT&T, and NCR. Many specific applications–like Harvard Presentation Graphics (Software Publishing, Mountain View, CA), MicroCADAM (CADAM, Inc., Burbank, CA), SuperImage (Computer Associates), and Freelance + (Lotus Development Corp., Cambridge, MA)–have embedded a CGM exporting capability in their products based on GSS*CGM.

Other companies–like Zenographics (Irvine, CA) and Presentation Technologies (Sunnyvale, CA)–have written their own CGM products. The Zenographics *Metafile* product is particularly notable, because it is a stand-alone CGM translator program. AutoCAD DXF files, Lotus PIC files, Hewlett-Packard HPGL files, and General Parametrics NAPLPS-based VideoShow files can all be converted into conforming CGM files for subsequent use by any application with a CGM importing capability. The Presentation Technologies ImageMate is targetted especially at driving their high-resolution camera system.

16.2 CGM Importers

16.2.1 On Mainframes, Minicomputers, and Workstations

Generally speaking, the same companies that offer CGM exporting capabilities through subroutine libraries also offer the capability for importing CGM files. In addition, some of these companies may also offer stand-alone, CGM interpreter applications that either drive a wide range of hardware or drive only a specific device or set of closely related devices. Logic Sciences (Houston, TX) and KMW Systems (Austin, TX) both have selected the CGM binary encoding as a data stream language for driving their high-performance, vector-to-raster converter hardware, which is used as front-ends for high-resolution raster plotters like those made by Benson and Versatec.

For workstations, only Wang has announced plans for providing CGM importing capability in its desktop publishing applications. However, it would not be surprising if companies like Interleaf and Texet were to announce such a capability sometime in 1988.

16.2.2 On Personal Computers and in Hardware

Companies offering remote slidemaking services–like MAGICorp (Elmsford, NY) and Brilliant Image (New York City, NY)–now accept CGM formatted pictures, in addition to accepting pictures in the more popular *de facto* industry standard formats, like Lotus PIC, HPGL, and AutoCAD DXF. They hope, by doing so, the range of applications capable of sending them pictures for enhancement and high-quality imaging will greatly expand. Their market should also expand to include imaging pictures generated by mainframe and minicomputer applications.

PC-based desktop publishing applications like Xerox Ventura Publisher (Morgan Hill, CA), Pansophic PageWorks, and Lotus Manuscript have built in to their latest releases support for importing CGM pictures, so that pictures created from a wide-range of applications can be used. Aldus Pagemaker (Bellingham, WA) does not yet directly support CGM, but Zenographics, again through its *Metafile* product, provides a translator from CGM files to MS-WINDOWS picture files that are acceptable as input to Pagemaker.

Some graphics peripheral companies, like Precision Image (Redwood City, CA), have chosen to supply their customers with stand-alone CGM interpreter applications that do an especially good job of creating CGM images on their output devices. Other companies, like Motorola (Phoenix, AZ) and CalComp/Sanders (Nashua, NH), have embedded CGI firmware in their graphics display boards and are working with software OEM suppliers like Nova Graphics International to provide a CGM translation and display capability.

16.3 CGM Editors

A few companies, principally targeting the graphic artist, picture-enhancement business, provide products that let CGM pictures be read in, modified and enhanced, and then written out again as CGMs. The companies and products in this category planning on exhibiting at GraphNet'88 include:

- Computer Associates SuperImage

- Genigraphics (Liverpool, NY) SG1 workstation

- Kinetic Presentations (Lexington, KY) Kinetic Graphics System, supplied by System One Software (Kansas City, MO)

- Pansophic/West End Films (Washington, DC) ArtWorks and ChartWorks

- Zenographics Mirage.

Pansophic also plans on demonstrating at GraphNet'88 a picture composition product that permits the scaling, cropping, and positioning of multiple CGM pictures into a single output image.

16.4 NCGA GraphNet'88

At NCGA's Computer Graphics'88, a multivendor systems integration demonstration, called GraphNet'88, will incorporate four application areas typically found in a multifaceted corporation: engineering/design, corporate communications/financial analysis, graphics arts, and computer-aided publishing. Graphics and pictorial information–drawings and charts–will be exchanged in digital format through the use of the CGM. The program will emphasize the relationships among different information activities within a corporation. The overall concept will illustrate information flow across standard interfaces to achieve an end product that is a composite of all functions. For example, a marketing brochure will be created from drawings coming from the engineering department and cost-benefit data graphs created from the corporate database and enhanced by in-house artists. The importance of standard interfaces for efficient information flow will be emphasized throughout the entire demonstration.

GraphNet'88 will show that separate and distinct operations within a company can share resources and information without costly proprietary solutions. The result will be an end product that is developed through use of multivendor systems integrated via standard interfaces. A successful demonstration should help to establish the validity of top-to-bottom exchange of digital information, which must be achieved to realize true computer-integrated manufacturing (CIM). The interchange of pictures and drawings is just a small part of the total solution, which must also include networking, file transfer, and office system standards.

Most of the companies mentioned in the previous sections have indicated their intent to participate in GraphNet'88.

16.5 Practical Considerations

Because the CGM standard does not specify minimum capabilities for CGM generators and interpreters, most–if not all–commercial implementations of the CGM differ among themselves in the elements that they can place in a CGM and the elements that they successfully interpret from a CGM. The TOP CGM Application Profile attempts to set minimum requirements for interpreters and maximum constraints on generators (see App. F), but its fairly recent publication (September 1987) means that it has not yet had a chance to influence the CGM implementations released for general sale and use.

In the remainder of this section, we briefly describe some of the current barriers to CGM interchange, give some hints concerning the use of CGMs generated outside your own local environment, and present a checklist of issues that an application developer must face when considering providing CGM support.

16.5.1 Barriers to Interchange

Most of the implementations on mainframes and workstations are nearly fully featured and consistent in their level of support. In part this is due to the fact that several of the major implementations are based on CGM generator and interpreter libraries marketed by Henderson Software (Boulder, CO). Developed by Lofton Henderson, editor of the ANSI and ISO CGM standard, these Fortran and C library implementations provide support for all three encodings of the CGM and are written assuming a GKS-like device interface.

Nevertheless, especially on personal computer implementations, there are a number of areas that stand in the way of completely blind interchange of

CGMs. Many of these issues are being addressed by future extensions planned for the CGM, as described in Chap. 17.

VDC Extent. The CGM standard states that the VDC extent is the *region of interest* of the picture. Some CGM generators always write a fixed set of values, say (-32768,-32768) (32767,32767), even when the picture is drawn in, say, the positive quadrant. When the CGM picture is imaged, the picture is displayed in the upper right hand corner of the display surface, with the rest of the surface blank. This is usually not the desired effect. CGM generators must be careful to place a good set of values for VDC extent in the CGM, so that this effect can be avoided. If the application driving the CGM generator has a concept similar to the GKS concept of "workstation window," this value should be used for the VDC extent.

Mapping from Colour to Black-and-White. Some CGM interpreters do a very poor job in mapping from multiple colours to black-and-white images. For example, all non-zero colour indices may be drawn in the foreground colour–not a very useful effect for a bar chart created with multicolour bars. Interpreters should either perform dithering to give grey-scale effects for solid colours or should substitute hatch patterns and different line styles for colours, when colour is not available as a distinguishing feature.

Fonts. Because there are no standards as yet for font names and font metrics, completely blind interchange of CGM files containing text is not possible. Instead, supplementary agreements and standards for such characteristics as character widths and kerning tables must be developed.

Attribute Support. Use of hatch styles, line types, and marker types outside the standardized set requires agreements outside the scope of the CGM. Not all styles will be supported, especially if heavy emulation is required on certain devices. Patterns may not be supported at all, because they are hard to render on certain classes of devices (e.g., pen plotters) and because storage of patterns occupies lots of memory.

Primitive Support. Like patterns, CELL ARRAY may not be supported because of the heavy demand for storage and the difficulty in proper rendering. RESTRICTED TEXT and APPEND TEXT may not be implemented, because not very many graphics packages have ever tried to implement these functions before. Similarly, "chord" close type for the circular arc and elliptical arc primitives may not be supported. Programmers simply do not have a base of experience and algorithms to draw from.

Text Model. The GKS/CGM text model, with its TEXT PATH, TEXT ALIGNMENT, CHARACTER SPACING, and CHARACTER EXPANSION FACTOR attributes, is not familiar to many applications. Consequently, many generators will not place these elements in the CGMs they produce and many interpreters may not properly handle all combinations of the text attributes.

16.5.2 Using Outside CGMs

The following list represents a set of "helpful hints" for those writing applications capable of importing CGMs created by other applications not under the developer's direct control.

- Watch out for incompatible physical file formats. On PCs and UNIX systems, binary encoded CGMs are usually written as a continuous stream of bytes, while on most other systems some sort of fixed-length or variable-length record structure is imposed.

- Watch out for missing information. For example,

  - colour table
  - colour value extents
  - font list.

- Watch out for misleading information. For example,

  - a VDC extent that is larger than the true region of interest
  - a metafile elements list that is incorrect (an element may be present in the metafile, but not mentioned in the list) or not very helpful (all possible CGM elements are listed, although not all are actually present in the metafile).

- Watch out for the size of buffers you need. For example, for

  - point lists
  - cell arrays, pattern tables, and colour tables
  - strings and data records.

- Watch out for use of partitioned elements and the use of the METAFILE DEFAULTS REPLACEMENT element.

The best strategy to follow is to encourage the use and acceptance of the TOP CGM Application Profile (see App. F).

16.5.3 Issues for the Application Developer

The principal issues facing a developer are outlined below:

- Which encodings should you use and support?

- How do you map between your application's internal object descriptions and the available CGM elements, while still maintaining picture fidelity?

- How rich a CGM do you generate, knowing that not all interpreters support all elements but realizing that the richer the use of CGM elements, the more likely that the resulting picture representation is of high quality? This question is important if you want to export your CGM files to other applications.

- How rich a CGM are you prepared to interpret (a rich interpreter is more difficult to implement than a lean one)? This question is important if you want to import CGM's from other applications.

- When and whether to use the APPLICATION DATA element to represent application-specific semantics and ESCAPE elements to access extended capabilities of certain devices or implementations? Generally speaking, you cannot rely on any other interpreter's being able to recognize and handle correctly these elements.

There is no "right answer" to these questions. Rather, the answer depends upon many factors including the nature of the application itself, the market dominance of the supplier, and cost and time-to-market considerations.

Chapter 17

Future Extensions to the CGM

As soon as the CGM was technically frozen in late 1985, there was pressure from various graphics user communities to specify additional elements. The sources of pressure are widespread and reflect diverse needs. The commercial acceptance of the CGM, described in the previous chapter, is fueling the demands for greater capability.

In this chapter, we will describe a few of the enhancements planned for the CGM by the ISO and ANSI standards group. We will also examine further needs, not yet covered by any approved graphics standards project.

17.1 The CGM as a GKS Metafile

In Chap. 15, we explained that the CGM was suitable for use as a GKS metafile (GKSM) only for GKS level 0 implementations. In 1985, ISO authorized a project to extend the capabilities of CGM to serve as a GKSM for all output levels of GKS. This project, known as **CGM Addendum 1**, reached the status of Draft Proposal in December 1987 (see App. C for an explanation of the stages of standards evolution). Also authorized for Addendum 1 is the addition of certain technically-frozen capabilities from the CGI Draft Proposal. When approved, CGM Addendum 1 will be closer to supporting the full CGI specification than the current version of the CGM is.

The principal elements added in Addendum 1 include:

- Segmentation support.

- Capabilities needed for dynamic picture regeneration.

- Device viewport control.

- An ability to override the font list and character set list on a picture by picture basis, rather than having these lists apply to all pictures in a metafile.

- Closed figure support.

- Pixel array and drawing mode support.

The new elements proposed for Addendum 1 are presented in the remainder of this section and in the following two sections. The style of presentation follows the conventions established in Chap. 13.

METAFILE CATEGORY *indicator.*

To permit existing metafile interpreters know whether a CGM they are trying to read conforms to the current CGM standard (ISO 8632) or the extended metafile specified in ISO 8632 Addendum 1, a new Metafile Descriptor element– METAFILE CATEGORY–has been created. Three categories–*cgm, gksm* and *cgmext1*–have been defined.

The default value is *cgm*. Consequently, if this element is absent from the Metafile Descriptor or if the category is given as *cgm*, the CGM conforms to the current CGM standard; that is, it contains elements specified in accordance with ISO 8632:1985. The *gksm* category implies that only those elements necessary for the CGM to be used as a GKSM are present in the metafile. Presence of the *cgmext1* category indicator means that any of the elements in the basic CGM or the Addendum 1 may be present in the metafile.

MAXIMUM VDC EXTENT *low-value, high-value.*

The parameters of this Metafile Descriptor element define a mapping of a sub-space of the VDC range specified by (low,low) and (high,high) and the virtual coordinate space of a graphics system, e.g., the NDC of a GKS implementation. The low value maps to the lower left corner of NDC and the high value to the upper right corner of NDC. The low value must be less than the high value.

The default values are 0,32767, if VDC TYPE is *integer*, and 0.0,1.0, if VDC TYPE is *real*.

DEVICE VIEWPORT *first-corner, second-corner.* 4.3

A Control Element. The default DEVICE VIEWPORT is implementation-dependent.

Chapter 17: Future Extensions to the CGM

DEVICE VIEWPORT SPECIFICATION MODE.   **4.3**

> *VSU-specifier, scale-factor*

A Control Element. The default mode is *fraction of default device viewport*.

DEVICE VIEWPORT MAPPING.   **4.3**

> *isotropy-flag, horizontal-alignment-flag, vertical-alignment-flag*

A Control Element. The default value is *forced, left, bottom*.

DEFERRAL MODE *indicator.*   **4.1**

A Control Element. The default DEFERRAL MODE is *asap*.

MAKE PICTURE CURRENT.   **4.1**

A Control Element.

PREPARE VIEW SURFACE *hardcopy-advance-indicator.*   **4.1**

A Control Element.

UPDATE *regeneration-flag.*

A Control Element.

MODIFY FONT LIST *starting-index, list of font-names.*

This Control Element modifies the font list specified in the FONT LIST element or the default font list. Only the specified entries in the font list are modified. One or more font names are replaced starting with the font name corresponding to the *starting -index* parameter. The modifications apply only to the current picture.

MODIFY CHARACTER SET LIST.

> *starting-index*
> *list of {character-set-type, designation-sequence-tail}*

This Control Element modifies the list of character set information given in the Metafile Descriptor via the CHARACTER SET LIST element or the default list. Only the specified entries are modified. The modifications apply only to the current picture.

LINE REPRESENTATION. 8.9

> *bundle-index*
> *type-indicator, width-specifier, colour-specifier*

The default value of this Attribute element is implementation-dependent.

MARKER REPRESENTATION. 8.9

> *bundle-index*
> *type-indicator, size-specifier, colour-specifier*

The default value of this Attribute element is implementation-dependent.

TEXT REPRESENTATION. 8.9

> *bundle-index*
> *font-index, precision-indicator*
> *character-expansion-factor, character-spacing, colour-specifier*

The default value of this Attribute element is implementation-dependent.

FILL REPRESENTATION. 8.9

> *bundle-index*
> *interior-style, colour-specifier, hatch-index, pattern-index*

The default value of this Attribute element is implementation-dependent.

EDGE REPRESENTATION. 8.9

> *bundle-index*
> *type-indicator, width-specifier, colour-specifier*

The default value of this Attribute element is implementation-dependent.

17.2 Global Segments

In the CGM Addendum 1, the entire CGI segmentation model is adopted. This not only permits the segmentation functions of GKS and CGI to be realized, but also permits support for segments outside of pictures.

In CGM Addendum 1, graphical output primitives and attribute setting elements may be grouped in segments as well as being used outside segments. Each segment is identified by a unique segment identifier. As in CGI, segments may be transformed, made visible or invisible, highlighted, ordered from front to back, made detectable or undetectable, and deleted–all within a picture. They can also be specified within Global Segments as part of the Metafile Descriptor. When specified in this manner, they can be copied into any picture in the metafile. Consequently, a single "pool" of segments can serve multiple pictures in the metafile. With this new feature, the CGM will be a very powerful candidate for storing and transmitting symbol libraries and drawings that employ symbol libraries (as we discussed in Chap. 12).

A Global Segment is delimited by the BEGIN SEGMENT and END SEGMENT elements. Global Segments are not, by default, defined for or known to individual pictures within the metafile. They must be accessed from within individual pictures by the COPY SEGMENT element. Local Segments are defined for a single picture by using the BEGIN SEGMENT and END SEGMENT elements after a BEGIN PICTURE element and before the next END PICTURE element. The effect within a picture of a COPY element referring to a Global Segment is identical to the effect of a COPY element referring to a Local Segment. Segments must be defined before they are referenced in any CGM element.

The entire set of Segment Elements are specified in the following, along with a few other new elements–SEGMENT PRIORITY EXTENT and PICK IDENTIFIER–that make sense only in the context of segments.

BEGIN SEGMENT *segment-identifier.* 7.3

A Delimiter element that may appear either in the Metafile Descriptor or when a Picture has been started, by BEGIN PICTURE.

END SEGMENT. 7.3

The Delimiter element that terminates the definition of a segment.

SEGMENT PRIORITY EXTENT *minimum-value, maximum-value.*

A Metafile Descriptor element whose parameters represent an extent that bounds the segment display priority values that will be found in the metafile. It need not represent the exact extent of the values found in the metafile.

The default values are 0, 7.

PICK IDENTIFIER *identifier.* 7.7

This Attribute element has no default value.

REOPEN SEGMENT *identifier.*   7.3

COPY SEGMENT *identifer, transformation-matrix.*   7.6

DELETE SEGMENT *identifier.*   7.6

DELETE ALL SEGMENTS.   7.6

RENAME SEGMENT *old-identifier, new-identifier.*   7.6

REDRAW ALL SEGMENTS.   7.5

IMPLICIT SEGMENT REGENERATION MODE *mode.*   7.5

The default mode is *suppressed*.

INHERITANCE FILTER *filter-selection-attribute-designator, setting.*   7.6

The default inheritance filter setting value for all attributes is *segment*.

SEGMENT TRANSFORM *identifier, transformation-matrix.*   7.4

The default segment tranformation matrix is the identity matrix.

SEGMENT VISIBILITY *identifier, mode.*   7.4

The default mode is *visible*.

SEGMENT HIGHLIGHTING *identifier, mode.*   7.4

The default mode is *normal*.

SEGMENT DISPLAY PRIORITY *identifier, priority-value.*   7.4

The default priority value is 0.

SEGMENT DETECTABILITY *identifier, mode.*   7.4

The default mode is *undetectable*.

SEGMENT PICK PRIORITY *identifier, pick-priority-value.*   7.4

The default pick priority value is 0.

17.3 New Elements from the CGI

The elements taken from the current version of the CGI and included in CGM Addendum 1 are described in this section.

BEGIN FIGURE. 8.5

This Control Element causes the metafile to enter the state "Figure Open; Region Closed," initiating construction of a compound closed figure. If the metafile is already in either of two "Figure Open" states, the previous portion of the closed figure boundary definition is discarded, and the metafile remains in the "Figure Open" state. That is, the effect is as if the boundary definition were started anew.

END FIGURE. 8.5

This Control Element causes the metafile to transition out of either the "Figure Open; Region Open" or "Figure Open; Region Closed" state and causes the compound closed figure primitive to be rendered.

If the metafile were in state "Figure Open; Region Open" and the last point of the last LINE function is not coincident with the current closure point, then the closed figure has not been explicitly closed and an implicit closure is performed by connecting the last point of the preceding LINE function to the current closure point. The visibility of this line segment is controlled by the IMPLICIT EDGE VISIBILITY element.

NEW REGION. 8.5

This Control Element is used only within the "Figure Open; Region Open" state for control of subregion construction within closed figures. The metafile goes into the state "Figure Open; Region Closed." The first point of the next LINE functions following a NEW REGION element becomes the current closure point, starting a new subregion.

IMPLICIT EDGE VISIBILITY *flag*. 8.5

This Control Element has a default value of *off*.

SAVE PRIMITIVE ATTRIBUTES *attribute-set-name*. 8.10

This is a Control Element.

RESTORE PRIMITIVE ATTRIBUTES *attribute-set-name*. 8.10

This is a Control Element.

DELETE ATTRIBUTE SET *attribute-set-name*.

This is a Control Element.

CIRCULAR ARC CENTRE BACKWARDS. 8.2

> *centrepoint*
> *start-vector, end-vector*
> *radius*

This is a Graphical Primitive element.

PIXEL ARRAY. 5.5

> *origin-point, number-of-columns, number-of-rows*
> *valid-x-range, valid-y-range*
> *x-scale, y-scale*
> *colour-specifiers*

This is a Graphical Primitive element.

DRAWING MODE *mode*. 5.4

The default value of this Attribute element is *replace* (mode 3); that is, $d' = s$.

17.4 3D Elements

In 1985, the ISO graphics committee (SC24) also authorized work to begin on extending the CGM standard so that it could serve as a GKSM for the GKS Extensions to Three-Dimensions (GKS-3D, ISO 8805). The scope of the GKS-3D project was discussed briefly in Chap. 1. This separate extensions work to CGM is known officially as **CGM Addendum 2**. In December, 1987, SC24 approved circulation of an initial draft CGM Addendum 2. However, at the time of the writing of this book, this draft was not yet available for perusal.

17.5 Other Requirements

In September 1987, the Eurographics Association and the US National Bureau of Standards sponsored a Workshop in Gaithersburg, Maryland, on "CGM in the Real World." About 20 participants were invited to discuss current use of the CGM and the future needs of various application areas. Areas represented included remote slidemaking for high-quality presentations, technical drawings and documentation, engineering drawings and architecture, automated raster-to-vector conversion systems, and desktop publishing.

The workshop concluded that, if the CGM were to become the principal method of graphics picture interchange, still more elements were needed to permit the use of CGM in a wide range of important governmental and industrial applications. At a meeting in October, 1987, the US graphics standards technical committee, X3H3, prepared an initial draft of a CGM Addendum 3 to address these concerns. This proposal was forwarded to ISO/IEC JTC1/SC24 for consideration at its December 1987 plenary meeting in Berlin. At that meeting, the proposal was referred to a group that will consider all of SC24's future work, including enhancements to GKS and CGM. The first meeting of that group is planned for April, 1988.

In the remainder of this section, we describe the purpose and scope of the proposed CGM Addendum 3, so that you can get the sense of where people feel future enhancements to CGM are needed. We also briefly list some of the suggested new elements, so that you have a more concrete understanding of these proposals. Because this work is in such a preliminary stage, you must read the rest of this section as only giving you an indication of future work. No agreement has yet been attempted, much less reached, in these areas.

17.5.1 Purpose

The purpose of CGM Addendum 3 is to extend the CGM to fulfill the picture transfer requirements of:

- Engineering drawing and technical illustration;
- Graphics arts quality pictures, including:
    - geometric graphics
    - raster images
    - text;
- Technical publishing.

An additional intent is to keep pace with the graphics requirements of office systems, especially those of ODA/ODIF (see Chap. 15).

The set of elements added to the CGM should include all elements necessary to meet those requirements and should comprise a minimal set sufficient to meet those requirements effectively.

17.5.2 Scope

The following list of capabilities has been identified as necessary to meet the requirements stated above:

- Advanced 2D graphics to include:
    - Bezier curves
    - Rational B-splines
    - Parametric spline curves
    - Line attributes of cap, mitre, and join
    - A composite line primitive
    - User-defined line types
    - User-defined hatch styles
    - Arbitrary text paths
    - Conics and conic arcs.

- Support for the text and font model of ISO 9541, *Information Processing–Font and Character Information Interchange.*

- Picture composition and control to include:
    - Clipping to an arbitrary boundary (i.e., general closed curve)
    - Shielding
    - Alignment.

- Additional colour models (beyond RGB); for example,
    - CIE
    - CMYB
    - Named colours.

- Additional raster graphics (scanned image) capabilities.

- Symbols: external references to standard libraries of named symbols.

17.5.3 Suggested New Elements

In the remainder of this section, we describe the new elements that have been proposed to meet the requirements stated. This list is neither complete, nor has it been subjected to much review and refinement within the graphics standards community. The list does, however, indicate the direction the CGM standard is likely to progress along in the next few years.

BEGIN COMPOUND LINE.

END COMPOUND LINE.

These Control elements delimit the definition of an entity that will have consistent line attributes and will be treated as a single "compound line primitive." The elements that make up the compound line can be any combination of non-closed line elements; e.g., POLYLINE and CIRCULAR ARC CENTRE, but not CIRCLE or ELLIPSE.

BEGIN COMPOUND TEXT PATH.

END COMPOUND TEXT PATH.

These Control elements delimit the definition of an entity that will provide the path along which a text string will be drawn. The same primitives allowed for COMPOUND LINE are permitted in the definition of a COMPOUND PATH.

Once defined, the compound text path replaces the text path as specified by the TEXT PATH and CHARACTER ORIENTATION elements. The skew of the characters is still specified by any skew that might be defined by the current character orientation, but the placement of subsequent characters is along the compound text path instead of in a straight line along the character up vector or character base vector.

BEGIN CLIP REGION.

END CLIP REGION.

These Control elements delimit the definition of an entity that will comprise a clipping region. When the clip indicator is *on*, only the portions of graphics elements inside or on the boundary of the clipping region are drawn. Once defined, the clipping region replaces any clipping region specified in a CLIP RECTANGLE element.

The elements that make up the clipping region can be any combination of closed or non-closed elements; e.g., POLYGON and CIRCLE are permitted along with the line primitives like POLYLINE and ELLIPTICAL ARC.

BEGIN SHIELD REGION.

END SHIELD REGION.

SHIELDING INDICATOR *flag*.

These Control elements delimit the definition of an entity that will comprise a shielding region and control whether shielding is performed. When the shield indicator is *on*, only the portions outside of the shielding region are drawn.

The same elements used to specify a clipping region may be used to specify a shielding region.

Enhanced Font Control. The following set of proposed Metafile Descriptor elements are intended to improve the CGM's ability to represent pictures containing high-quality, graphics art text. The abbreviation FCS means Font Coordinate System.

FONTMETRIC DEFINITION LIST.

    font-index, list-of-character-metrics

For each character of the specified font used in the CGM, basic character metrics may be specified. These include left and right bearing, character height, and offset of the character from the baseline.

CHARACTER KERNING MODE *mode*.

Mode may take on one of the values *none, pair, sectored*.

CHARACTER KERNING TABLE *data-record*.

The data specified in this element will be dependent upon which, if any, kerning styles are supported. The most prevalent form of kerning is character pair kerning.

FCS TYPE *indicator*.

The indicator specifies the data type of the font coordinate space. Font coordinate space may be different than VDC space because higher precision may be necessary to accurately specify the fontmetric data. If the indicator is *integer* or *real*, the remaining FCS elements may be specified. However, if the indicator is *VDC*, then the font coordinate space will map to VDC space and take on the type (*integer* or *real*) of the VDC space. In this case, none of the following FCS elements apply.

FCS INTEGER PRECISION.

FCS REAL PRECISION.

These elements are analogous to VDC INTEGER PRECISION and VDC REAL PRECISION.

FCS EXTENT *first-corner, second-corner.*

The two corners define a rectangular extent in font coordinate space that marks a *font window*. Each character within a font must be contained entirely within this window.

New CGM Attributes. The following Attribute elements have been proposed so that an extended CGM could provide the detailed control over appearance demanded by current technical illustration and desktop publishing applications.

DEFINE LINE TYPE.

linetype-index, dash-unit-selector, dash-repeat-length, adaptive-flag list-of-dash-elements

This element defines a linetype and associates it with a line type index for future use in the CGM. The first element in the list of dash elements specifies the length of the first dash, the second element the length of the first space, the third element the length of the second dash, and so on.

The unit of measure for length is specified by the dash unit selector, which can take on the values *VDC, mm, native device units,* and *abstract*. A value of *abstract* indicates that the implementation can treat the lengths specified as relative values and can normalize them to any suitable lengths that maintain the approximate ratios specified for dashes and spaces.

If the adaptive flag is *yes*, every vertex in the specification of the primitive should be made to fall on an inked portion of the line.

DEFINE HATCH STYLE.

hatch-index, style-indicator, hatch-space-units-selector
angle-vector, duty-cycle-length
list-of-hatch-elements

This element defines a hatch style and associates it with a hatch index for future use in the CGM. The first element in the list of hatch elements specifies the width of the first hatch line, the second element the width of the first gap between lines, the third element the width of the second line, and so on.

The unit of measure for duty cycle length is specified by the hatch space units selector, which can take on the values *VDC, mm, native device units,* and *abstract*. A value of *abstract* indicates that the implementation can treat the widths specified as relative values and can normalize them to any suitable widths that maintain the approximate ratios specified for lines and gaps.

A value of VDC means that the hatching transforms with segment tranform and anisotropic tranforms (as if the hatching were made up of DISJOINT POLYLINE elements); otherwise, the hatching is like "wallpaper" that shows through a polygon-shaped hole–everything is specified in device units and hatching is done in device space.

The angle parameter is specified as the x and y components of a vector. The angle is measured between the positive x-axis of the appropriate coordinate system and the vector provided.

LINE CAP *indicator.*

The supported line caps include:

- *Butt*: The line is squared off at the endpoint; there is no projection beyond the endpoint.

- *Round*: A semicircular arc with diameter equal to the line width is drawn around the endpoint and filled in. The drawn line thus projects beyond the endpoint.

- *Projecting square*: The line is squared off at a distance equal to half the line width beyond the endpoint.

LINE JOIN *indicator.*

The supported line joins include:

- *Mitre*: The outer edges of the two adjoining line segments are extended until they meet at a point.

- *Round*: A circular arc with diameter equal to the line width is drawn around the vertex between the adjoining segments and filled in, producing a rounded corner.

- *Bevel*. The adjoining line segments are terminated with a butt cap, and the resulting triangular notch is filled in.

EDGE CAP *indicator.*

Butt, round, and *projecting square* edge caps are supported.

EDGE JOIN *indicator.*

Mitre, round, and *bevel* edge joins are supported.

MITRE LIMIT *scale-factor.*

Mitred corners can extend very far beyond the line vertex if the angle between the adjoining line segments is small. Mitre length is defined to be the distance from the point at which the inner edges of the adjoining line segments meet to the point at which the outer edges meet. If mitre length exceeds the mitre limit, the joining line segments are rendered with a bevel join instead of a mitre join.

Mitre limit is specified as a scale factor applied to the current line width and the current edge width. Mitre limit applies to line elements and to the edges of filled areas.

New Graphical Primitives. These Primitive element definitions follow the IGES standard (ANSI Y14.26M-1981). Further review of the STEP (and PDES) work is required before these specifications can be accepted.

CONIC ARC *start-point, end-point, A, B, C, D, E, F.*

A conic arc is defined by the endpoints and the six parameters that satisfy the following equation:

$$Ax^2 + Bxy + Cy^2 + Dx + Ey + F = 0$$

CONIC ARC TRANSFORMATION MATRIX *matrix.*

PARAMETRIC SPLINE CURVE.

> *curve-type, degree-of-continuity, number-of-segments*
> *break-point-list-for-polynomial*
> *X-coordinate-polynomial-list*
> *Y-coordinate-polynomial-list*

Curve type may be any of the following types: linear, quadratic, cubic, Wilson-Fowler, modified Wilson-Fowler, B-spline.

RATIONAL B-SPLINE CURVE.

> *upper-index-of-sum, degree-of-basis-function*
> *curve-open-flag, equation-type-flag, periodic-flag*
> *knot-sequence-list, weight-list, control-point-list*
> *start-parameter, end-parameter*

If the beginning and ending points of the curve are identical, the curve open flag is set to *closed*; otherwise, it is set to *open*.

If all of the weights are not equal, the equation type flag is set to *rational*; otherwise, all of the weights cancel and the equation type becomes *polynomial*.

COMPRESSED PEL ARRAY.

> *encoding type, pel-path, line-progression*
> *pel-spacing, spacing-ratio*
> *number-of-pels-per-line, number-of-lines*
> *pel-array*

This element permits the storage and transfer of images encoded in one of two CCITT standard formats: Recommendation T.4 (Group 3 facsimile) or Recommendation T.6 (Group 4 facsimile). Facsimile pictures do not contain colour or grey-scale information. Only one-bit-per-pixel images can be represented.

PEL ARRAY CLIP RECTANGLE.

> *X1, Y1, X2, Y2*
> *first-corner, second-corner*

This element specifies the rectangular area of pels in a decoded pel array that is to appear in the picture represented by the CGM.

The first four values form two coordinate pairs–(X1,Y1) and (X2,Y2)– corresponding to the first and last pels to appear in the picture. For example, (6,2) would specify the seventh pel in line 3, given that (0,0) specifies the first pel on the first line.

The two corner points specify the pel array clip rectangle in VDC space. The first pel specified above will appear at the first corner and only those portions of the decoded pel array from the COMPRESSED PEL ARRAY element inside or on the boundary of the pel array clip rectangle will be drawn.

Colour model support. No draft proposals for these new elements have yet been suggested.

External symbol reference. No suggestions for supporting references to external symbols has yet been advanced. However, the mechanisms used for the PHIGS Archive File will be studied.

PART IV

Appendices

Appendix A

Glossary

acknowledgement An action of a Logical Input Device that signals to the operator that an input operation has been completed.

anisotropic mapping A mapping in which the scale factors applied along each axis are not equal. This term is often used in reference to the mapping from VDC to physical device units. See **isotropic mapping**.

arming (a trigger) An action by the Virtual Device that enables a trigger to be "fired" by the operator.

aspect ratio The ratio of the width to the height (x to y) of a rectangular area, such as a window or a viewport. For example, an aspect ratio of 0.5 indicates an area twice as high as it is wide.

BITBLT BIT-aligned BLock Transfer. Transfer of a rectangular array of pixel information from one location in a bitmap to another location in the same or a different bitmap. An operation may be performed by the Virtual Device to combine the information of the source and destination during this transfer.

bitmap A region of computer memory, which can be treated as if it were a rectangular array of pixels.

blind interchange A mode of interaction between a service and its client in which the client requests services without recourse to interactive negotiation before use or acceptance of response during use. This mode of interchange may result from the service's inability to respond, the client's lack of interest in listening, or limitations in the communications path between client and service.

block In the context of event input, blocking prevents the entry of event reports into the event queue.

boundary The mathematical locus that defines, in abstract VDC space, the limits of a region to be filled (for fill area primitives and closed figures). The visual appearance of interior style *hollow* consists of a depiction of the boundary obtained after clipping has been taken into account. The boundary is distinct from the edge.

break action An action of the operator that signifies that an input operation should be aborted (that is, completed without normal result).

character set The set of displayable symbols mapped to individual character codes in a text string. A character set is independent of the font or typeface.

client An entity that uses the services of the CGI; the computer software that calls CGI functions or exchanges data with the Virtual Device, as contrasted with the human **operator**.

client-defined bitmap A bitmap that is created at the request of the client. Client-defined bitmaps cannot be displayed, except by transferring them to a displayable bitmap.

clipping The process of removing any portion of a graphical image that extends beyond a specified boundary.

conjugate diameter pair (CDP) A pair D,d of diameters of an ellipse such that a tangent to the ellipse at each endpoint is parallel to the other diameter.

constituency profile A subset of the CGI functions, minimal support requirements for them, and restrictions on their behaviour, chosen to satisfy the needs of a particular constituency of users. A constituency profile provides a complete and consistent set of functions independently of any other profile.

data interface An interface between software modules and/or devices comprising one or more packets containing opcodes and data, or a stream of bits or characters, as contrasted with a subroutine call interface.

Appendix A: Glossary 229

data stream encoding
A specific representation of the syntax of the CGI suitable for use over a data interface that defines the sequence of bits or bytes representing the CGI functions and their parameters.

device-dependent
A system or portion of a system that contains logic, algorithms, or data that are consistent with the behaviour of a specific graphical device.

device-independent
A system or portion of a system that contains logic, algorithms, or data that do not require nor represent knowledge about the behaviour of any particular graphical device.

device coordinates
The coordinates native to a device; device-dependent coordinates; physical device coordinates.

direct colour
A colour selection scheme in which the colour values are specified directly, without requiring an intermediate mapping via a colour table.

displayable bitmap
A particular type of bitmap corresponding to special memory of certain devices and which is displayable on the view surface. Displayable bitmaps are considered attributes of the Virtual Device and are not created by the client.

echo
Feedback to an operator of the value of the measure of a Logical Input Device.

echo area
A rectangular region on the display surface, which may be used for messages or other input echoes during an input operation.

echo input
A mode of input in which the current value of a measure is returned when the operator performs an action, such as firing a trigger, but in which echoing occurs on a separate output device managed by the client of the CGI.

echo type
The method of echoing the current value of a Logical Input device's measure. The echo type also determines the method of prompting and acknowledgement of an input operation.

effective viewport
The smaller viewport resulting from forced isotropic mapping from the VDC extent to the device viewport.

error class	A category of errors, all of which elicit the same detection, error reaction, and error reporting behaviour by the CGI.
error detection	The process of discovering that an error has occurred.
error logging	Writing of error messages to a special device or file. This is not a feature of the CGI, but may be performed by the client using the CGI (e.g., by GKS).
error queue	A First-In-First-Out (FIFO) data structure maintained by the CGI that contains the list of error reports.
error reaction	Behaviour of the virtual device in response to errors that are detected.
error report	Consists of an error code and a CGI function identifier.
error reporting	A behaviour of the CGI that saves an error report in the error queue, so that it can be made available to the client of the CGI.
escape functions	Graphical functions that describe device-dependent or system-dependent elements used to construct a picture, but that are otherwise not standardized.
event	An input operation that was completed by an operator action, such as firing a trigger, and was asynchronously entered into the event queue for later retrieval by the client of the CGI.
event queue	A data structure maintained by the CGI containing the sequence of event reports for a Virtual Device, in order of occurrence of the events.
event report	Data from an input event saved the event queue. The exact nature of the data depends upon the Logical Input Device class causing the event.
external functions	Functions present in some graphics standards that communicate information not directly related to the generation of a graphical image.

Appendix A: Glossary 231

firing (a trigger) An action by the operator that indicates to a Logical Input Device a significant moment in time, associated with request or event mode input.

font As used in the CGI and CGM standards, the typeface or style of characters, independent of other text attributes such as size or rotation.

full-depth bitmap A bitmap having the same number of bits per pixel as the physical device is capable of displaying.

graphics pipeline The directional flow of graphical information from an application program to the display surfaces which it is using, or to the application program from the input devices with which the human operator is generating input actions or events.

indexed colour A colour selection scheme in which the colour index is used to retrieve colour values from a colour table.

inquiry The means by which a client of the CGI may ascertain the level of support and the capabilities provided by the Virtual Device and by the CGI implementation and also the currently settings and values active in the Virtual Device.

isotropic mapping A mapping invariant with respect to direction; equal scaling in all orthogonal representational dimensions.

Logical Input Device A component of an INPUT or OUTIN CGI, consisting of a measure and other state information plus a set of associated triggers.

mapped bitmap A bitmap whose pixels can assume only the two abstract values *foreground* and *background*, both of which are mapped to actual colours of the client's choice when the bitmap is involved in an operation.

measure The value of a Logical Input Device.

metafile A mechanism for retaining and transporting graphical data and control information. This information contains a device-independent description of one or more pictures.

metafile generator The process or equipment that produces a metafile.

metafile interpreter   The process or equipment that reads a metafile and interprets the contents to produce again the picture represented in the metafile.

modelling coordinates   Local world coordinates tied to some object being modelled by the client and viewed by the graphical system.

negotiation   The interchange of inquiry and response by which a client of a set of services determines which capabilities are provided by the service and what the characteristics of the service are.

normalized device coordinates (NDC)   Coordinates specified in a real device-independent coordinate system, normalized to some range (in GKS, from 0.0 to 1.0).

non-retained data   Any graphical objects not contained within a segment.

pixel   The smallest element of a display surface that can be independently assigned a colour or intensity.

prior agreement   A process whereby the generator of a metafile and the recipient of the metafile come to some understanding regarding the content or format of the metafile, that understanding *not* being recorded in the metafile itself. In a blind interchange environment, prior agreement can be used to overcome limitations of exchange standards.

prompting   An action taken at the beginning of an input operation which informs the operator that the triggers associated with the measure have been armed and that an input operation has been initiated.

raster   A rectangular array of cells.

regeneration   Redisplay of an image from stored segments for purposes of updae or renewal. Regeneration may be performed to reflect changes in the description of an image, as from a change to segment attributes, or to recover an image previously overlaid or otherwise made invalid.

Appendix A: Glossary   233

region In the context of closed figures or the POLYGON SET function, an area which is explicitly closed (that is, the end point connected to the first point), which is a subset of the full area being filled. Regions can be nested (e.g., the hole in a "donut"), disjoint (e.g., the dot and the stem of the letter "i"), or overlapping. The boundaries of all regions are considered together when applying the interior test for filling a closed figure or POLYGON SET.

remote echoing The process performed by a client of two CGI Virtual Devices of producing an input echo display on a Virtual Device different from that from which the input value is obtained.

segment A collection of graphical functions that can be manipulated as a unit. Once functions are grouped into segments, they are referred to as segment elements.

segment storage The location in the Virtual Device where the segments are stored.

skewed Oblique or slanting; non-perpendicular. Used to describe stroke precision text when the character orientation vectors are non-perpendicular, cell arrays, when the three defining points form a parallelogram rather than a rectangle, and a segment transformation that causes rectangles to become parallelograms.

state list The collection of information that characterizes the instantaneous operating state of a CGI Virtual Device.

timeout The termination of an input operation following the lapse of a specified time period.

tracking A form of echoing which couples the measure of an input device to a display below the CGI (that is, within the CGI Virtual Device). Tracking is enabled or disabled as a mode.

trigger A physical or logical input device that an operator may use to indicate significant moments in time; when this moment occurs, the trigger is said to have been "fired" by the operator. A trigger can be fired only after it has been "armed."

trigger association   The relationship between a trigger and a Logical Input Device, such that the firing of the trigger satisfies request or event mode input for that LID. Triggers can be associated with LIDs by the client, or they may be non-dissociable.

VDC range   The subset of VDC space consisting of the set of all positions representable in the declared coordinate type, precision, and encoding format of the CGI or CGM.

VDC space   A two-dimensional Cartesian coordinate space of infinite precision and extent. Only a subset of VDC space, the VDC range, is realizable across a CGI or representable in a CGM.

Virtual Device   An idealized graphics device that presents a set of graphics capabilities to graphics software or systems via the Computer Graphics Interface; an implementation of the CGI.

Virtual Device Coordinates (VDC)   Coordinates specified in a device-independent coordinate system, either integer or real. The coordinate system of the abstract virtual device managed by the CGI.

world coordinates   Coordinates specified in a device-independent coordinate system, whose units are selected by and are meaningful to the client.

Appendix B

Bibliography

B.1 Standards Documents

The official standards documents referred to in this book include:

Computer Graphics Interfacing Techniques for Dialogues with Graphical Devices (CGI), ISO DP 9636, 6 December 1986; also, dpANS X3.161.

Computer Graphics Metafile for the Storage and Transfer of Picture Description Information (CGM), ISO 8632-Parts 1 through 4: 1987; also, ANSI/X3.122-1986.

Graphical Kernel System (GKS), ISO 7942, 15 August 1985; also, ANSI X3.124-1985, 24 June 1985.

Graphical Kernel System for Three Dimensions (GKS-3D), ISO DIS 8805, July 1987.

GKS Metafile (GKSM), Annex E of ISO 7942, 15 August 1985; also, Appendix E of ANSI X3.124-1985, 24 June 1985.

Initial Graphics Exchange Specification (IGES), Version 3.0, National Bureau of Standards Report NBSIR 86-3359, April 1986.

Presentation Entities for the Product Definition Exchange Specification (PDES), ISO TC184/SC4/WG1 N53, 4 November 1985.

Programmer's Hierarchical Interactive Graphics System (PHIGS), ISO DIS 9592, December 1987; also, dpANS X3.144.

The STEP File Structure, ISO TC184/SC4/WG1 document 4.2.2 (working paper), 7 February 1986.

These documents are available from a variety of sources:

> The published ANSI standards (viz., GKS and CGM) and the ISO documents (CGI, CGM, GKS, GKS-3D, PHIGS) can be obtained from ANSI, 1430 Broadway, New York, NY 10018. Outside the United States, ISO documents can be obtained from the national standardization organization (e.g., BSI in the UK, AFNOR in France, DIN in Germany, and JIS in Japan).
>
> The draft ANSI standards (CGI, GKS-3D, and PHIGS) can be obtained from the X3 Secretariat, CBEMA, 311 First Street, Suite 500, Washington, DC 20001.
>
> The IGES and PDES documents can be obtained from the IGES Committee Chairman, Mr. Bradford Smith, National Bureau of Standards, Gaithersburg, MD.

B.2 Books

Adobe Systems, Inc., *PostScript Language Reference Manual*, Addison-Wesley, Reading, Massachusetts, 1986.

Adobe Systems, Inc., *PostScript Language Tutorial and Cookbook*, Addison-Wesley, Reading, Massachusetts, 1985.

Bono, P., and Herman, I. (eds.), *GKS Theory and Practice*, Springer-Verlag, Heidelberg, 1987.

Brown, M., and Heck, M., *Understanding PHIGS*, Megatek Corporation, San Diego, 1985.

Enderle, G., Grave, M., and Lillehagen, F. (eds.), *Advances in Computer Graphics I*, Springer-Verlag, Heidelberg, 1986.

Enderle, G., Kansy, K., and Pfaff, G., *Computer Graphics Programming, GKS–The Graphics Standard*, Springer-Verlag, Heidelberg, 2nd ed. 1987.

Foley, J., and van Dam, A., *Fundamentals of Interactive Computer Graphics*, Addison-Wesley, Reading, Massachusetts, 1982.

Hearn, D., and Baker, M.P., *Computer Graphics*, Prentice-Hall, Englewood Cliffs, New Jersey, 1986.

Hopgood, F.R.A., Hubbold, R., and Duce, D. (eds.), *Advances in Computer Graphics II*, Springer-Verlag, Heidelberg, 1986.

Hopgood, F.R.A., Duce, D., Gallop, J., and Sutcliffe, D., *Introduction to the Graphical Kernel System*, Academic Press, 1986 (second edition).

Hopgood, F.R.A., Duce, D., Fielding, E., Robinson, K., and Williams, A. (eds.), *Methodology of Window Management*, Springer-Verlag, Heidelberg, 1985.

Kessener, R., Peters, F., and van Lierop, M. (eds.), *Data Structures for Raster Graphics*, Springer-Verlag, Heidelberg, 1986.

McKay, L., *GKS Primer*, Nova Graphics International, Austin, Texas, 1984.

McKay, L., *CGI/CGM Primer*, Nova Graphics International, Austin, Texas, 1987.

National Computer Graphics Association, *Standards for the Computer Graphics Industry*, Fairfax, Virginia, 1986.

Rogers, D., and Adams, J., *Mathematical Elements for Computer Graphics*, McGraw-Hill, New York, 1976.

Rogers, D., *Procedural Elements for Computer Graphics*, McGraw-Hill, New York, 1985.

Salmon, R., and Slater, M., *Computer Graphics Systems & Concepts*, Addison-Wesley, Reading, Massachusetts, 1987.

B.3 Journal Articles

Arnold, D., "The Computer Graphics Interface and CAD applications," *CAD*, Vol. 19, No. 8 (October 1987), pp. 444-450.

Arnold, D., Duce, D., and Reynolds, G., "An Approach to the Formal Specification of Configurable Models of Graphics Systems," in *Proceedings of Eurographics '87*, Amsterdam, August 24th-28th 1987, pp. 439-464.

Arnold, D., and Reynolds, G., "The Use of Modularity and Configurability in the Comparison of Graphics Systems Designs," to appear in a book from the NATO International Advanced Study Institute on *Theoretical Foundations of Computer Graphics and CAD*, Lucca, Italy, July 4th-17th, 1987.

Arnold, D., Reynolds, G., and Hall, G., "GKS Programming in a PHIGS Environment," in *Computer Graphics Forum*, Vol. 4, No. 4 (December 1985), pp. 349-358.

Arnold, D., "The Importance of a Correct Approach to the Design of Metafiles Standards," in *Proceedings of Eurographics '82*, North Holland (September 1982), pp. 93-102.

Arnold, D., "Device Independence via Device Controllers," in *Computer Graphics 81* (Proceedings of the Conference held in London, October 25th-27th 1981), Online Publications Ltd., Northwood Hills, Middlesex, pp. 367-381.

Arnold, D., "The Requirement for Process Structured Graphics Systems," in *Computer Graphics*, Vol. 15, No. 2 (July 1981), ACM-SIGGRAPH, pp. 163-173.

Bono, P., "A Survey of Graphics Standards and Their Role in Information Interchange," *IEEE Computer*, Vol. 18, No. 10 (October 1985), pp.63-75.

Bono, P.,"Chips for the High-End," *Computer Graphics World*, Vol. 10, No. 7 (July 1987), pp.71-78.

Bono, P., "Software Standards: Which Ones are Here to Stay?," *The S. Klein Computer Graphics Review*, Inaugural Issue (Spring 1986), pp.94-100.

Bono, P. (ed.), "Special Issue on Graphics Standards," *IEEE Computer Graphics and Applications*, Vol. 6, No. 8 (August 1986).

Bresenham, J., "Ambiguities in Incremental Line Rendering," *IEEE Computer Graphics and Applications*, Vol. 7, No. 5 (May 1987), pp. 31-43.

Carson, G.S., and McGinnis, E., "The Reference Model for Computer Graphics," *IEEE Computer Graphics and Applications*, Vol. 6, No. 8 (August 1986), pp. 17-23.

Henderson, L., Journey, M., and Osland, C., "The Computer Graphics Metafile," *IEEE Computer Graphics and Applications*, Vol. 6, No. 8 (August 1986), pp. 24-32.

Powers, T., Frankel, A., and Arnold, D., "The Computer Graphics Virtual Device Interface," *IEEE Computer Graphics and Applications*, Vol. 6, No. 8 (August 1986), pp. 33-41.

Puk, R., and McConnell, J., "GKS-3D: A Three-Dimensional Extension to the Graphical Kernel System," *IEEE Computer Graphics and Applications*, Vol. 6, No. 8 (August 1986), pp. 42-49.

Shuey, D., Bailey, D., and Morrissey, T., "PHIGS: A Standard, Dynamic, Interactive Graphics Interface," *IEEE Computer Graphics and Applications*, Vol. 6, No. 8 (August 1986), pp. 50-57.

Skall, M., "NBS's Role in Computer Graphics Standards," *IEEE Computer Graphics and Applications*, Vol. 6, No. 8 (August 1986), pp. 66-70.

Sparks, M., and Gallop, J., "Language Bindings for Computer Graphics," *IEEE Computer Graphics and Applications*, Vol. 6, No. 8 (August 1986), pp. 58-65.

Appendix C

The Standards-Making System

C.1 Standards Bodies

ANSI. Founded in 1918 and headquartered in New York City, the American National Standards Institute is the coordinating organization for America's federated standards system. Its membership includes over 900 companies and 200 trade, technical, professional, labour, and consumer organizations.

ANSI does not itself develop standards. Rather, in cooperation with its members, it identifies what standards are required, provides a set of model procedures that standards-writing organizations may follow to attain industry-wide consensus standards, and makes the resulting national and international standards available for purchase by industry, government, and the public.

ISO Representative. As the official US member, ANSI manages, coordinates, finances, and administratively supports US Participation in the International Organization for Standardization (ISO). It helps govern ISO through membership on its council, executive committee, and technical board, and actively participates in the work of some 1900 ISO technical committees, subcommittees, and working groups.

ANSs and FIPS. As a private, nonprofit organization operating in the public interest, ANSI's income is derived mainly from membership dues and from the sale of American National Standards. ANSs are developed and used voluntarily. They may become mandatory only when adopted or referenced by government. In the information processing field, many ANSs are adopted as Federal Information Processing Standards through the National Bureau of Standards, an agency of the US Department of Commerce. Only a few FIPSs have testing and validation services associated with them, often administered by NBS or other governmental agencies. Examples are the Fortran and Cobol compiler validation services.

X3 and CBEMA. X3 is the standards development committee accredited by ANSI for information processing. The committee is administered by CBEMA, the Computer Business Equipment Manufacturers Association, located in Washington, D.C. X3 has about 30 technical committees, each with about 15 to 80 members.

X3H3. Within X3, technical committee X3H3 is responsible for all computer graphics standards. Currently more than 100 participants, representing about 70 companies, regularly attend X3H3 meetings. Represented on X3H3 are such industry stalwarts as AT&T, CalComp, Digital Equipment Corporation, Evans and Sutherland, Hewlett-Packard, IBM, Intel, National Semiconductor Corporation, Prime, Tektronix, Texas Instruments, Unisys, and Wang. Also active are large end users like Boeing, General Motors, Hughes, and McDonnell Douglas, and governmental organizations like NBS, Los Alamos National Lab, and Sandia National Lab.

JTC1 and SC24. The international counterpart to X3 is ISO/IEC Joint Technical Committe 1 (JTC1), which first met in November, 1987, succeeding ISO/TC97. Also in the fall of 1987, all computer graphics standards projects were assigned to a new subcommittee, SC24. Previous to that, graphics work took place in Working Group 2 of Subcommittee 21, Open Systems Interconnection, of TC97, Information Processing. The official designator of the new graphics subcommittee is *ISO/IEC JTC1/SC24*.

Included in JTC1 as separate subcommittees are Character Sets and Information Coding (SC2), which covers teletext, videotex, picture and image coding, audio coding, and facsimile; Networking Services (SC6); Text and Office Systems (SC18), which covers office document architecture, office document interchange format, intergrated text and graphics content architectures, page description languages, and font naming and description; Open Systems Interconnection (SC21), which covers OSI architecture and reference models, data bases, operating systems, virtual terminal, and file transfer; and Programming Languages (SC22).

US TAGs. Each of these international subcommittees and working groups has a US counterpart within X3. Called Technical Advisory Groups, the primary task of these committees is to develop US standards, but they must also prepare the US position on international standards. This is a partial list of information processing TAGs and their corresponding ISO committee: X3H3 for SC24 (graphics); X3H2 for SC21/WG3 (data base); X3T5 for SC21/WG1, WG4, WG5, and WG6 (OSI); X3L2 for SC2 (Coding); X3V1 for SC18(Text and Office Systems); and several X3Jx committees, each with its own corresponding working group within SC22, including X3J1 for PL/I, X3J2 for Basic, X3J3 for Fortran, X3J4 for Cobol, X3J6 for Pascal, X3J10 for Ada, and X3J11 for C.

X3/SPARC. Overseeing all these technical committees for X3 is the Standards Planning and Requirements Committee. All new project proposals must be approved by SPARC before being voted on by X3. Likewise, all technical committee actions relating to the advancement of a proposed ANS must be reviewed by SPARC before they can be acted upon by X3 and ANSI. This process is designed to ensure that the standard meets the requirements as originally specified in the project proposal.

C.2 The ANSI Process

We will now describe each stage in the development of an ANS for computer graphics. The duration of each stage is a function of a number of factors. The principal factors are the number of formal steps that must be followed and the degree of consensus within both X3H3 and X3. The time ranges given for each stage are for a typical graphics project. Graphics standards are long documents (100 pages minimum to 600 pages or more) and so may take more time to develop than standards in other areas of information processing. Furthermore, up to now, each standard has been a new one–a factor that contributes to the time it takes to develop consensus.

SD-3. To start a new graphics standards project, X3H3 must draft and approve a project proposal (known as an SD-3, or Standing Document 3). The SD-3 must be approved by SPARC and is then subject to a vote of X3. Any negative comments resulting from the X3 vote must be responded to by X3H3 before technical work can proceed. This stage can take six months or more.

Working Drafts. X3H3 prepares a series of working drafts that are circulated and commented upon by X3H3 members. For graphics, this stage typically takes several years.

dpANS. When X3H3 believes that the proposed standard is sufficiently stable, it votes to forward the draft for public review in order to solicit opinions from outside the committee. If approved, SPARC reviews the document to see that it has met its goals and falls within the scope outlined in the project proposal. X3 then conducts a 30-day ballot (with a possible 15-day reconsideration period) on forwarding the draft to ANSI for announcement of the public review period.

ANSI needs about three to four weeks lead time before public review starts, in order that official notification can be given in ANSI's publication, *Standards Action*. At this point, a document number is assigned (for example, CGM is X3.122) and the proposal is promoted to the status of draft proposed American National Standard, or dpANS. It can easily take six to

10 months from the first X3H3 ballot on public review to the start of the public review period.

Public Review. The initial public review period for X3 draft standards is four months; subsequent public review periods are two months. After each public review, X3H3 prepares responses to the written comments that were submitted and then votes on whether to approve the responses. If substantial technical changes are made to the document as a result of this process, a new public review cycle begins. This cycle may invite comment on the entire document again, or it may be restricted to those changes made to the previous draft. This stage can take eight months or more depending on the number of public review cycles. We expect most X3H3 standards, because of their size and complexity, to require at least two public reviews before final approval.

Final Approval by BSR. When X3H3 has approved a document in response to a public review that results in no more technical changes to the dpANS, X3 commences a six-week ballot on forwarding the dpANS to the ANSI Board of Standards Review for acceptance by ANSI. The BSR does not judge technical merit but must be assured that ANSI procedures were followed and that there is sufficient consensus on the dpANS among the companies and organizations likely to be affected. If BSR approves, it authorizes ANSI to publish the X3 document as an ANS. This final stage can take six to nine months, depending upon how long it takes the document editor to put the document in a format that is acceptable to ANSI.

C.3 The ISO Process

While similar in intent to the ANSI process, the ISO process differs in many particulars, in the time scale for each stage, and in the voting procedures. Once again, the range of time given for each of the stages represents typical times expected for graphics standards with JTC1. For the same reasons already mentioned for ANSI, these times are probably somewhat longer for graphics projects than for many of the other JTC1 development projects.

NWI. In ISO, a new project is started when a subcommittee (like SC24) or a member body (like ANSI or BSI) drafts a New Work Item proposal and submits it to JTC1 for a three-month letter ballot. Each member country has one vote to decide if it accepts the definition of the work item, if it supports the work item, and if it will commit resources to work on it. X3H3 recommends the US position on graphics NWIs, but it is X3 (as TAG to JTC1) that casts the vote on whether to support the recommendations. The US position is forwarded by X3 to JTC1 via ANSI. An NWI is often accompanied by a base document; X3H3 provided the base documents for the CGI and CGM NWIs. After an NWI is approved, the project will be assigned to a Working Group of SC24. This stage can take five to eight months.

Working Drafts and Rapporteur Groups. From the base document, the SC24 Working Group prepares one or more working drafts (WDs) that are circulated for comment by SC24 member bodies. This comment period is usually three months. X3H3 prepares the US comments and forwards them to ANSI via X3 for submission to SC24. SC24 Working Groups manage their projects by creating Rapporteur Groups (subgroups of the WG) who may hold meetings in between the meetings of the WG, by assigning Rapporteurs to lead them, and by assigning Document Editors for each international standard being developed. This stage can take 6 to 18 months, depending on how complete the base document is and how much consensus there is among SC24 member bodies.

DP. When the working draft is essentially complete and most major issues have been resolved, SC24 can register the document as a Draft Proposal. This is accomplished by resolution at an SC24 meeting or by a three-month SC24 letter ballot. X3H3 prepares the US vote and forwards the vote to SC24 via X3 and ANSI. If successful, an ISO number is assigned to the proposed standard (for example, CGM is ISO 8632; at the draft proposal stage, it was known as DP 8632).

Immediately upon registration, the same document is usually circulated for a three-month DP approval and comment ballot among SC24 member bodies. X3H3 prepares the US vote and forwards it to SC24 via X3 and ANSI. Member body comments must be responded to either by an editing committee, by SC24 during a meeting, or by the appropriate SC24 WG during a meeting. Changes will be made to the document, where appropriate, to achieve or improve consensus. Additional DP cycles, requiring three-month ballots within SC24, may be needed. It is the goal of SC24 that this stage not take more than 12 to 14 months.

DIS. When consensus has been reached (that is, the document is considered technically stable) and the DP has been put into a format acceptable to ISO, it is circulated by the ISO Central Secretariat for a six-month combined voting ballot by the ISO member bodies of both JTC1 and SC24. The document is now called a Draft International Standard and its designator is changed accordingly (for example, CGM was DIS 8632). X3H3 recommends the US vote and comments to X3; X3 actually casts the US ballot. X3 forwards the formal US vote to JTC1 via ANSI. The DIS stage can take 9 to 12 months after the text is received by ISO/CS.

IS. Comments from the DIS ballot must be responded to either by an editing committee appointed by the SC24 Secretariat (and typically including the Document Editor and the Rapporteur in charge of the standard), by SC24 during a meeting, or by the appropriate SC24 WG during a meeting. If the document is technically changed in a substantial way as a result of the DIS vote, another DIS ballot (only three months, this time) will be required. In general, multiple DIS rounds are to be avoided; that is why a graphics standard will not reach the DIS stage if SC24 still has technical concerns about the content of the standard. The final International Standard text is then submitted to the ISO Central Secretariat by the SC24 Secretariat. When the document is approved by ISO Council, it can then be published by ISO. One final time the designator changes form (for example, CGM is known as ISO 8632:1985).

C.4 Standards Status

The tentative working group structure approved by ISO/IEC JTC1/SC24 at its first plenary meeting in Berlin, West Germany, on 1-3 December 1987, is shown in Fig. C.1 and its programme of work summarized in Table C.1.

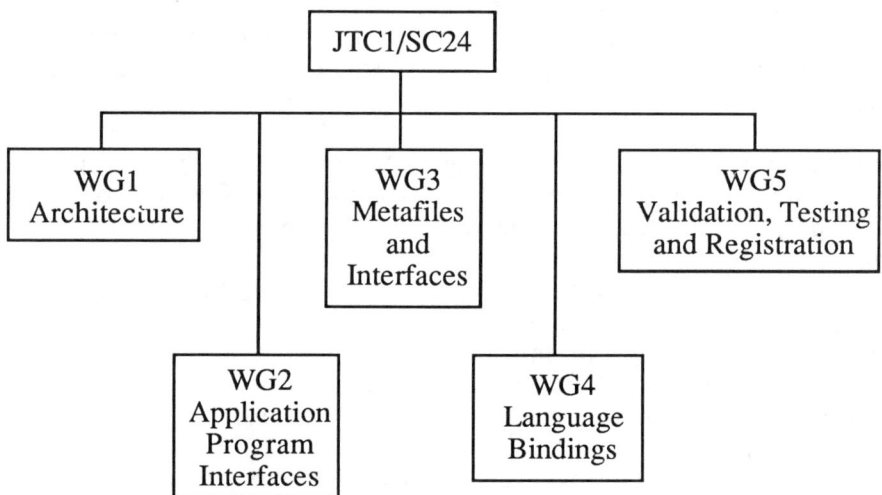

Fig. C.1. Proposed Working Group Structure for ISO/IEC JTC1/SC24

Table C.1. Programme of Work for ISO/IEC JTC1/SC24

Project	Latest Doc. No	Actual/Expected Completion Date
GKS	ISO 7942	1985
GKS-3D	DIS 8805	1988

GKS Language Bindings
    FORTRAN
    Pascal
    ADA
    C
	
	DIS 8651-1
	DIS 8651-2
	DIS 8651-3
	DD 8651-4
		
		1988
		1988
		1988
		1989

GKS-3D Language Bindings
    FORTRAN
    Pascal
    ADA
    C
	
	DP8806-1
	-
	-
	-
		
		1988
		not yet registered
		not yet registered
		not yet registered

PHIGS	DIS 9592 Parts 1-3.	1988

PHIGS Language Bindings
    FORTRAN
    Pascal
    ADA
    C
	
	DIS 9593-1
	-
	DIS 9593 -3
	-
		
		1989
		Not yet registered
		1989
		Not yet registered

CGM
    Basic Standard
 	
    CGM Add. 1
 	
    CGM Add. 2
	
	ISO 8632
	Parts 1-4
	DPAD 8632
	Parts 5-8
	-
		
		1987
		
		1989
		
		Not yet registered

CGI
    Functional Standard
 	
    CGI Data Encodings
 	
    CGI Library Bindings
	
	DP 9636
	Pts 1-6
	-
	
	-
		
		1990
		
		Not yet registered
		
		Not yet registered

Conformance Testing of Implementations of Graphics Standards	-	Not yet registered
Reference Model of Computer Graphics	-	Not yet registered

Appendix D

CGI Description Tables and State Lists

D.1 Device Description Table

The device description table define the configuration of a given CGI. It is hierarchical, with various groups of description elements being present as needed to elaborate higher level description elements.

Hard/Soft Copy Class may take one of the enumerated values *hard* or *soft*. Device Class can be OUTPUT, INPUT or OUTIN, and the device identification will be an implementation dependent string.

The types, precisions, and general information group is present for any class of device and includes information on supported VDC types and supported precisions for the various data types supported by the device. It also includes physical parameters such as display surface and input surface extents and data regarding the error stack.

Further information will depend on the device class and while the document recognises that all classes may eventually require a class specific table. There is currently only a table for OUTPUT and OUTIN device classes.

The device class specific information provided for devices capable of output contain entries regarding hardware and technology dependencies.

Name	Range	Type
For each Control Primitive:		
Support Flag	(Yes,No)	E
Device Identification:		
Device Class	(Output, Input, Outin)	E
Device Identification	impl. dep.	S

Name	Range	Type

OUTPUT and OUTIN Device Information:

Entries in this group do not exist for devices of classes INPUT.

Name	Range	Type
Hard/Soft Copy Class	(Hard, Soft)	E
Raster or vector display	(Vector, Raster, Other)	E
(Vector =vector display, Raster=raster device, Other=other device type; for example, both Vector and Raster)		
Background Colour Capability	(None, IRG,IMM)	E
Dynamic Modification for Device Transform	(IRG,IMM)	E
Device Physical Coordinate Units	(Integer, Real)	E
Device Bottom Left Corner		DP
Device Top Right Corner		DP
Display Surface Width	mm	R
Display Surface Height	mm	R

Types, Precisions and General Information:

Entries in this group exist for all device classes.

Name	Range	Type
Supported VDC Types	(Integer, Integer-and-Real)	E
Number of Supported VDC Integer Precisions	(1...n)	I
List of Supported VDC Integer Precisions	*see the note†*	
Number of Supported VDC Real Precisions	(1...n)	I
List of Supported VDC Real Precisions	*see the note†*	
Number of Supported Integer Precisions	(1...n)	I
List of supported Integer Precisions	*see the note†*	
Number of Supported Real Precisions	(1...n)	I
List of supported Real Precisions	*see the note†*	
Number of Supported Index Precisions	(1...n)	I
List of Supported Index Precisions	*see the note†*	
Number of Supported Colour Precisions	(1...n)	I
List of Supported Colour Precisions	*see the note†*	
Number of Supported Colour Index Precisions	(1...n)	I
List of Supported Colour Index Precisions	*see the note†*	

†Note - Because the precision specifications are defined in the binding or encoding of the CGI, these entries are designated implementation specific.

Supported Controls:

Name	Range	Type
List of Device Viewport Specification Units	Some of (fraction of display surface, mm with scale factor, physical device units)	E
List of Deferral Modes Supported	(ASTI, BNI or ASAP)	nE
Maximum Depth of Error Stack	(0...n)	I
Number of ESCAPEs supported	(0...n)	I
List of ESCAPE function IDs supported	impl dep	nI
No. of GET ESCAPEs Supported	(0...n)	I
List of GET ESCAPE function IDs supported	impl dep	nI

D.2 Output Description Table

Name	Range	Type
For each Output Primitive:		
Support Flag	(Yes,No)	E

Maximum Support Levels for Output Functions:

NB. Minimum is defined by the standard and, therefore, does not need to be described in the Description Table for the implementation.

Name	Range	Type
Number of points in POLYLINE	(≥128,-1 means unbounded)	I
Number of points in DISJOINT POLYLINE	(≥0,-1 means unbounded)	I
Number of points in POLYGON	(≥0,-1 means unbounded)	I
Number of points in POLYGON SET	(≥0,-1 means unbounded)	I
Number of points in POLYMARKER	(≥128,-1 means unbounded)	I
Number of points in CLOSED FIGURE	(≥0,-1 means unbounded)	I
Number of chars in TEXT Primitive	(≥80, means unbounded)	I
Fill Capability for FILL Primitives	(Yes,No)	E
CELL ARRAY Support Level	(Parallelogram Only, Intermediate, Full)	E

Approximations:

Name	Range	Type
CELL ARRAY support	(parallelogram only intermediate (non-skewed) full)	E
Compound TEXT string support	(simple only, intermediate†, full)	E
Compound Closed figure support	(none intermediate†, full)	E

† *compound primitives may be assembled but are rendered using the state of the attributes on completion of the compound definition.*

List of GDPs (may be empty)

For each GDP		
GDP Identifier		I
Number of Sets of Attributes	(0...5)	I
List of Sets of Attributes	(Line, Marker, Text, Fill, Edge)	nE

D.3 Attributes Description Table

Name	Range	Type

For each Attibute function:

Support Flag	(Yes,No)	E

Maximum Support Levels for Attribute Functions:

NB. Minimum is defined by the standard and, therefore, does not need to be described in the Description Table for the implementation, organised by Primitive Class.

Lines:

Number of Settable Line Bundles	(≥ 20)	I
Number of Predefined Line Bundles	(≥ 5)	I
Table of Predefined Line Bundles	See State List	
List of Available Line Types	($-i \ldots -1, 1 \ldots j$, where $i+j=n$)	nI
List of Available Line Widths	($0 \ldots n$; 0 means continuous)	nI
Nominal Line Width	(>0)	DC
Minimum Line Width	(>0)	DC
Maximum Line Width	(>0)	DC
Dynamic Modification Line Attributes	(IRG,IMM)	E

Markers:

Number of Settable Marker Bundles	(≥ 20)	I
Number of Predefined Marker Bundles	(≥ 5)	I
Table of Predefined Marker Bundles	See State List	
List of Available Marker Types	($-i \ldots -1, 1 \ldots j$, where $i+j=n$)	nI
List of Available Marker Sizes	($0 \ldots n$; 0 means continuous)	I
Nominal Marker Size	(>0)	DC
Minimum Marker Size	(>0)	DC
Maximum Marker Size	(>0)	DC
Dynamic Modification of Marker Attributes	(IRG, IMM)	E

Text:

Number of Settable Text Bundles	(≥ 20)	I
Number of Predefined Bundles	(≥ 6)	I
Table of Predefined Bundles		
List of Text Fonts	($1 \ldots n$)	I
Dynamic Modification of Text Attributes	(IRG, IMM)	E
List of Text Font Description Tables	See State List	

NB. CGI font names and descriptions will follow the lead of ISO DP9541, being developed by ISO/IEC JTC1/SC18, the Text and Office Systems Subcommittee.

Edge:

Number of Settable Edge Bundles	(≥ 20)	I
Number of Predefined Edge Bundles	(≥ 6)	I
Table of Predefined Edge Bundles	See State List	
List of Available Edge Types	($-i \ldots -1, 1 \ldots j$, where $i+j=n$)	nI
List of Available Edge Widths	($0 \ldots n$; 0 means continuous)	I
Nominal Edge Width	(>0)	DC
Minimum Edge Width	(>0)	DC
Maximum Edge Width	(>0)	DC
Dynamic Modification of Edge Attributes	(IRG, IMM)	E

Appendix D: CGI Description Tables and State Lists   253

Name	Range	Type

Fill:
Number of Settable Fill Bundles	(≥10)	I
Number of Predefined Fill Bundles	(≥5)	I
Table of Predefined Fill Bundles	See State List	
List of Available Interior Styles	(Some of empty, hollow, solid, pattern, hatch, bitmap)	nE
List of Available Hatch Styles	(-i...-1,1...j, where i+j=n)	nI
Number of Available Pattern Styles	(≥0)	I
List of Available Pattern Indices	(1...n)	nI
List of Predefined Pattern Representations		
Pattern Size Support Level	(none,unskewed,full)	E
Dynamic Modification of Fill Attributes	(IRG, IMM)	E
Preferred Pattern Resolution		2I
Maximum Pattern Resolution		2I

Colour:
Number of Simultaneous Colours	(2...n)	I
Number of Available Colours	(2...n)	I
Colour Selection Mode Supported	(Index only,Direct & Indirect)	E
Colour Table Support	(No, Yes)	E
Dynamic Modification Accepted for Colour Table	(IRG, IMM)	E
Number of Available Intensities (R,G,B)		3xI
Background Colour Capability	(No, Delayed, Immediate)	E
Colour Overwrite Capability	(No, Delayed, Immediate)	E
Monochromatic Device	(No,Yes)	E

Miscellaneous Output Control:
Range of Supported Attributes Set Names	(binding dep)	
Maximum number of simultaneously stored Attribute sets	(10...n)	I

D.4 Raster Description Table

Name	Range	Type

For each Raster function:

Name	Range	Type
Support Flag	(Yes,No)	E
Number of Displayable Bitmaps	(1...n)	I
List of Displayable Bitmap Names		nBN
Bitmap formats supported	(Full Depth, Mapped, Both)	E
Number of bits per pixel		I
Table of Support for Drawing Mode and Transparency	(Supported, Not Supported)	16x2xE
Support for all drawing modes and transparency	(all, some, none)	E
Size of pixel (eg in mm)		2xR
Preferred Bitblt Pattern Size in Pixels		2xI
Default display bitmap name		BN
Default drawing bitmap name		BN
Default Drawing Mode		I
Default Mapped Bitmap Foreground Colour		CI/CD

For each displayable bitmap:

Name	Range	Type
Bitmap name		BN
Type	(Mapped, Full depth)	E
Number of pixels (Width and Height)		2xI

D.5 Segmentation Description Table

Name	Range	Type

For each Segmentation function:

Name	Range	Type
Support Flag	(Yes,No)	E
Number of Display Priorities Supported	(0...n)	I
Number of Pick Priorities Supported	(0...n)	I
Number of Allowable Segment Identifiers	(0...n)	I
Number of Simultaneously Existing Segments	(1...n)	I
Maximum Length of Simulate Pick List	(1...n)	I
Dynamic Modification Accepted for:		
Segment Transformation	(IRG,IMM)	E
Display Priority	(IRG,IMM)	E
Visibility (visible => invisible)	(IRG,IMM)	E
Visibility (invisible => visible)	(IRG,IMM)	E
Highlighting	(IRG,IMM)	E
Delete Segment	(IRG,IMM)	E
Adding Objects to Open Segment	(IRG,IMM)	E

D.6 Input Description Table

The Virtual Device Input Description Tables give, for an OUTIN or INPUT device, the implementation and device dependent capabilities for input.

Name	Range	Type
For each Input function:		
Support Flag	(Yes,No)	E
Number of CHOICE devices	(0...n)	I
Number of LOCATOR devices	(0...n)	I
Number of PICK devices	(0...n)	I
Number of STRING devices	(0...n)	I
Number of STROKE devices	(0...n)	I
Number of VALUATOR devices	(0...n)	I
Number of GENERAL devices	(0...n)	I
Number of AREA devices	(0...n)	I
Timeout capability	(FULL, LIMITED)	E
Timestamp implementation	(CLOCK, TRIGGER COUNT, NA)	E
Units of Timestamp		E
For each logical input device:		
List of Echo Types supported		nIX
List of Prompt Types Supported		nIX
List of Acknowledgement Types Supported		nIX
For CHOICE input devices:		
Maximum number of alternatives	(1...n)	I
Bottom-left corner		DP
Top-right corner		DP
Width		I
Height		I
For PICK input devices:		
Maximum number of pickable segments	(1...n)	I
For STRING input devices:		
Maximum string buffer size	(1...n)	I
For STROKE input devices:		
Maximum number of stroke points	(1...n)	I
Bottom-left corner		DP
Top-right corner		DP
Width		I
Height		I
For AREA input devices:		
Colour capability	(YES,NO)	E
Number of levels	(1...n)	I
Maximum bits per pixel	(1...n)	I
Maximum no. of pixels in x,y	(1...n)	2xI
For GENERAL input devices:		
Maximum data record size	(1...n)	I
List of associable triggers		nIX
Number of nondissociable triggers		I[1]
List of default associable triggers		nIX[2]

[1] Non-dissociable triggers are the first entered in the list of available triggers.
[2] This list includes one entry per available trigger.

D.7 Echo Output Description Table

The Echo Output Description Table occurs once, for an OUTIN or INPUT device, which supports the Echo Output Functionality. As for all the description tables, it contains the static data that cannot be changed by the client of the CGI.

Name	Range	Type
Group 1–Maximum number of Echoes:		
Maximum number of choice echoes	(-1...n)	I
Maximum number of locator echoes	(-1...n)	I
Maximum number of pick echoes	(-1...n)	I
Maximum number of string echoes	(-1...n)	I
Maximum number of stroke echoes	(-1...n)	I
Maximum number of valuator echoes	(-1...n)	I
Maximum number of area echoes	(-1...n)	I
Maximum number of general echoes	(-1...n)	I
Group 2–Echo, Prompt, and Acknowledgement Types Supported:		
Echo types supported for choice		nIX
Echo types supported for locator		nIX
Echo types supported for pick		nIX
Echo types supported for string		nIX
Echo types supported for stroke		nIX
Echo types supported for valuator		nIX
Echo types supported for area		nIX
Echo types supported for general		nIX
Prompt types supported		nIX
Acknowledgement types supported		nIX
Group 3–String and Stroke limits:		
Maximum string buffer size	(1...n)	I
Maximum number of points in stroke value	(1...n)	I
Maximum general input data record size	(1...n)	I
List of supported output format identifiers		
Maximum no. of pixels for AREA Input device	(1...n)	I

D.8 Output State List

Name	Range	Type	Default
Output State	(active, text open, figure open (region closed) figure open (region open)		

Specification Modes:

Name	Range	Type	Default
List of Attribute Set Names	(0...n)	nASN	(empty)
Line Width Spec Mode	(VDC,Scaled)	E	Scaled
Edge Width Spec Mode	(VDC,Scaled)	E	Scaled
Marker Size Spec Mode	(VDC.Scaled)	E	Scaled
Colour Selection Mode	(Direct,Indexed)	E	Indexed
Colour Value Extent	2xCol Spec	Impl Dependent	
Auxiliary Colour	CD or CI	(CD,CI)	Impl Dep
Colour Selection Mode for Aux Col		E	Indexed
Transparency	(OFF,ON)	E	ON
Colour Table	(CI,nCD)	Impl Dep	Dev Dep Aux Col=0 Dev Dep Fore Col=1
Current Aspect Source Flags	(Individual,Bundled)	nE	n(Individual)
Implicit Edge Visibility	(Off,On)	E	Off
Current Background Colour		CD	
Number of Line Bundle Entries		I	5
For every Line Bundle			
Line Bundle Index		IX	1
Line Type		I	1
Line Width	LWMode	(VDC,R)	VDC,1/1000 Max Length
Line Width Spec Mode Used	(absolute, scaled)	E	scaled
Line Colour	CSMode	(CD,CI)	CI, 1 or Fore
Colour Selection Mode	(CD,CI)	E	CI
Individual Line Type		I	1
Individual Line Width	LWMode	(VDC,R)	VDC,1/1000 Max Length
Line Width Spec Mode Used	(absolute, scaled)	E	scaled
Individual Line Colour	CSMode	(CD,CI)	CI, 1 or Fore
Colour Selection Mode	(CD,CI)	E	CI
Current Line Bundle Index		IX	1
Number of Marker Bundle Entries		I	5
For every Marker Bundle			
Marker Bundle Index		IX	1
Marker Type		IX	3
Marker Size	MSMode	(VDC,R)	1/100 of Longest or 1.0
Marker Size Spec Mode	(absolute, scaled)		scaled
Marker Colour	CSMode	(CD,CI)	CI,1 or Fore
Colour Selection Mode	(CD,CI)	E	CI
Individual Marker Type		IX	3
Individual Marker Size	MSMode	(VDC,R)	1/100 of Longest or 1.0
Marker Size Spec Used	(absolute, scaled)	E	scaled
Individual Marker Colour	CSMode	(CD,CI)	CI,1 or Fore
Colour Selection Mode			CI
Current Marker Bundle Index		IX	1

258   Part IV: Appendices

Name	Range	Type	Default
Number of Text Bundle Entries		I	2
For every Text Bundle			
Text Bundle Index		IX	1
Text Font Index		IX	1
Text Precision	(String, Character, Stroke)	E	String
Character Expansion Factor		R	1.0
Character Spacing		R	0.0
Text Colour	CSMode	(CD,CI)	CI, 1 or Fore
Colour Selection Mode	(CI,CD)	E	CI
Individual Text Bundle Index		IX	1
Individual Text Font Index		IX	1
Individual Text Precision	(String, Character, Stroke)	E	String
Individual Character Expansion Factor		R	1.0
Individual Character Spacing		R	0.0
Individual Text Colour	CSMode	(CD,CI)	CI, 1 or Fore
Colour Selection Mode	(CI,CD)	E	CI
Current Text Bundle Index		IX	1
Geometric Text Attribute Table			
Current Character Height	CHMode	(VDC,R)	VDC,1/100 longest side
Character Orientation		4xVDC	(0,1,1,0)
Text Path	(Right,Left,Up,Down)	E	Right
Horizontal Text Alignment	(Left,Centre,Right, Normal,Continuous)	E	Normal
Vertical Text Alignment	(Top,Cap,Half,Base, Bottom,Normal,Cont)	E	Normal
Continuous Horizontal Alignment		R	1.0
Continuous Vertical Alignment		R	1.0
Current Font List	Imp. dependent	nS	dev dep
For every Font			
Character Box		2xVDC	
Inter Character Spacing		VDC	
Inter Line Spacing		VDC	
Character Placement		2xVD	
Font Definition			
Current Character Set List: for each			
Type	(94,96,94 Multibyte, 96 Multibyte, Complete)	nE	94 char
Designator		S	
Current Character Set Index		IX	1
Current Alternate Character Set Index		IX	1

Appendix D: CGI Description Tables and State Lists

Name	Range	Type	Default
Number of Fill Bundle Entries		I	5
For Every Fill Bundle:			
Fill Bundle Index		IX	1
Interior Style	(Hollow,Solid,Pattern, Hatch,Empty)	E	Hollow
Fill Colour	CSMode	(CD,CI)	CI,1 or Fore
Colour Selection Mode	(CI,CD)	E	CI
Hatch Index		IX	1
Pattern Index		IX	1
Fill Bitmap		IX,P	
Current Fill Bundle Index		IX	1
Individual Interior Style	(Hollow,Solid,Pattern, Hatch,Empty)	E	Hollow
Individual Fill Colour	CSMode	(CD,CI)	CI,1 or Fore
Colour Selection Mode	(CI,CD)	E	CI
Individual Hatch Index		IX	1
Individual Pattern Index		IX	1
Pattern Table:			
List of:			
nx,ny		2I	1,1
local colour precision	(binding dep)		
colour selection mode	(CD,CI)	E	CI
pattern		nx*ny(CI or CD)	
solid,index1			
Fill Bitmap		IX,2P	
Current Fill Reference Point		P	(0,0)
Current Pattern Table			
Current Pattern Size		2I	
Number of Edge Bundle Entries		I	5
For Every Edge Bundle:			
Edge Bundle Index		IX	1
Edge Type		IX	1
Edge Width	EWMode	(VDC,R)	VDC,1/1000 Max Length
Edge Width Spec. Mode	(absolute, scaled)	E	scaled
Edge Colour	CSMode	CI,CD	CI,1 or Fore
Colour Selection Mode	(CI,CD)	E	CI
Current Edge Bundle Index		IX	1
Individual Edge Type		IX	1
Individual Edge Width	EWMode	(VDC,R)	VDC,1/1000 Max Length
Edge Width Selection Mode	(absolute, scaled)	E	scaled
Individual Edge Colour	CSMode	CI,CD	CI,1 or Fore
Colour Selection Mode	(CI,CD)	E	CI
Individual Edge Visibility	(Off,On)	E	Off

D.9 Control State List

The control state list contains the details of the current state of the device, and, while it is not strictly hierarchical, the format of some entries may be conditioned by the states of other entries. For example, the data types will depend on the appropriate type settings.

Name	Range	Type	Default
CGI State	(initialised)	E	initialised (or no entry)
Device View Surface State	(Clean, Dirty)	E	Dirty
Deferral Mode	(ASTI, BNI, ASAP)	E	ASTI
VDC Type	(integer, real)	E	integer
VDC Integer Precision			Impl. Dep.
VDC Real Precision			Impl. Dep
Integer Precision			Impl. Dep.
Real Precision			Impl. Dep
Index Precision			Impl. Dep
Colour Precision			Impl. Dep
Colour Index Precision			Impl. Dep
VDC Extent		2P	(0,0),(32767,32767)
Device Viewport Specification Units	("fraction of display surface," "millimetres" with scale factor, "physical device units")	E	fraction of display surface
Device Viewport Mapping:			
Isotropy	(not forced, forced)	E	forced
Horizontal Alignment	(left, centre, right)	E	left
Vertical Alignment	(bottom, centre, top)	E	bottom
Device Viewport		2DP	(0,0),(1.0,1.0)†
Clip Indicator	(clip rectangle, view surface off)	E	clip rectangle
Clip Rectangle		2P	(0,0),(32767,32767)
Error Stack Depth	(0...n)	I	0
Error Stack		ER	(empty)*
Number of Error Reports Lost	(0...n)	I	0
Oldest Error Report		ER	(empty)*
Character Coding Technique	(basic 7 bit, basic 8 bit, extended 7 bit, extended 8 bit)	E	basic 7 bit

† *The aspect ratio of the default device viewport should match that of the display surface.*

* *Although a separate entry, as well as on the stack, the oldest error need not be held twice in the state list. The two entries ensure direct inquirability via either route under the rules for inquiry functionality.*

D.10 Raster State List

Name	Range	Type	Default
Current Display Bitmap Name		BN	From desc table
Current Drawing Bitmap Name		BN	From desc table
Current Drawing Mode		I	From desc table
Current Mapped Bitmap Drawing Colour		CI.CD	From desc table
Number of Client-defined bitmaps		I	0
List of Client-defined bitmap names		nBN	
For each Client-defined bitmap			
Bitmap name		BN	
Type	(Mapped, Full depth)	E	
VDC Extent		2xP	
Viewport		2xVSP	
Bottom-left Pixel		DP	
Top-Right Pixel		DP	
VDC Extent		2P	(0,0),(32767,32767)
Device Viewport Specification Units	("fraction of display surface," "millimetres" with scale factor, "physical device units")	E	fraction of display surface
Device Viewport Mapping:			
Isotropy	(not forced, forced)	E	forced
Horizontal Alignment	(left, centre, right)	E	left
Vertical Alignment	(bottom, centre, top)	E	bottom
Device Viewport Spec. Units in which the current viewport was last specified		E	
For each Bitmap:			
Pixel Values		mxnxCI/CD	

D.11 Segmentation State List

Name	Range	Type	Default
Identifier of Open Segment		SN	
Number of Segment Identifiers	(0...n)	I	0
Set of Defined Segment Identifiers		nSN	(null)
Pick Identifier	(0...n)	I	0
Implicit Segment Regeneration Mode	(Suppressed, Allowed)	E	Suppressed
Inheritance Filter	1 flag for each class		
For each stored Segment and the Open Segment:			
Segment Identifier		SN	
Segment Transformation Matrix:			
Scale & Rotation Portion		2x2xR	identity
Translation Portion		2x1xVDC	identity
Visibility	(Visible, Invisible)	E	Visible
Highlighting	(Normal, Highlighted)	E	Normal
Display Priority		I	0
Detectability	(Undetectable, Detectable)	E	Undetectable
Pick Priority		I	0

D.12 Logical Input Device State List

For each device identified by Input Device Class (Choice, Locator, Pick, String, Stroke, Valuator) and input device index (IX).

Name	Range	Type	Default
Input device state	(Released, Ready, Request Pending, Echo Request Enabled, Echo Request Pending, Echo Request Completed, Events Enabled)	E	Released
Echo state	(Echo On, Echo Off)	E	Echo On
Echo type	(1...N)	IX	impl. dep.
Prompt state	(Prompt On, Prompt Off)	E	Prompt On
Prompt type		IX	impl. dep.
Acknowledgement state	(Ack On, Ack Off)	E	Ack On
Acknowledgement type		IX	impl. dep.
Echo Area		2DP	impl.dep.
Echo Data Record		D	impl.dep.

Data depending on Input Device Class:

Name	Range	Type	Default
For Pick devices			
Pick Aperture		2xVDC	impl. dep.
Maximum number of pickable segments		I	impl. dep.
For String devices			
Maximum string length		I	impl.dep.
For Stroke devices			
Maximum number of points		I	impl.dep.
x,y intervals		P	impl.dep.
Time interval		I	impl.dep.
Echo window			
Echo viewport			
Viewport specification units		E	
Echo Extent		P	
For Valuator devices			
Minimum value of range		V	impl.dep.
Maximum value for range		V	impl.dep.
For Locator devices:			
Echo window	(0,1)	4R	(0,0,1,1)
Echo viewport		2DP	
Viewport Specification units		E	
Echo Extent		P	
For AREA devices:			
x,y resolutions		2I	
Colour	(YES,NO)	E	
Threshold value		I	
Bits per pixel		I	
Window		2DP	
Input Device Data Record		D	

D.13 Event Queue State List

Name	Range	Type	Default
Event Queue State	(Released, Empty-No-LID-Enabled, Empty-LID-Enabled, Not-empty, Overflow)	E	Released
Event Block State	(Blocked, Not Blocked)	E	Not Blocked

D.14 Echo Entity State List

An Echo Entity State List will be required to exist following the function INITIALIZE ECHO OUTPUT. It is, thus, applicable only to OUTPUT or OUTIN class CGIs which support the Remote Echoing Functionality. This state list contains only that data which may be varied by the client of the CGI and that the CGI is required to make available to the client by inquiry. It should not be taken as a complete statement of the data required to implement an Echo Entity.

Name	Range	Type	Default
Group 1 - Echo, Prompt and Acknowledgement States			
Echo State	(Echo On, Echo Off)	E	Echo On
Echo Type		IX	impl.dep.
Prompt State	(Prompt On, Prompt Off)	E	Prompt On
Prompt type		IX	impl.dep.
Acknowledgement state	(Ack On, Ack Off)	E	Ack On
Acknowledgement type		IX	impl.dep.
Group 2 - Echo Area			
Echo Area		2DP	
Group 3 - Echo Data Record			
Echo Data Record (Contents and structure vary according to Input Class)		D	

Appendix E

CGI Functions and Parameterization

E.1 Introduction and Conventions

All CGI functions are listed in this appendix, in the order that they appear in the draft CGI standard. Parameters for each function are also provided, so that you can get an idea of the purpose of each function. A parameter list of () indicates that the function takes no parameters.

E.2 Part 2 Functions

E.2.1 Virtual Device Management

INITIALIZE ()
RESET TO DEFAULTS ()
TERMINATE ()
MAKE PICTURE CURRENT ()
SET DEFERRAL MODE (ASTI, BNI or ASAP)
PREPARE VIEW SURFACE (Force Hardcopy Advance Flag)
END PAGE ()
BACKGROUND COLOUR (RGB Colour Value)

E.2.2 Coordinate Space Control

VDC TYPE (Real or Integer)
VDC PRECISION FOR INTEGER POINTS (encoding dependent)
VDC PRECISION FOR REAL POINTS (encoding dependent)
VDC EXTENT (two corners)
DEVICE VIEWPORT (two corners)
DEVICE VIEWPORT SPECIFICATION UNITS
    (fraction, mm plus scale factor, or Device Units)
DEVICE VIEWPORT MAPPING
    (Isotropy Flag, Horizontal and Vertical Alignments)
CLIP RECTANGLE (two corners)
CLIP INDICATOR(Clip Rectangle, Effective Viewport, or Off)

E.2.3 Error Handling

POP ERROR STACK (Number of Reports, Reports)
EMPTY ERROR STACK ()
ERROR HANDLING (error class,flag: On/ Reporting Off/ Detection Off)

E.2.4 Miscellaneous Control

INTEGER PRECISION (encoding dependent)
REAL PRECISION (encoding dependent)
INDEX PRECISION (encoding dependent)
COLOUR PRECISION (encoding dependent)
COLOUR INDEX PRECISION (encoding dependent)
MESSAGE (Action Required Flag, Message)
APPLICATION DATA (ID,Record)
ESCAPE (ID,Record)
GET ESCAPE (ID,Record,Validity Flag, Output Data Record)

E.3 Part 3 Functions

E.3.1 Graphical Primitives

POLYLINE (point list)
DISJOINT POLYLINE (point list)
CIRCULAR ARC 3 POINT (starting, intermediate, ending point)
CIRCULAR ARC CENTRE (centrepoint,start and end vectors, radius)
CIRCULAR ARC CENTRE BACKWARDS (")
ELLIPTICAL ARC (centrepoint, two CDPs, start and end vectors)
POLYMARKER (point list)
TEXT (location, flag:*final* or *not-final*, string)
RESTRICTED TEXT (extent rect., location, flag:*final* or *not-final*, string)
APPEND TEXT (flag:*final* or *not-final*, string)
POLYGON (point list)
POLYGON SET (list of {edge-out-flag,point})
RECTANGLE (two points)
CIRCLE (centrepoint, radius)
CIRCULAR ARC 3 POINT
    CLOSE (starting, intermediate, ending point,*pie* or *chord* close)
CIRCULAR ARC CENTRE
    CLOSE (centrepoint,start and end vectors, radius,*pie* or *chord* close)
ELLIPSE (centrepoint, two CDPs)
ELLIPTICAL ARC CLOSE
    (centrepoint, two CDPs, start and end vectors,*pie* or *chord* close)

CELL ARRAY
   (three corner points, grid dimensions, local colour precision, colours)
GENERALIZED DRAWING PRIMITIVE (ID, point list, data record)

E.3.2 Attribute Functions

LINE BUNDLE INDEX (integer)
LINE TYPE (solid, dash, dot, dash dot, dash dot dot)
LINE WIDTH (Specifier)
LINE COLOUR (Descriptor)
LINE REPRESENTATION (Index, Line Type,Line Width, Line Colour)
MARKER BUNDLE INDEX (integer)
MARKER TYPE (dot, plus, asterisk, circle, cross)
MARKER SIZE (Specifier)
MARKER COLOUR (Colour Descriptor)
MARKER REPRESENTATION
   (Index, Marker Type, Marker Size, Marker Colour)
TEXT BUNDLE INDEX (integer)
TEXT FONT INDEX (integer)
TEXT PRECISION (string, character, or stroke)
TEXT COLOUR (Descriptor)
TEXT PATH (Right, Left, Up or Down)
TEXT ALIGNMENT(horizontal, vertical, two continuous values)
TEXT REPRESENTATION (Index, Text Font,Text Precision,
   CharacterExpansion Factor, Character Spacing,Colour)
CHARACTER EXPANSION FACTOR(deviation from normal aspect ratio)
CHARACTER SPACING (Spacing in Character Heights)
CHARACTER HEIGHT (baseline to capline distance in VDC)
CHARACTER ORIENTATION (Character Up Vector, String Base Vector)
CHARACTER SET INDEX (integer)
ALTERNATE CHARACTER SET INDEX (integer)
FILL BUNDLE INDEX (integer)
INTERIOR STYLE (Empty,Hollow, Solid, Pattern, Hatch, or Bitmap)
FILL COLOUR (Descriptor)
HATCH INDEX (one of six patterns)
PATTERN INDEX (integer)
FILL REFERENCE POINT (Point in VDC)
PATTERN TABLE (Index, X&Y counts,
   Local Colour Precision, Array of Colour Descriptors)
PATTERN SIZE (Pattern Height Vector, Pattern Width Vector)
FILL REPRESENTATION(Index, Interior Style,Colour,
   Hatch Index, Pattern Index, Fill Bitmap, Bitmap Region)

EDGE BUNDLE INDEX(integer)
EDGE TYPE (same as line type)
EDGE WIDTH (Specifier)
EDGE COLOUR (Descriptor)
EDGE VISIBILITY (*on* or *off*)
EDGE REPRESENTATION
    (Index, Edge Type, Edge Width, Edge Colour)

E.3.3 Output and Attribute Control Functions

COLOUR SELECTION MODE (Direct or Indexed)
COLOUR VALUE EXTENT (Min Colour Value, Max Colour Value)
AUXILIARY COLOUR (Colour Descriptor)
TRANSPARENCY (*on* or *off*)
COLOUR TABLE (starting index, List of Colours)
LINE WIDTH SPECIFICATION MODE (VDC or scaled)
EDGE WIDTH SPECIFICATION MODE (VDC or scaled)
MARKER SIZE SPECIFICATION MODE (VDC or scaled)
ASPECT SOURCE FLAGS (List of {ASF Type; Individual or Bundled})
FONT LIST (List of Font Names)
CHARACTER SET LIST
    (List of {Character Set Type,†Designation Sequence Tail})
BEGIN FIGURE ()
END FIGURE ()
NEW REGION ()
IMPLICIT EDGE VISIBILITY (*on* or *off*)
SAVE PRIMITIVE ATTRIBUTES (Attribute Set Name)
RESTORE PRIMITIVE ATTRIBUTES (Attribute Set Name)
CHARACTER CODING ANNOUNCER (coding technique)
GET TEXT EXTENT (text position,string,validity,
    concatenation point, text extent parallelogram)

    †One of 94 Character Sets; 96 Character Sets;
        94 Character Multi-byte Sets; Complete Code.

E.4 Part 4 Functions

E.4.1 Segment Manipulation

GET NEW SEGMENT IDENTIFIER (Segment ID, Validity Flag)
OPEN SEGMENT (Segment ID)
REOPEN SEGMENT (Segment ID)
CLOSE SEGMENT ()
COPY SEGMENT (Segment ID, Copy transform)

DELETE SEGMENT (Segment ID)
DELETE ALL SEGMENTS ()
RENAME SEGMENT (Old Segment ID, New Segment ID)
REDRAW SEGMENT (Segment ID)
REDRAW ALL SEGMENTS ()
IMPLICIT SEGMENT REGENERATION MODE (Suppressed or Allowed)
PICK IDENTIFIER (Pick Identifier)

E.4.2 Segment Attributes

SEGMENT TRANSFORM (Segment ID, Scaling and Rotation, Translation)
SEGMENT VISIBILITY (Segment ID, Visible or Invisible)
SEGMENT HIGHLIGHTING (Segment ID, Normal or Highlighted)
SEGMENT DISPLAY PRIORITY (Segment ID, integer display priority)
SEGMENT DETECTABILITY (Segment ID, undetectable or detectable)
SEGMENT PICK PRIORITY (Segment ID, integer pick priority)

E.4.3 Segment Interrogations

SIMULATE PICK (Pick point, pick aperture, no. of segments hit,
   list of segments hit, status–*valid* or *invalid*)
INHERITANCE FILTER (Filter selection attribute designator;
   setting: *state-list* or *segment*)

E.5 Part 5 Functions

E.5.1 Logical Input Device Functions

INITIALIZE LOGICAL INPUT DEVICE (class,index)
RELEASE INPUT DEVICE (class,index)
SET ACKNOWLEDGEMENT STATE (class,index,*on* or *off*)
PUT CURRENT xxx† MEASURE (index,measure value, validity)
SET ECHO DATA (class,index,echo type,prompt type,
   acknowledgement type, echo area, data record)
SET ECHO STATE (class,index,*on* or *off*)
SET xxx† DEVICE DATA (class,index,*rest of data varies by class*)
SET PROMPT STATE (class,index,*on* or *off*)
ASSOCIATE TRIGGERS (class,index, list of triggers)
REQUEST xxx†
   (index,timeout,timeout exponent,status,validity,trigger,value)
SAMPLE xxx† (index, validity, value)
INTIALIZE ECHO REQUEST (class, index, timeout, timeout exponent)
ECHO REQUEST xxx† (index,status,validity,trigger,value)

INITIALIZE EVENT QUEUE (initial time stamp)
RELEASE EVENT QUEUE ()
ENABLE EVENTS (class, index)
DISABLE EVENTS (class, index)
BLOCK EVENT QUEUE ()
UNBLOCK EVENT QUEUE ()
FLUSH EVENTS ()
FLUSH DEVICE EVENTS (class, index)
AWAIT EVENT
    (timeout, timeout exponent, class, index, timestamp, event queue state)
DEQUEUE xxx† EVENT (status, event report)
AWAIT EVENT QUEUE TRANSFER
    (timeout, timeout exponent, event queue state, event reports)
RETRIEVE OVERFLOW EVENT (class, index, trigger index, timestamp)

E.5.2 Echo Output Functions

INITIALIZE xxx† ECHO OUTPUT (echo index, value, acknowledgement
    type, prompt type, echo type, echo area, echo data record)
RELEASE ECHO OUTPUT (class, echo index)
SET ACKNOWLEDGEMENT OUTPUT STATE
    (class, echo index, state)
SET ECHO OUTPUT STATE (class, echo index, state)
SET PROMPT OUTPUT STATE (class, echo index, state)
UPDATE xxx† ECHO OUTPUT (echo index, new value)

† The "xxx"'s represent functions which exist for each device class
(CHOICE, etc.), but the parameterisation is obviously different due to
the data types used, etc.

E.6 Part 6 Functions

E.6.1 Output and Attributes

PIXEL ARRAY (origin, number of columns and rows,
    valid array range, x and y scale, array of colour specifiers)
MAPPED BITMAP FOREGROUND COLOUR (specifier)
FILL BITMAP (name, region)

E.6.2 Raster Control Functions

CREATE BITMAP (bitmap extent, *mapped* or *full-depth*, name)
DELETE BITMAP (bitmap name)
SELECT DRAWING BITMAP (bitmap name)
DISPLAY BITMAP (bitmap name)
DRAWING MODE (mode: one of sixteen codes)
SOURCE DESTINATION BITBLT
    (source bitmap, source origin, destination origin, x and y offsets)
TILE THREE OPERAND BITBLT
    (pattern bitmap and region, source bitmap and origin,
    destination origin, x and y offsets, drawing-mode-3: one of 256 values)
PATTERN SOURCE BITBLT (*note: not expected in next draft*)
    (pattern bitmap and region, source bitmap and origin,
    destination origin, x and y offsets)

E.6.3 Raster Inquiry Functions

GET PIXEL ARRAY (origin, number of columns and rows,
    validity flag, valid x and y ranges, array of colour specifiers)
GET PIXEL ARRAY DIMENSIONS (region, number of columns and rows)

Appendix F

TOP CGM Application Profile

F.1 What is an Application Profile?

As we discussed in Chap. 12, the CGM standard itself specifies only the syntax and semantics of a metafile. The standard does not place *any* constraints on the behaviour of CGM generators and interpreters, although Annex D of the standard does suggest how CGM interpreters might process particular elements.

An application profile is a set of guidelines that define implementation constraints and performance characteristics. Application profiles specify characteristics of an implementation that go beyond the conformance requirements of the base standard. Application profiles used in conjunction with the base standard can promote interchange of data between systems employing different implementations of the CGM.

CGM implementations adhering to the TOP CGM application profile will be able to be integrated into other application processes, such as compound document interchange.

F.2 The Technical Office Protocols Organization

The TOP CGM application profile was developed by the TOP Graphics Subcommittee, under the auspices of the MAP/TOP Users Group. To obtain a complete copy of the TOP Version 3.0 Implementation Release, contact:

>Society for Manufacturing Engineers
>One SME Drive
>P.O. Box 930
>Dearborn, MI 48121
>United States of America

The current draft of TOP Version 3.0 was issued in September, 1987. The final draft is expected to be issued in June, 1988, after comments have been considered and errors have been noted and fixed.

F.3 TOP Version 3.0

The TOP Version 3.0 CGM Application Profile defines the conformance characteristics or permissable combinations for all possible data streams that are specified in the profile. Additional requirements for transmitting, receiving, interpreting, and handling valid CGM data streams are also defined. Because the specification of such implementation constraints is usually outside the scope of an ISO standard, this application profile has been developed to insure uniform implementation of the CGM, especially where interchange of CGM files in an open systems environment is desired.

The TOP CGM Application Profile specifies conformance in terms of *permissable* and *basic* values. Permissable values are the range of values of CGM elements as specified in ISO 8632:1985. Basic values are a subset of the permissable values. For example, permissable values of MARKER TYPE include all non-zero integers, while the basic values include only the standardized enumerated values of 1 to 5.

TOP defines a conforming *basic metafile* as one that contains no elements or parameter values outside of the basic set. Similarly, TOP defines a conforming *basic interpreter* as one that correctly interprets any conforming basic metafile. Conforming basic interpreters may have additional capability. Finally, TOP defines a conforming *basic generator* as one that produces only conforming basic metafiles or one that can be reliably directed to function in a mode of producing basic metafiles.

Any TOP CGM conforming basic interpreter should correctly parse and ignore any elements and parameter values that it does not support.

TOP Version 3.0 specifies an application profile only for the Binary Encoding of the CGM; the other encodings may be the subject of future application profiles.

The current version of the Application Profile specifies that the basic form for the command header and the string parameter header be the long form. Because of comments from the using community, it is likely that this constraint will be removed in the final version of the TOP CGM Application Profile. Considerable savings in file size can be obtained when the short forms are used.

Appendix F: TOP CGM Application Profile   275

F.4 Constraints on the Metafile Contents

Recall that the basic set is defined by limitations on the set of permissable values. Where a CGM element is not mentioned, it is implied that the basic set includes all the values permitted in the CGM.

Delimiter Elements.

Element	*Basic Values*
no-op	An arbitrary sequence of up to 32767 octets.

Metafile Descriptor Elements.

Element	*Basic Values*
metafile description	The sub-string "TOP/BASIC-1" should be included in the description string.
integer precision	16
real precision	0, 9, 23 (for floating point) and 1,16,16 (for fixed point)
index precision	16
colour precision	8 and 16
colour index precision	8 and 16
maximum colour index	255
font list	four simultaneous fonts are permitted. The font names are selected from 16 Hershey font names specified in the profile.
character set list	0,4/2 (selects 7-bit ASCII, X3.4) 1,4/1 (selects 8-bit ASCII, X3.134/2, which is equivalent to ISO 8859/1)
character coding announcer	0 and 1

Picture Descriptor Elements.

Element	*Basic Values*
scaling mode	All permissable values, but implementers should use care in specifying the value of the metric scaling factor to ensure that it has sufficient resolution to specify the intended accuracy.

Control Elements.

Element	*Basic Values*
VDC integer precision	16 and 32
VDC real precision	0, 9, 23 (floating point) and 1, 16, 16 (fixed point)

Graphics Primitive Elements.

To ensure portability and predictable results, TOP conforming basic metafiles may not contain any Generalized Drawing Primitive (GDP) elements.

Attribute Elements.

Element	*Basic Values*
line bundle index	1-5
line type	1-5
marker bundle index	1-5
marker type	1-5
text bundle index	1-2
text font index	1-4
character set index	1-2
alternate character set index	1-2
fill bundle index	1-5
hatch index	1-6
pattern index	1-8
edge bundle index	1-5
edge type	1-5
pattern table	pattern table index:1-8 nx: 1-16 ny: 1-16
colour table	starting colour index: 0-255

Escape Elements.

To ensure portability and predictable results, only two ESCAPE elements are permitted to appear in a TOP conforming basic metafile. The ESCAPE elements that have been defined by the TOP CGM Application Profile are *Disable Clearing of View Surface* and *Device Viewport*. The former escape permits the overlapped display of multiple pictures in a metafile, such as might occur with a PC-board layout drawing, where each layer is placed in a separate picture within the CGM. The latter escape is identical to the CGI function and CGM Addendum 1 element of the same name.

External Elements.

Element	*Basic Values*
message	action required flag: 0

CGM Defaults.

The CGM specifies a complete set of defaults. In a few cases, these defaults are not sufficient for TOP requirements. However, any TOP conforming basic metafile must be a legal CGM. Consequently, each TOP deviation from the CGM defaults requires that the affected element (that is, the element with a different default value) either

or
> appear in the Metafile Defaults Replacement Element

> be explicitly specified in the appropriate places in the CGM.

The elements that need setting are:

> TEXT PRECISION: set the precision value to 2 (stroke);

> COLOUR TABLE: set the starting colour table index to 2 and repeat the following list of colour values for the remaining 254 entries:

index	values	meaning
2	255,0,0	red
3	0,255,0	green
4	0,0,255	blue
5	255,255,0	yellow
6	255,0,255	magenta
7	0,255,255	cyan
8	0,0,0	black
9	255,255,255	white

> MAXIMUM COLOUR INDEX: set to 255;

> CHARACTER SET LIST: set to (0,4/2) (1,4/1).

Miscellaneous Constraints.

In the CGM, the COLOUR TABLE element has an unspecified effect when it appears in a picture, subsequent to any graphical primitive elements. In a TOP conforming basic metafile, the COLOUR TABLE element should appear prior to any graphical primitive elements to insure that interpreting systems without dynamic colour update capabilities can render the intended effect.

F.5 Constraints on Generators and Interpreters

TOP specifies that all of the guidelines of ISO 8632, Annex D, Guidelines for metafile generators and interpreters, shall be adhered to by TOP CGM generators and interpreters. In particular, the minimum interpreter capabilities of Annex D.5, plus any explicit additional capabilities already mentioned should be the minimum supported capabilities.

TOP also gives a few more specific guidelines. These are described in the following paragraphs. The first one is highlighted, because it clarifies a potential ambiguity in the CGM standard itself.

In the text of the CGM standard, it is not apparent what the default value for the precision of the floating point real parameter of the SCALING MODE element is. TOP conforming generators and interpreters shall assume that the real precision for this parameter is (0,9,23).

The METAFILE DEFAULTS REPLACEMENT element shall not be partitioned. In addition, no part of any element within this element shall be partitioned. As a result of the commenting process, TOP may also be revised to specify that one METAFILE DEFAULTS REPLACEMENT element should be used for *each* default value being replaced.

For the RESTRICTED TEXT element, the minimum capability of a TOP basic conforming interpreter shall be to render the complete restricted text string (that is, with APPEND TEXT elements permitted), scaled isotropically (that is, the specified aspect ratio for the text is not distorted), such that the text string fits into the text extent parallelogram provided with the RESTRICTED TEXT element.

Data Structure Constraints. The following constraints represent *maximum* allowed capabilities for TOP conforming basic metafile generators and *minimum* allowed capabilities for TOP conforming basic metafile interpreters:

Maximum colour array dimension	1,048,576 for CELL ARRAY (i.e., one 1Kx1K image) 1024 for PATTERN TABLE (i.e., 4 16x16 patterns) 256 for COLOUR TABLE (i.e., entries 0-255).
Maximum point array length	1024 points (i.e., pairs of coordinates).
Maximum string length	256 for all string parameters except data records; 32,767 for data records.

Appendix F: TOP CGM Application Profile 279

Default bundle tables. The bundle representations are not settable in ISO 8632:1985, although this deficiency is being addressed by CGM Add 1. The TOP CGM Application Profile specifies default values for each of the bundle table entries. These defaults are summarized in the following.

Line and Edge Bundles	Five bundles distinguished by line types 1 through 5; line width always 1; line colour always 1.
Marker Bundles	Five bundles distinguished by marker types 1 - 5; marker size always 1; marker colour always 1.
Text Bundles	Two bundles distinguished by character expansion factors 1.0 and 0.5; text precision always *stroke*, character spacing always 0.0; text colour always 1.
Fill Area Bundles	Five bundles distinguished by hatch indices 1 -5; interior style always *hatch*; fill colour always 1; pattern index always 1.

These values are compatible with the default bundle table values specified in ISO 8613-8, Geometric Graphics Content Architecture, described in Chap. 15.

CGM Transfer Format. Operating system dependencies for file formats can often be a greater barrier to interoperability than differences in interchange formats. To ensure CGM interoperability, some conventions for file formats are required.

The TOP Version 3.0 CGM Application Profile specifies that the CGM should be formatted into fixed length 80 octet records. If the record length is less than 80 octets, even octet records are required. When the files are transferred on magnetic tape, the 80 octet records should be formatted into blocks of 800 octets.

This latter TOP CGM requirement has not been very popular with implementers, especially those using MS-DOS™ (on IBM PCs and compatibles) and on UNIX™ systems where CGMs can be created and interpreted as a single continuous stream of octets, with no record structure required. This requirement may change in the final version of the CGM Application Profile as a result of comments received by the TOP organization.